D0992195

n. 7 ✓

'85

○

CURRICULUM THEORY IN ADULT AND LIFELONG EDUCATION

RADICAL FORUM ON ADULT EDUCATION SERIES
Edited by Jo Campling, Hillcroft College

Curriculum Theory in Adult and Lifelong Education

Colin Griffin

CROOM HELM
London & Canberra

NICHOLS PUBLISHING COMPANY
New York

092959

© 1983 Colin Griffin
Croom Helm, Provident House, Burrell Row,
Beckenham, Kent BR3 1AT

British Library Cataloguing in Publication Data

Griffin, Colin
   Curriculum theory in adult and lifelong education. –
   (Radical forum on adult education)
   1. Adult education – Curricula
   I.   Title   II. Series
   374'.001   LC5219
   ISBN 0-7099-1120-3

First published in the United States of America 1983
by Nichols Publishing Company, Post Office Box 96,
New York, NY 10024

Library of Congress Cataloging in Publication Data

Griffin, Colin.
   Curriculum theory in adult and lifelong education.

   Bibliography: p.
   Includes index.
   1. Adult education – Curricula – Philosophy.
2. Continuing education – Curricula – Philosophy.
I. Title.
LC5219.G683   1983   374'.01   83-4173
ISBN 0-89397-162-6

Printed and Bound in Great Britain

CONTENTS

EDITOR'S INTRODUCTION

The purpose of this series is to provide a forum of discussion for the whole field of adult and continuing education. With increasing pressure on traditional areas of secondary and higher education and changing employment patterns, there is a growing awareness that the continuing education of adults has a vital role to play in our society. All the books in the series are about radical thinking and practice in education in Britain and abroad. The authors are concerned with education in its widest sense, and, by implication, with the inadequacy of traditional views of education as a process which concerns only the young and which takes place only in the formal sectors.

A major focus of the series is on the consequences of social change and the need to formulate an educational response to new technologies and new economic, social and political conditions as they affect *all* members of our society. The growth and distribution of knowledge is rapidly making traditional models of education obsolete, and new learning technologies are being developed which give a greater potential than ever before to the possibilities of education as an instrument of social change, but only if we change radically our conceptions of education itself and adopt a critical view of the uses to which it could be put.

At the same time that educational ideals become more attainable through the growth of knowledge and learning technologies, economic, social, political, sexual and racial conflicts remain undiminished and often find expression in educational inequalities and injustices. The series aims to explore this paradox, to identify obstacles in the way of realising the full potential of education for all and to describe some of the initiatives being taken in the United Kingdom and abroad to try to overcome them.

This book is about the failure of traditional ideas and concepts to generate an adequate theory of adult and lifelong education, despite the fact that some fairly large claims are being made out for its significance as an object of legislation and social policy in many countries of the world. The consequent need for a curriculum theory of adult and lifelong education is set out: one which is concerned with the aims, content and methods of adult learning, and which is located in a context of knowledge, culture and power. As with schooling, a curriculum theory of adult education is one which analyses its practices as a definition, distribution and evaluation of knowledge.

Adulthood is a culturally and politically problematic category: 'provision' is increasingly polarising around concepts of 'compensatory' or 'continuing/recurrent' education. Most effort seems to have been put into 'distancing' adult education from schooling through various attempts to identify distinctive 'adult characteristics'. However, any general theory of adult education must focus upon curriculum processes, however widely defined, and must not be confused with psychological theories of how adults learn, nor with descriptions of the organisation of provision, nor even with hypotheses about participation among a population. Within the dominant curriculum paradigm of schooling, political and ideological analysis have now become very important. In the case of adult education, the parochialism of 'adult characteristics' analysis has effectively depoliticised its curriculum practices and failed to account for them in relation to the definition, distribution and evaluation of knowledge.

Curriculum theory of adult and lifelong education should be concerned with the ways in which it reproduces or transforms the curriculum categories of schooling, and therefore, with generating a critical view of knowledge and modernisation processes rather than with the uncritical one which prevails. Recent developments in curriculum theory, particularly the radical critique of educational progressivism, have not found much reflection in the adult sector, where innovation rather than curriculum development seems to be the rule. Despite the alleged influence of writers such as Illich and Freire, whose work is critically reviewed, the dominant paradigm of adult education is still one based upon 'adult characteristics' rather than one based upon the transformation of the curriculum categories of schooling.

Three formulations of the 'adult characteristics' approach are reviewed, and each found inadequate as a real description of adult learning in curriculum terms: adult knowledge, adult teaching methods (or andragogy), and adult organisation for provision. A professional ideology of adult education is identified as one centred around the ideas of needs, access and provision. This is analysed as a liberal/progressive ideology which fails to account critically for the problem of how educational processes are effective in defining, distributing and evaluating knowledge. The idea, for example, of curriculum development as a process of accommodation to 'adult needs' or to technological growth and modernisation is challenged as a profoundly conservative view of knowledge, society and change. Paradoxically, much of adult education reproduces the curriculum categories of progressive schooling in spite of its evident potential to transform them. For example, the developing UNESCO concept of lifelong education as curriculum integration and evaluation is analysed in this way. Crucial distinctions are made between educational legislation and social policy, and between educational innovation and curriculum development. More often than not, these distinctions are hopelessly blurred. Similarly, major elements of professional ideology, such as those of needs or access, are based upon a failure to distinguish between the institutional agents and the social agencies of knowledge and change. Even Illich and Freire, it is argued, do not properly account for key problems in the social construction of knowledge. The work of Ettore Gelpi, however, comes much closer to providing some idea of the construction of knowledge in the social relations of production, and thus offers us, uniquely so far, the groundwork of a curriculum theory of adult learning.

This provocative book challenges both received opinion and some currently fashionable ideas, and should stimulate discussion and controversy amongst all those concerned with the education of adults.

Jo Campling
Series Editor

(Jo Campling is Lecturer in Social Policy at Hillcroft College)

1 DEVELOPMENTS IN CURRICULUM THEORY

Introduction

The meaning of 'curriculum' is nowadays wholly bound up with that of 'education' itself, although in its Latin origins it had to do with the course over which a race was run, and this association with competition has not been entirely lost. What 'curriculum' stands for in modern times, however, is a course of study pursued in an educational institution such as a school. Indeed, 'curriculum studies' and 'curriculum theory' tend nowadays to be pursued almost exclusively in the context of the school,[1] which is a measure of the extent to which, in modern societies, education has come to be synonymous with schooling and childhood learning.

Conventional usage apart, however, there is clearly nothing in the meaning of curriculum to preclude its relevance in educational contexts other than those of schools. Its most fundamental reference is, after all, to the content and processes of learning rather than to the historically and culturally contingent educational institution of the school. The dominance of the school has become reflected in a dominant paradigm of the curriculum, a consequence of which has been the general neglect of curriculum studies and curriculum theory in what might variously be described as post-school, post-initial or post-compulsory education. Such an association of curriculum with childhood has not only reinforced the dominant paradigm but has to some extent at least impoverished the general theory of adult, continuing or lifelong education. A dominant paradigm of adult education studies is that of the 'structures of provision', about which more is now being written.[2] Nevertheless, the arguments which are going to be pursued here are based upon the assumption that no general theory of adult or lifelong education is possible which does not have the context and processes of adult learning as a primary object; no general theory is possible, that is, which lacks the dimension of curriculum analysis. For the importance of the curriculum is that of education itself, and those who have been seriously concerned with education have necessarily found it of interest:

The reason for their interest is simple: the content of education, the curriculum, is at the heart of the educational enterprise. It is the

11

means through which education is transacted. Without a curriculum education has no vehicle, nothing through which to transmit its messages, to convey its meanings, to transmit its values. It is mainly because of the crucial role which the curriculum plays in educational activities that it is worthy of study.[3]

In fact, this view reveals a further aspect of the dominant, school-based paradigm of the curriculum: its primary concern with content and with the way in which it is defined in terms of teacher-pupil relations. Accordingly, the messages, meanings and values which are the content of educational experience and therefore crucial to its understanding have become almost completely dependent upon a view of the teaching – rather than learning – function. This explains not only a widespread and growing interest in curriculum matters but also the fact that learner-centred education has sometimes seemed a rather revolutionary idea, not least to parents. For what has been referred to as the dominant paradigm of curriculum is not merely an idea in the minds of theorists but reflects a set of widespread cultural beliefs about education. It would be a major social, as well as theoretical, achievement to revise the dominant or school-based paradigm of curriculum in the industrialised societies, and it cannot be said that those who have attempted this have had much success, except for the creation of a rather negative, anti-school rhetoric.[4] All this does suggest, however, that the greatest scope for curriculum development exists in the non-school sectors of education systems – just those sectors, paradoxically, where interest in curriculum matters seems at its lowest.

So far, it has been suggested that the meaning of 'curriculum' has been shaped by schooling as a universal institution of modern societies rather than by any purely logical or conceptual features of the term. But even within the school context there is no universal agreement as to what should be included in its meaning, and it is possible to take a narrower or a wider view. The narrower view is that when we talk of the curriculum we are talking about courses and subjects which comprise the intended outcomes of teaching, the knowledge and skills which it is the business of education to transmit. It is the most influential view of the curriculum, and needs to be considered further.

Curriculum and Knowledge

Many of those who have written about the curriculum argue for the usefulness of an analytic distinction between the aims, content and methods of education, even though they tend to admit that, in practice, such distinctions are meaningless. They are also likely to agree that a theory of education is necessarily a theory of practice. One reason for this seeming contradiction is that problems of the aims, content and methods of education have separately given rise to arguments and controversies in the areas of philosophy, sociology and politics, and it is mainly in these areas that the most important recent developments have occurred. Not the least interesting of such controversies have been those over the content of education, where there are major differences between those taking a more philosophical or a more sociological view of knowledge.

That the content of education consists of public knowledge would seem a reasonable starting-point for a theoretical, or indeed for a common-sense, account of the matter. To say that someone has learned something does, after all, seem to entail a demonstrable new capacity on the part of the learner. It further entails that something identifiable has been learned, so that one has learned this and not that. And this would be true however the content of education is defined: even if real education is, as some would say, 'learning how to learn', the demonstrableness of the capacity is a condition of saying that learning has occurred. In this sense of a demonstrable capacity, the content of learning is public.

Traditional curriculum theory, developed in the context of the school, has stressed this sense in which the content of education is public, together with the sense in which the teaching or instructional function is at the heart of the matter. In his classic text on *Basic Principles of Curriculum and Instruction*, Ralph W. Tyler set out the essentially public processes by which these principles are elucidated, although in practice such principles have been decided in a more narrowly professional than widely public setting. In the context of the school at least, curriculum theorists who take public knowledge to be the content of education have not always made it clear how this public knowledge is mediated through the teaching and instructional functions. Thus Tyler identified four fundamental questions which needed to be answered as a prior condition of curriculum analysis and development, and which express the sense in which the curriculum should be an object of public debate:

1. What educational purposes should the school seek to attain?
2. What educational experiences can be provided that are likely to attain these purposes?
3. How can these educational experiences be effectively organized?
4. How can we determine whether these purposes are being attained?[5]

In effect, these are four question of a rather different order and they progress from a more public to a more professional issue. Classical curriculum theory failed to elucidate adequately the sense in which knowledge, as the content of education, was really *public*. It was, as will be seen, left to philosophers and sociologists to explore the issue of public knowledge in a more satisfactory way.

In the case of Tyler and later curriculum theorists in the school-oriented tradition of analysis[6] the role of the teacher is so crucial that the issue of public knowledge seems to revolve around it. It is hardly surprising, therefore, that the so-called 'objectives model' of the curriculum has been of such importance in recent years. According to this, in Tyler's words:

Since the real purpose of education is . . . to bring about significant changes in the students' patterns of behaviour, it becomes important to recognize that any statement of the objectives of the school should be a statement of changes to take place in students.[7]

This kind of passage demonstrates the practical impossibility of separating the content of education from its aims, objectives and purposes, particularly when the content is conceived wholly in terms of its potential for bringing about behavioural changes in learners. But, more significantly, we are thereby enabled to see more clearly an important meaning of public knowledge in the minds of the classical curriculum theorists. For behavioural change is more demonstrably public than knowledge: in this way learning can be proved to have taken place. It is difficult to avoid the conclusion that in the case of 'objectives model' curriculum theory, however liberally interpreted, there exists the possibility of confusing public knowledge as the content of education with public accountability on the part of professional educators. The case for this kind of analytic distinction is surely much greater than that which can be made between the content and the aims of education. In other words, to be able to demonstrate that learning has taken place is important to educators in terms of their public role, but this does not prove that knowledge itself is in any other sense 'public'. In order to pursue the issue of knowledge in these senses we have to look at the kinds of philosophical and sociological theories of knowledge upon which curriculum theory depends.

Now just as in traditional school-curriculum analysis the idea of public knowledge has become uncritically linked with the public accountability of education systems through demonstrable learning-objectives models, so the philosophical issues in this tradition have become linked with the issue of knowledge as school subjects. In other words, the content of school education is not knowledge in general but knowledge of particular subjects or skills or areas at a specific level or in a specific balance which constitutes a curriculum at any point in the education system. But is it of the nature of knowledge to be organised in this way or are we talking about the social conventions to do with knowledge in any particular society? Philosophers and sociologists have given a range of answers to the question.

As for the philosophical position about knowledge and the curriculum, the most influential view has tended to be that of P.H. Hirst and R.S. Peters. Curriculum planning, they argue, involves determining the aims, ends or objectives of the enterprise:

> Secondly there is the crucial point that if we examine carefully the character of the central objectives sought by progressives, we find that they, as much as those sought by traditionalists, are necessarily related to the acquisition of certain fundamental forms of what we have loosely called public modes of experience, understanding and knowledge.[8]

The logic of education, Hirst and Peters are saying, makes the public nature of its content inevitable, regardless of the kinds of aims that are envisaged for it. The same logic leads on to an 'objectives model' for the curriculum:

> We shall take the term 'curriculum' to be the label for a programme or course of activities which is explicitly organized as the means whereby pupils may attain the desired objectives, whatever these may be.[9]

In acknowledging the importance of Bloom's taxonomy of educational objectives[10] Hirst and Peters, however, point out that such a taxonomy in the cognitive, affective and psycho-motor domains provides 'no awareness of the fundamental, necessary relationships between the various kinds of objectives that can be distinguished'. Again we are made aware of the difficulty of abstracting the content of education from the complexities of practice. Nevertheless, Hirst and Peters are clear that educational objectives must have to do with those 'desirable states of mind' to which distinct, public modes of experience and knowledge are fundamental. Furthermore, they argue, it is cognitive objectives that must be the most fundamental of all, for these are the objectives which come within the domain of knowledge and experience. This is the core of the philosophical argument for the essentially public nature of the content of education:

> Let us begin by noting that there can be no experience or knowledge without the acquisition of the relevant concepts. Further, it is only when experience and thought, which necessarily involve the use of concepts of some sort, involve those shared in a public world, that the achievements with which we are concerned are possible. Without shared concepts, there can be no such distinctions as those between fact and fantasy, truth and error. Only where there is public agreement about the classification and categorization of experience and thought can we hope for any objectivity with them.[11]

Hirst and Peters identify seven irreducible conceptual areas of knowledge and experience: logic and mathematics; the physical sciences; concepts essential to interpersonal experience and knowledge; moral judgement and awareness; aesthetics; religion; philosophy. This constitutes a fundamental division of modes of experience and knowledge and between them there exist 'radical differences of kind', despite the fact that there is an important pattern of interrelationships between them too. The curriculum implications of this view of 'conceptual domains' for educational objectives are fairly obvious in terms of, say, balance or specialisation: these are the kind of curriculum objectives which seem, from the authors' point of view, philosophically defensible. However, they do not make the claim that the forms of knowledge and experience could be directly translated into school subjects, and different patterns of 'curriculum units' may well achieve the desired result of introducing learners to the discrete and public modes of knowledge and experience. However, this philosophical conceptualisation of the content of education does inevitably have rather negative consequences for curriculum integration and related non-traditional teaching practices organised around themes, topics or projects rather than around 'subjects' as traditionally conceived:

> In less competent hands, project and topic work can only too easily degenerate into pursuits which, however interesting, have little or no educational value . . . there would seem to be an ever present danger that this form of curriculum organization be allowed to determine what educational objectives it shall serve.[12]

On the whole, therefore, this view of the curriculum content, from a philosophical account of the public modes of knowledge and experience, constitutes a reasoned defence of the flexible subject-structured curriculum, at least in the face of what Hirst and Peters describe as 'a doctrinaire insistence on integrated curriculum units', which may be 'seriously miseducative'. In terms of a theory of knowledge, the idea of a more integrated and less subject-structured curriculum raises problems whose solutions are yet to be found.[13]

One of the most influential cases for the content of education as public knowledge was put by Paul H. Hirst in his essay on 'Liberal Education and the Nature of Knowledge'.[14] Hirst argued very succinctly for the view of education as something that was 'based fairly and squarely on the nature of knowledge itself, a concept central to the discussion of education at any level'. Education, according to this view, is a process without much social or concrete historical reference: vocational or other specialist learning is not strictly to count as education at all. Its content is determined by knowledge itself which Hirst describes as taking various forms, each of which is characterised by distinct conceptual, logical and methodological features. The implications of this for the curriculum of liberal education are clear: the organisation of the curriculum must be related in some way to the organisation of knowledge itself into its various discrete forms. It is also clear, however, that Hirst is talking about public manifestations of knowledge and perhaps exploring its social as well as its intrinsic organisation:

> As stated earlier, by a form of knowledge is meant a distinct way in which our experience becomes structured round the use of accepted public symbols. The symbols thus having public meaning, their use is in some way testable against experience and there is the progressive development of series of tested symbolic expressions. In this way experience has been probed further and further by extending and elaborating the use of the symbols and by means of these it has

become possible for the personal experience of individuals to become more fully structured, more fully understood.[15]

In what Hirst describes as the 'developed forms of knowledge'
certain distinguishing characteristics can be identified: central concepts
peculiar in character to the form; a distinctive logical structure, means
whereby it may be tested against experience; the further development
of techniques for exploring experience and testing the distinctive
expressions of the form.

Hirst's account of the forms of knowledge has attracted much attention and some criticism, and the reasons for this are not far to seek.
For example, does he — and others who use it — mean by the term
'public' what might otherwise be called 'social'? What value-judgements
underlie the idea of the 'structured personal experience of individuals'?
What is the status of 'undeveloped' forms of knowledge? Philosophical
analysis, it is often said, is a 'second-order' activity and therefore para-
sitic upon, rather than critical of, concrete historical practice. In this
instance, it might be argued that Hirst offers a reflection of dominant
curriculum values rather than an analytic account of the forms of
knowledge which they assume: his subject is the tradition of curriculum
practice as much as the traditions and forms of public knowledge.

Hirst's is certainly an analysis of knowledge which very closely
reflects what was described earlier as the dominant paradigm of the
curriculum organised around 'school-knowledge' and the teaching function:

> Acquiring knowledge of any form is therefore to a greater or less
> extent something that cannot be done simply by solitary study of
> the symbolic expressions of knowledge, it must be learnt from a
> master on the job. No doubt it is because the forms require partic-
> ular training of this kind in distinct worlds of discourse, because
> they necessitate the development of high critical standards according
> to complex criteria, because they involve our coming to look at
> experience in particular ways, that we refer to them as disciplines.
> They are indeed disciplines that form the mind.[16]

But is this really the language of 'public knowledge' or is it the
language ('master', 'standards', 'disciplines') of the public accountability of teachers, from which the dominant paradigm of the school-
knowledge curriculum has been constructed? Of course, Hirst is not
suggesting that the forms of knowledge constitute the curriculum as

such, and he allows for the ways in which distinct disciplines or forms of knowledge exist alongside other important classifications of knowledge. These he describes as 'fields' of knowledge, 'formed by building together round specific objects, or phenomena, or practical pursuits, knowledge that is characteristically rooted elsewhere in more than one discipline'. Such fields of knowledge may be theoretical or practical and may include elements of what Hirst calls moral knowledge. In the end, however, his position rests upon the forms of knowledge as these find expression in curriculum disciplines: 'It is the distinct disciplines that basically constitute the range of unique ways we have of understanding experience if to these is added the category of moral knowledge'.[17]

The contributions of philosophers such as Hirst in terms of the forms of knowledge, or Phenix in terms of 'realms of meaning'[18] have been associated with the so-called classical model of the curriculum.[19] According to this, the curriculum must give expression to the nature of knowledge itself in such a way that its public forms determine educational objectives. Romantics have, on the other hand, tended to argue for a less structured and objectives-oriented view of education as a process of a rather more indeterminate kind, which characteristically involves learners rather than knowledge-objectives as the primary focus of attention.

But the classical knowledge-based view of education as an induction into public forms or traditions of knowledge, meaning and discourse has stimulated the further issue of whether the distinction between content and aims of education is of any substantive use. Few would deny that in practical terms this is the case and that the content of education must to some extent be determined by factors other than that of the logic of knowledge itself:

> ... in practice all things are not in fact equal and decisions about the content of courses cannot be taken without careful regard to the abilities and interests of the students for whom they are designed.[20]

Curriculum and Culture

The aims, as well as the content of education, have been traditionally an area of philosophical concern, and the same influential writers who have argued the case for the knowledge-content of education have argued the case for the desirable or worthwhile states of mind associated with forms of knowledge and experience as aims of education. R.S. Peters is perhaps best known in this connection for having treated concepts of education in the style of analytic philosophy. One important consequence of his approach was to demonstrate that analysis of 'education' revealed the intrinsic nature of its aims. Beyond that, Peters argued,[21] to look for one agreed aim of education would be absurd given the distinct criteria represented in the concept of the 'educated man'. However, the 'public' nature of education, which has emerged as a cornerstone of the philosophical content-and-aims case, is still clearly present in Peters' analysis:

> Aims can also relate to principles immanent in procedures of educa-
> tion, such as the importance of freedom and individual self-
> origination. It was argued, however, that if these are to be aims of
> *education*, they can be understood only against a background in
> which the general criteria involved in being educated are taken for
> granted. This is an important point to make against some child-
> centred educators who emphasize principles of procedure with a
> seemingly cavalier disregard for matters of direction and content.[22]

The aims of education are to be understood only by reference to what it means to be an educated person in a particular public tradition. Peters claims to make no substantive pronouncements and only to be analysing a concept of 'education':

> It was, however, suggested that this involves certain formal criteria
> — commitment to modes of thought and conduct that are regarded
> as worth while in themselves, which involve some depth of under-
> standing, and which are not pursued with cavalier disregard for other
> ways of looking at the world. A curriculum is largely composed of
> such activities and forms of awareness.[23]

Questions about what is or is not worth while raise further ethical problems and invoke such principles as freedom and respect for persons which are, Peters argues, 'built-in to procedures of education'. But this philosophy may not approach too near substantive prescriptions, and certainly he makes clear its limited role: 'Philosophy has an important contribution to make to practical wisdom; but it is no substitute for it.'

Thus in the context of both the knowledge-content of the curric-ulum and the aims of education, the abstractions of conceptual analysis give us little sense of the way in which the 'public' relates to the 'social'. The criteria which govern the use of a concept of an 'educated man' do not arise directly out of its analysis, any more than the curriculum arises directly out of the forms of knowledge. Strictly speaking, Peters and Hirst would accept this. But by having recourse to an idea of 'public' traditions or modes of experience[24] they imply that there are limits to what could properly count as the content of the curriculum or the aims of education, and there can be no doubt that theirs is an extremely influential view of the matter. At the same time there are, as Peters says, no agreed aims of education. Nevertheless, in the end, some aims come to prevail, as do some models of the curriculum, and the social processes by which these things happen are important to understand. It is not simply that the style of philosophising would need to be less one of conceptual analysis and more one of prescriptive ethics (Peters suggests Utilitarianism) but rather that an uncritical concept of 'public' forms, traditions or discourses constitutes a fundamental weakness of much philosophical analysis of content and aims of education. It becomes, in other words, quite difficult to separate public forms and criteria from the public accountability of teachers.

The content and aims of education come into a closer relationship when curriculum is approached from a more sociological view, concerned as this is with the social relations of education rather than with its concepts. Here the primary concern is with the way in which, out of the variety of possibilities which the forms and fields of knowledge and the variety of aims which 'education' permit, the curriculum takes shape in historical and social conditions. In practice it is social forces that determine it, although in view of the distinction between the 'public' and the 'social' which is inherent in the way that philosophers and sociologists employ these terms, the connection is not perhaps as obvious as some assume. Stenhouse, for example, puts it like this:

> The school has the task of making available to the young a selection of society's intellectual, emotional and technical capital. It is this capital which I have characterized as 'public traditions'. In our society, schools teach a variety of public traditions. Among the most important are bodies of knowledge; arts; skills; languages; conventions; and values. These traditions, seen from one point of view, exist as social facts; and they are therefore subjects of study for the social scientist.[25]

He goes on to say that: 'The anthropologist and the sociologist use the term *culture* to designate what I have called above "public traditions".' It is certainly true that sociologists concerning themselves with the curriculum have regarded the idea of culture as an important key to understanding, although they have not generally used it as a term synonymous with 'public traditions'.

Sociological thinking about the curriculum focuses upon certain key social processes, as distinct from a philosophical view of it which focuses upon conceptual characteristics of 'knowledge' or 'education'. This has been captured very succinctly by Denis Lawton:

> It seems to me that the school curriculum (in the wider sense) is essentially *a selection from the culture of a society*. Certain aspects of our way of life, certain kinds of knowledge, certain attitudes and values are regarded as so important that their transmission to the next generation is not left to chance in our society but is entrusted to specially-trained professionals (teachers) in elaborate and expensive institutions (schools). Not everything in a culture is regarded as of such importance, and in any case, time is limited, so *selection* has to be made. Different schools may make different kinds of selection from the culture:teachers may have different lists of priorities, but all teachers and all schools make selections of some kind from the culture.[26]

So the idea that the curriculum consists of 'a selection from the culture of a society' opens up a wider range of possibilities for thinking about the curriculum than does the philosophy of knowledge alone, although it does not supersede it as some have supposed. In this way knowledge is located in the social structure, and attention is directed towards what is selected to count as knowledge for educational purposes in a particular context of culture. The problem of what can and what cannot be known in absolute terms remains a philosophical issue, whereas in educational practice — and indeed in the practice of everyday life — knowledge remains selective and relative, and inextricably linked with the purposes to which it can be put. In other words, treating the curriculum as a selection from a culture makes it impossible to distinguish substantively between the aims, content and methods of education: the culture determines not only what is to count as educational knowledge but also the reasons why it should be learned and the legitimate processes by which we learn it. It is not therefore the analytic distinctions of knowledge but the substantive relations of practice that give rise to such issues as that of education versus training, or education versus indoctrination. Such issues arise out of the social processes of knowledge and the social purposes and methods of education itself.

In locating the curriculum in the social structure and among social processes, the sociological approach also stresses the role of professional people, such as teachers, who play a large part in the selection from the culture which comes, in the end, to be made. In this context too the way is opened to the study of the curriculum in terms of class, status and power, and thus to relate it to broader themes of educational provision and policy. In recent years the curriculum focus has grown ever sharper both in the academic content of education theory and in the implementation of social policies of education, in the realisation that, in the end, it is the issue of curriculum content in relation to aims and methods which must be resolved as a condition of resolving all the others.

So an important consequence of the sociological approach to the curriculum has been to raise it as a social and political issue, rather than to leave it as something analyticaly related to the concept of 'education' itself. The sociological approach has, in fact, raised the issue of the curriculum to that level of ideological controversy which often takes the form of 'progressivism' versus 'traditionalism' in educational debate, by implying that in engaging in such debates people are expressing what are essentially political views rather than merely technical positions on the subject.

Nevertheless, the more extreme views about education and the curriculum arise in the first instance from the earliest attempts to ground educational issues in sociological theory. Eggleston, for example, sets out the inevitability of thinking of the ways in which knowledge is defined, distributed and legitimated in all societies, once a sociological view of the curriculum begins to be assumed.[27] And although some earlier sociologists, such as Mannheim, had suggested the importance of a sociology of knowledge for a sociology of education, it is only relatively recently that this has culmimated in a sociological study of what is taught in schools. External factors of rapid social and technological change have led to the focus upon what was previously the 'taken-for-granted' curriculum, which flowed directly from a concept of 'education' based upon an uncritical idea of 'public' knowledge. In fact, what was taken for granted was very much a source of practical problems for generations of teachers, pupils and parents. Perhaps one reason for the resurgence of a sociological view of the curriculum is that it can be related quite closely to these kinds of problems; in response, the sociology of the school is represented in a growing body of literature.[28] Schooling has become a social and political issue, rather than a merely technical one, in societies undergoing rapid change and transformation:

> In consequence the curriculum has come to be seen more clearly as an important instrument, if not the most important instrument, in the process whereby the school helps the young to assume adult roles. More importantly, the curriculum is also viewed as a central factor in the establishment and maintenance of the power and authority structures both of the society and the school. In consequence sociologists have become interested not only in curriculum content, method and evaluation, but also in the origins and support of the implicit and explicit values that are embodied in the curriculum. They are interested in how the curriculum is legitimated, in why decisions, both overt and covert, are made as they are and in the social factors that determine the choice of subjects and their content and method.[29]

The 'values that are embodied in the curriculum' have been described as the 'selection from the culture', and they are certainly what sociologists would describe as cultural values. However, the culture of a society permits a variety of values to co-exist, and there is a danger of assuming that culture has some kind of independent existence; independent, that is, of the institutional structure and material base or economy of a particular society. Nor are the ways in which knowledge is defined, distributed and legitimated always unambiguous. What is clear is that different groups, sometimes characterised as subcultures, gain access to different kinds of knowledge and that these knowledges are differentially ranked in a hierarchy of status or legitimacy. G.H. Bantock claimed that the failure of a traditional educational system such as that of Britain arose precisely because the cultural conditions from which it derived made it irrelevant to those of a modern mass society.

In modern conditions, Bantock argued for a form of popular education which would reflect the onset of a popular culture.[30] By popular, said Bantock, 'I intend in the first place a general reference to those children with whom our present schooling would appear to have failed.' It has failed, he suggests, because the tradition of education as an induction into public forms of knowledge and experience bears no relation to the characteristics of working-class culture. Bantock's point is one against what was earlier described as an uncritical concept of 'public' derived as much from a professional view of accountability as from a philosophical analysis of knowledge; a concept which entirely fails to capture the social diversity of the forms of knowledge and experience. A popular education, argues Bantock, could only succeed if it reflected the curriculum implications of working-class culture and stressed the affective rather than the cognitive domain of learning. What is wanted is not a kind of watered-down high-culture education for all, but rather a curriculum reflecting practical, concrete and specific life situations of home, work and leisure. It should have reference to human relations and to the role of the popular media in people's lives; it should be an education of the emotions and for artistic creativity and leisure pursuits. Such an education, according to Bantock, would reflect communally-oriented experience rather than the socially-isolated and literary education of tradition. Clearly this is a very different view of the curriculum from that derived out of the 'public knowledge' analysis of Hirst and Peters, which stressed the centrality of conceptual and cognitive learning not to the exclusion of the rest but in such a way as to make it a precondition of worthwhile states of mind and experience. In so far as the 'public knowledge' view underpins that of a liberal education then its curriculum principles seem quite opposed to that of a popular education.

These arguments about culture in the context of education have revolved often around the issue of whether it is possible to speak of a 'common culture' in a complex modern society or whether there exists rather a plurality of cultural sources and possibilities arising out of class, ethnic, demographic or generational diversity. It is an issue which has been extensively discussed, especially in the context of a common curriculum, by Denis Lawton.[31] He takes the view that class differences, at least, are affective rather than cognitive and have to do with attitudes and values rather than knowledge, and that this gives no grounds for a separate curriculum of 'popular' education:

> [social class differences], although important, do not today allow us to identify a distinctively working-class culture. A heritage of knowledge and beliefs which includes mathematics, science, history, literature and, more recently, film and television is shared by all classes. Real differences in social class sub-cultures should not obscure this communality of heritage.[32]

Lawton's view turns out to be one of a more sociologically informed 'public knowledge' account of the curriculum, and with others he has been critical of the view that knowledge is socially constructed and therefore in a sense culturally relative and the further view that rationality itself is merely a convention. In this connection he is concerned, as have been many curriculum theorists, with the work of M.F.D. Young.[33]

Curriculum and Control

Since 1970 or thereabouts curriculum theory has been further stimulated through attempts to synthesise issues of knowledge and culture into an essentially political account of the role of the curriculum in social change and social control. Working within sociological and Marxist perspectives, writers associated with Young began to examine and question the taken-for-granted or common-sense assumptions of curriculum theory and practice. The definition, distribution and evaluation of knowledge, they tended to argue, was inevitably a political process and constituted a way of looking at the class relations of capitalist society. In this way some explicit connections were made between education and social control.[34]

In terms of knowledge the view was taken that, far from constituting a universal structure of public forms accessible to logic and rationality, it reflected the capacity of a ruling class to determine the definition, distribution and evaluation of knowledge itself. This could be done, it was argued, in such a way that knowledge was still widely regarded as constituted by public forms and therefore universally accessible. The reality, however, was taken to be the impossibility of public forms of knowledge in a class society which lacked any structural basis for a common culture. Power, rather than culture, came to constitute the focus of argument in curriculum studies, and the transformation of education was seen to be closely related to the possibility of the transformation of society. As far as curriculum theory was concerned, the 1970s represented a great age of model-building as theorists worked out the implications of the issues in knowledge, culture and power which had come to the fore. It proved a convenient, if rather abstract, way of dealing in broad terms with issues being raised simultaneously on various levels of discourse: philosophical, sociological and political. Thus there were devised classical and romantic models,[35] along with received and reflexive ideological models,[36] whilst theorists writing more from a teaching orientation derived research models of curriculum development.[37] In the public mind it tended to appear simply as an issue between traditional and progressive models of teaching method, although of course in terms of curriculum theory much more than method was at stake.

Michael F.D. Young himself explored the territory in these terms in the course of setting out his own view of the issue. This he presented in an article on 'Curriculum Change: Limits and Possibilities'.[38] According to such a view, curriculum change and social change are indivisible, although he is still seeing the issue in terms of the school curriculum and the role of the teacher:

> I am concerned with the problems of change in education — with developing a theory or theories that may enable those involved in education to become aware of the ways of changing their or their pupils' or students' educational experience, even if this leads us to conceive of teachers' struggles as not independent from other struggles in the work places and communities where people live.[39]

Young takes two familiarly opposed models of the curriculum as his starting-point: the 'public traditions' of knowledge account founded in the philosophical analysis of Hirst and Peters, and the learner-centred and more problematic account of the curriculum founded in phenomenology. His own terms for these models are, respectively, 'curriculum as fact' and 'curriculum as practice': the commodity view of knowledge as contrasted with a view of the curriculum as rooted in the 'intentions and actions of men'. But Young argues that either model may be a form of mystification: one because it seems to give the curriculum an existence independent of human relations, the other because it seems to reduce this social reality to 'the subjective intentions and actions of teachers and pupils'. Neither, he is saying, does justice to the ways in which knowledge is conceptualised in concrete historical conditions — the ways in which the 'public forms' come to find expression in cultures and social structures and take on familiar appearance as subjects or disciplines.

According to Young, the 'curriculum as fact' describes precisely that process by which, as was argued earlier, 'public forms of knowledge and experience' can be confused with the public accountability of teachers and learners:

> a view of 'curriculum as fact' expresses many of the prevailing assumptions or theories of practitioners, both teachers and pupils. In that most of what passes for curriculum theory, whether of that name or derived from philosophy, psychology or sociology, con-

firms such assumptions, it can do little more than redescribe a world that teachers and pupils already know.[40]

No possibilities for change are presented in the 'curriculum as fact': it leaves teachers and learners alike powerless in the face of education 'as a thing' and without the means to understand it as a collective production of social relations.

But the view of the 'curriculum as practice', although countering that of the structures of knowledge, also has serious weaknesses. Locating the reality of the curriculum in teachers' classroom practice will confront them, says Young, with the limits on their possibilities of action as well as those of a theory which lacks the capacity to locate such limits in concrete historical conditions. A genuinely *critical* theory must take as its starting-point people's everyday views of the world, and the idea of the 'curriculum as fact' is, Young argues, just such a view. Failure to do this constitutes a major weakness of the view of curriculum as practice.

A critical account of curriculum — one which *is* concerned with the possibilities of change in education — will therefore transcend the dichotomies of fact and practice and it suggests to Young three directions to follow. The first is concerned with the need for a practical change in the relations between theorists and those teachers and learners who are the object of theory: the validity of theory must be measured in terms of changes and transformations in teacher and pupil practice. The second direction is to take into account the ways in which conventional and received accounts of the curriculum are sustained not only by the classroom practices of teachers and learners but by everyone involved in education:

> If the educational experience of both teachers and pupils is to become a realistic possibility of human liberation, then this is going to involve many others who have no direct involvement with the school, and much action by teachers and pupils that would not be seen as either confined to school or in conventional terms necessarily educational at all.[41]

The third direction set by Young for a 'social transformation' curriculum lies in the importance of a historical perspective: to understand the economic and political character of education and transcend the received view of it, it is necessary to understand it as an outcome of conflicts and struggles rather than as the evolution of 'public' forms and traditions of knowledge and experience.

It is significant that the problem of the curriculum has been seen as a central one in radical education theory and in the so-called 'new' sociology of education with which Young's name has been prominently associated. The apparently diverse roots of these recent developments lie in a humanistic Marxism as well as in a phenomenological view of knowledge and experience. Many of the most important contributions to the debate have therefore taken the form of analysing education under capitalism. This has certainly had the effect of directing attention to the economic system as one of the 'received' elements in education theory and practice, and has therefore succeeded in bringing about a political debate about the curriculum as a form of social control in capitalist societies. So the second of Young's directions for a 'social transformation' curriculum has been followed in the pursuit of all those ways in which schooling gives expression to the relations of production under capitalism. But it is doubtful whether the first of his directions has seen much progress: the relations between theorists and the objects of their theorising, teachers and learners, have, if anything, grown even further apart.[42]

However, Marxist analysis has, especially in the United States, notably contributed to a critique of liberal and progressive ideologies of 'open access' or compensatory education programmes by placing them in a wider class and political context. S. Bowles and H. Gintis, for example, analysed schooling in terms of the way in which it reproduces capitalist relations of production.[43] They meant by this that the educational system, as it is reformed in directions of openness and relevance to people's needs, constitutes an imprtant way in which the class conflict inherent in capitalism is managed and deflected. It is a view sharing the logical characteristics of all the 'social control' ideas of education and is similar in outcome to that of Althusser's view of education as the dominant ideological state apparatus.[44] In detail there are considerable differences between such views in terms of the state, the economy and ideology, but taken together they provide a critical theory of the received view of education and the curriculum.

Bowles and Gintis, for example, trace the connection between progressive, learner-centred and needs-based education (with its corollaries of testing and counselling) and the acceptance by learners of their own situations as a true reflection of their merit rather than of an exploitative system of social relations. The consciousness of emerging new classes, such as a 'white-collar proletariat', is manipulated through the education system so that they are effectively prepared to accept their subordinate roles in the occupational system. In other words, under capitalism, the hierarchies of schooling serve to legitimate in people's minds the hierarchies of the workplace, controlling as it were their aspirations and neutralising conflicts which would otherwise threaten the stability of the system.

Bowles and Gintis showed some ways in which schooling reproduces the economic relations of production under capitalism, although they achieved this in a rather deterministic way, assuming a fairly uncomplicated relationship between the economy and the value-system or culture of a society. The account of social and cultural reproduction associated with Bourdieu provides a somewhat different view of this relationship.[45] He is concerned with the same processes but adopts a rather different theoretical perspective by considering how far the educational and other cultural systems achieve an apparent autonomy from the economic base of society, as opposed to the economic determination of Bowles and Gintis. The issue, as it was for Michael Young, was one of exploring people's everyday view of the world as a real view rather than one of false class consciousness or some other kind of reduction inherent in economic determinism. What are the processes according to which people come to accept the connection between social selection for elite membership and 'natural' talent or ability as a universal one, whereas it may only be demonstrable in individual instances? In Bourdieu's terms these are cultural processes having some degree of independence from the economic and social processes; they stand for the taken-for-granted or received systems of value and belief, and they confer legitimacy upon the economic and social processes themselves. The significance of a concept of a 'common culture' is therefore very different in Bourdieu's mind from, say, a belief such as Lawton's in a common culture grounded in public forms of knowledge. The only way to explain the selection functions of education systems is therefore to explain the ways in which an elite culture takes on a reality as a common culture in society at large.

The name given to such educational and cultural processes was that of social and cultural reproduction.[46] In this way, in societies such as our own, the material interests of a dominant class are served by an educational system which imposes universal meaning and legitimacy upon a so-called 'common culture'. It is possible also to distinguish social from cultural reproduction as mutually reinforcing elements of an identical process of transmission. For by cultural reproduction is meant a transmission of values in the whole content of socialisation, which is constituted by both the home and the school in the kind of society under consideration. This is an element in a wider process of social reproduction which describes the way in which material conditions, technology and manpower and so on, are themselves the object of the education system. The 'social capital' which is reproduced therefore represents the conditions of material life of society. What 'cultural capital' stands for is the kind of significances, meanings and values which have been traditionally associated in society with its material conditions. The transformation of 'public forms of knowledge and experience' into 'cultural capital' has in fact come to represent a major ideological shift in the theory of the curriculum. The significance of the curriculum for Bourdieu was largely in terms of the part it plays in cultural reproduction rather than in the somewhat wider context of social reproduction. This distinction may be a highly abstract one but in fact it is reinforced to some extent by the differences of emphasis between the kinds of sociological research into the French education system, engaged in by Bourdieu, and that into the British system. In the latter case the curriculum has been considered as an instrument rather of social reproduction, and there has been more emphasis upon the problem of education and social mobility and recruitment rather than upon the cultural significance of the curriculum. Perhaps the form of the 'cultural capital' of British society does not give us such ready access to an idea of 'culture' as does that of French society. The predominantly empirical and analytic public forms of knowledge which characterise the British tradition may make it more difficult to think in terms of a curriculum which both serves a multitude of real individual interests and yet at the same time really constitutes an instrument of cultural reproduction.

The connection between the curriculum and ideology and between the curriculum and power has in recent years become a major theoretical issue. Michael W. Apple, in his book *Ideology and Curriculum*, has concentrated upon the ideological role of school knowledge in the processes of social and cultural reproduction:

> . . . one of our basic problems as educators and as political beings . . . is to begin to grapple with ways of understanding how the kinds of cultural resources and symbols schools select and organise are dialectically related to the kinds of normative and conceptual consciousness 'required' by a stratified society.[47]

The idea of the curriculum as a 'selection from the culture of a society' has led inexorably to a much closer examination of the selection as a process, and one related to other social and cultural processes in society. The original idea tended towards a fairly abstract view of 'education', together with a rather static concept of 'public' forms of knowledge and modes of experience, and a relatively unproblematic role for teachers engaged in the process of selection. 'Public' knowledge, it was suggested, could be associated with a professional concern for accountability as well as with a philosophical concept of objectivity or rationality. In any case, the dimensions of power and control in both knowledge and society are much more at issue in curriculum theory than they once were, and the original objective of the 'new' sociologists of education, which was to question the received or professional accounts of the curriculum, continues to be pursued.

According to Apple, three aspects of an education system need to be understood as somehow determined by the structural relations of society. These are the school as an institution, the knowledge forms and the educator him- or herself. This is not to be done in a narrow sense of economic determinism or a direct kind of social control but rather one having regard to the concept of hegemony as contributed most notably by Gramsci. Thus, as an alternative to the more simplistic forms of economic determinism or social control, Apple argues that:

> . . . there is a somewhat more flexible position which speaks of determination as a complex nexus of relationships which, in their final moment, are economically rooted, that exert pressures and set limits on cultural practice, including schools. Thus, the cultural sphere is not a 'mere reflection' of economic practices. Instead, the influence, the 'reflection' or determination, is highly mediated by forms of human action. It is mediated by the specific activities, contradictions, and relationships among real men and women like ourselves — as they go about their day-to-day lives in the institutions which organize these lives.[48]

The idea of control is inherent in the 'constitutive principles, codes, and especially the commonsense consciousness and practices underlying our lives'. Hegemony itself, therefore, according to Apple, 'refers to an organized assemblage of meanings and practices, the central, effective and dominant system of meanings, values and actions which are *lived*'. Reflecting upon the work of Raymond Williams, he is thinking of schools, along with other institutions, as agents of cultural and ideological hegemony because they are not so much agents of a public as of a 'selective' tradition; ideology, hegemony and selective tradition now represent major analytic categories of curriculum analysis. As in the case of Bowles and Gintis, Apple sees 'progressivism' in education as a fairly superficial development, one which largely leaves untouched the 'latent ideological content' of the curriculum:

> The movement, say, in social studies towards 'process orientated' curriculum is a case in point. We teach social 'inquiry' as a set of 'skills', as a series of methods that will enable students 'to learn how to inquire themselves'. While this is certainly better than the more rote models of teaching which prevailed in previous decades, at the same time it can actually depoliticize the study of social life.[49]

A theme running through these recent developments in curriculum theory is clearly that of the need to 'politicise' the issues, and to consider knowledge and culture in terms of social class and social control. It has been a very influential theme, although in an important sense it has divorced curriculum theory from the more practical or technical concerns of teachers and policy-makers as they have continued to go about the business of curriculum development in schools and education systems. Issues of, for example, science and mathematics teaching, or of the desirability of a common curriculum, have continued to be pursued. More often than not, however, these are seen as issues in the context of school organisation rather than in that of the politics of knowledge, and there is a recurrent tendency to reduce the political content of education wherever possible. But some issues, such as the education of 'socially disadvantaged' groups, obtrude politics and in these cases curriculum issues can be directly related to the kind of theoretical developments which have been sketched above. In these cases the wider issues of knowledge, culture and power become inescapable unless the most superficial treatment of them is to result.

To some educationalists the association of power and the curriculum seems to have gone too far and taken some wrong directions. Such a critic is William Taylor, in his acknowledgement that 'There has been a pretty sharp shift in recent years from authority talk to power talk about education.'[50] In common with writers such as Stenhouse and Lawton, and addressing a largely professional audience, Taylor tends to see the issue particularly in terms of the consequences of the shift of emphasis for the teacher and the teacher's role:

> In some circles in this country and in the United States, to talk about the authority of the teacher, the authority of the subject, the

authority of the parent (within the home, of course), is distinctly démodé. The disenchanted, demythologised, demystified world of the professional educator makes better sense in terms of power talk — a world of coercion, compulsion, oppression, force, manipulation, indoctrination, ideology — rather than in the language of particular forms of authority.[51]

Authority, which is constituted by the legitimate exercise of power, seems to Taylor to be an inescapable condition of social life, handed down from one generation to the next by way of public traditions of knowledge and experience. This being the case, it is not possible to avoid the limitations upon our freedom of action which are constituted by traditional beliefs and practices: 'we must begin from where we are'. Much recent discussion of the curriculum, argues Taylor, ignores this basic fact, particularly in the case of what he calls 'the New Criticism'. As a result, and perhaps out of a misguided sincerity and concern, this kind of theorising 'undermines institutional structures and practices that sustain possibilities of individual freedom and democratic pluralism, and is very imprecise about the structures and practices that would characterise post-capitalist social and political life'. He goes on[52] to summarise the kinds of criticisms of radical curriculum theory which have been voiced in recent years.

In the first place there are the philosophical arguments about knowledge, and the view that relativism tends to collapse into solipsism and the paradoxical dependence of reality upon our concepts of it. By a parallel logic, 'demystification' and 'demythologising' also tend to collapse into a kind of crude 'debunking' exercise, in which evidence and rational argument have little part to play. It may also be doubted whether differences and forms of discrimination can always be directly linked to the particular interests of groups or classes in society, as is implied by a critique of education systems in capitalist societies. The role of teachers has been defended against a view of them as instruments of control and as agents of 'middle-class values' which have been assumed to be identical with 'western culture'. The traditional 'mainstream' sociology, with its emphasis upon the importance of socialisation, has been temporarily eclipsed and along with this a loss of objectivity has occurred, making for a tendency to romanticise working-class culture.

Other criticisms of radical curriculum theory listed by Taylor are that it casts doubt upon the possibility of knowledge by reducing it to the property of a dominant class and by attributing a 'false consciousness' to those who disagree with such an analysis. This is related to an unsupported assumption of a degree of alienation and disaffection among significant numbers of the working class in capitalist countries. Critics of radical theory say it has neglected the potentially relevant historical and comparative perspective which a critique of capitalist society requires, and also any contrary evidence regarding the role of liberal ideology in maintaining such a society. In more practical terms, radical curriculum theory has been charged with a failure to provide the possibility of objective criteria of performance, so that it becomes impossible to evaluate achievement, and on these terms the whole business of curriculum development is rendered problematic. Finally, exponents of the 'New Criticism' have themselves been criticised for a failure to respond constructively to these kinds of charges, seeking refuge instead in pleas of prejudice and victimisation.

These are the kinds of criticisms of, and doubts about, the radical theories which Taylor outlines. The new approach, he would agree, does not constitute a single monolithic view — it has evolved and it contains significant differences of emphasis and ideology — but nevertheless criticisms of it have arisen from a wide range of perspectives not always on the political right. The strength of its appeal, he suggests, lies in the intellectual influence of Marxism, its focus on classroom practice, its rather simplistic and all-embracing perspective, its fashionable appeal in social terms, its idealistic settings, and finally in its appeal as a form of esoteric knowledge to those who occupy the lowest statuses in the hierarchy of the education system. Taylor's own view is that we can get little further in understanding the politics of the curriculum unless we can reintroduce the notion of authority — the public forms and the traditional forms of authority in knowledge, culture and politics. Above all, the notion of authority which these public and traditional forms confer upon the teacher in the classroom.

Summary

The purpose of this chapter was to demonstrate the concerns of curriculum theory within what was described at the outset as the dominant paradigm of schooling. It is clear that these concerns are with knowledge, culture and power, and that recently they have found expression in such terms as ideology, reproduction and social control. At the same time as theoretical issues at this level were being debated, curriculum analysis and development was taking place in practice, in system, school and classroom. Sometimes these levels of theory and practice came into relation, but often they did not. Radical curriculum theory tends to resist the reduction of substantive theoretical and ideological issues to the level of mere techniques: this is the basis of its criticism of progressive education. Nevertheless, as its critics agree, it has influenced educational thinking, especially amongst teachers themselves. It seems that the idea of the curriculum as content has proved far too narrow a conception of the education process to contain the theoretical issues which have now been raised about it, nor has it proved practical to divorce the issue of the curriculum content from that of its aims and methods.

Notes and References

1. Colin Richards, *Curriculum Studies: An Introductory Annotated Bibliography* (Nafferton: Studies in Education, 1978).

2. For a recent example, see Derek Legge, *The Education of Adults in Britain* (Milton Keynes: Open University Press, 1982).

3. Philip H. Taylor and Colin Richards, *An Introduction to Curriculum Studies* (Windsor: NFER Publishing Company, 1979), p. 11.

4. Ivan Illich, *Deschooling Society* London: Calder and Boyars, 1971).

5. Ralph W. Tyler, *Basic Principles of Curriculum and Instruction* (Chicago: University of Chicago Press, 1949), p. 1.

6. See, for example, Lawrence Stenhouse, *An Introduction to Curriculum Research and Development* (London: Heinemann, 1975).

7. Tyler, *Basic Principles of Curriculum*, p. 44.

8. P.H. Hirst and R.S. Peters, *The Logic of Education* (London: Routledge and Kegan Paul, 1970), p. 60.

9. Ibid.

10. B.S. Bloom, *Taxonomy of Educational Objectives* (London: Longman, 1956).

11. Hirst and Peters, *Logic of Education*, p. 62.

12. Ibid., p. 71.

13. See Richard Pring, 'Curriculum Integration', *The Philosophy of Education*, ed. R.S. Peters (London: Oxford University Press, 1973).

14. In *Philosophical Analysis and Education*, ed. R.D. Archambault (London: Routledge and Kegan Paul, 1965).

15. Ibid., p. 128.

16. Ibid., pp. 129-30.

17. Ibid., p. 131.

18. P. Phenix, *Realms of Meaning* (New York: McGraw-Hill, 1964).

19. See Denis Lawton, *Social Change, Educational Theory and Curriculum Planning* (London: Hodder and Stoughton, 1973), Chapter 2.

20. Hirst and Peters, *Logic of Education*, pp. 134-5.

21. R.S. Peters, 'Aims of Education – A Conceptual Inquiry', *The Philosophy of Education*, ed. R.S. Peters (London: Oxford University Press, 1973), pp. 27-9.

22. Ibid., p. 27.

23. Ibid., p. 28.

24. For an example of the source in empirical philosophy of the idea of 'public' traditions see Michael Oakeshott, *Rationalism in Politics* (London: Methuen, 1962).

25. Stenhouse, *Introduction to Curriculum Research*, p. 6.

26. Denis Lawton, *Class, Culture and the Curriculum* (London: Routledge and Kegan Paul, 1975), pp. 6-7.

27. John Eggleston, *The Sociology of the School Curriculum* (London: Routledge and Kegan Paul, 1977), Chapters 1 and 2.

28. For a recent example see S.J. Ball, *Beachside Comprehensive: A Case Study of Secondary Schooling* (Cambridge: Cambridge University Press, 1981).

29. Eggleston, *Sociology of the School Curriculum*, p. 6.

30. G.H. Bantock, 'Towards a Theory of Popular Education', *The Curriculum: Context, Design and Development*, ed. R. Hooper (Edinburgh: Oliver and Boyd, 1971).

31. Lawton, *Class, Culture and the Curriculum*, Chapter 3.

32. Ibid., p. 114.

33. Michael F.D. Young (ed.), *Knowledge and Control* (London: Collier-Macmillan, 1971).

34. Rachel Sharp and Anthony Green, *Education and Social Control* (London: Routledge and Kegan Paul, 1975).

35. Lawton, *Social Change, Educational Theory and Curriculum Planning*, op. cit. Chapter 2.

36. Eggleston, *Sociology of the School Curriculum*, Chapter 4.

37. Stenhouse, *Introduction to Curriculum Research*, Chapter 9.

38. Reprinted in *Schooling and Capitalism: A Sociological Reader*, ed. R. Dale *et al.* (London: Routledge and Kegan Paul/Open University Press, 1976).

39. Ibid., p. 185.

40. Ibid., p. 187.

41. Ibid., p. 190.

42. See, for example, H. Cohen and A. Miller, 'Curriculum Theory and Practice: Some Guidelines for Discussion', *Curriculum*, vol. 1., no. 1 (Spring 1980).

43. Samuel Bowles and Herbert Gintis, *Schooling in Capitalist America: Educational Reform and the Contradictions of Economic Life* (London: Routledge and Kegan Paul, 1976).

44. Louis Althusser, 'Ideology and the Ideological State Apparatuses: Notes Towards an Investigation', *Education: Structure and Society*, ed. B.R. Cosin (Harmondsworth: Penguin Books/Open University Press, 1972).

45. Pierre Bourdieu, 'Systems of Education and Systems of Thought', *Knowledge and Control*, ed. Michael F.D. Young.

46. Pierre Bourdieu and Jean-Claude Passeron, *Reproduction in Education, Society and Culture* (London: Sage Publications, 1977).

47. Michael W. Apple, *Ideology and Curriculum* (London: Routledge and Kegan Paul, 1980), p. 2.

48. Ibid., p. 4.

49. Ibid., p. 7.

50. William Taylor, 'Power and the Curriculum', *Power and the Curriculum: Issues in Curriculum Studies*, ed. C. Richards (Nafferton: Studies in Education, 1978).

51. Ibid., p. 7.

52. Ibid., pp. 10-11.

2 ADULT EDUCATION THEORY AND THE CURRICULUM

Introduction

Adult, continuing or lifelong education is not often conceptualised in terms of knowledge, culture and power. Indeed, it is not often conceptualised in curriculum terms at all. That is not to say that curriculum matters are not of concern here, for indeed much work has been done in the area of teaching and learning methods and many innovations have been achieved in this sector of education. However, conceptualisation has tended to be at the level of technique and strategy rather than that of educational theory, as has been the case with school education. If anything, conceptualisation in adult and continuing education has increasingly reflected a view of it as a form of social policy rather than of education as such, and this perhaps constitutes one reason for a general absence of curriculum theorising about it. Thus the primary conceptual framework of adult and continuing education has been constructed in terms of needs, access and provision rather than in terms of knowledge, culture and power, and this conceptual framework will be explored further in the next chapter. Some fairly ambitious claims are sometimes made for adult education and its capacity to ameliorate social problems or contribute to their solution, and it would generally be seen as a progressive force in society. But such claims and such a view of it depend for verification upon a more theoretical view of adult and lifelong education in a curriculum context of knowledge, culture and power. Otherwise there is the danger of an inadequately argued educational radicalism in the context of social conservatism, which is a conceptual style sometimes represented in the 'structures of provision' approach to adult education. That educational progressivism is not necessarily connected with social structural change, and indeed may actually constitute a form of social control in conditions of political reaction, has been argued with some success in recent years in the context of schooling. Arguments in this area of conceptualisation need working through if adult and continuing education is to be located in the social structure and in theoretical and ideological terms, rather than in unexamined borrowings from social policy and organisation theory. It is, of course, possible to deny that adult education sufficiently resembles school education for them to draw upon the same kind of

38

conceptual frameworks. In practice, however, few would adopt such a position, preferring instead to construct a framework of 'adult characteristics' and accepting that any educational situation, properly so called, is one in which teaching or learning are intended outcomes.

This chapter is concerned with 'adult characteristics' as a basis of adult education theory, and it is hoped to demonstrate that it would be difficult, if not impossible, to derive a curriculum theory of adult education from any 'adult characteristics' approach as such. And yet if we are to treat adult education *as* education and make informed judgements about its social functions and potential then the kinds of conceptualisation that are made in the area of school education — conceptualisations of the curriculum — are inevitable. It is in these terms that it is necessary to investigate the relation between what has been called the dominant paradigm of the school curriculum and the ways in which we conceptualise adult learning and teaching. In other words, the question is one of whether it is possible to speak of a distinctive body of principles, theories and practices constituted by adult, as contrasted with school, education, but to do this not in terms of adult characteristics but in terms of curriculum theory itself.

Adult Education Theory

It is certainly assumed that a distinctive body of principles, theories and practices constitutes some form of adult education knowledge in something of the sense in which Hirst himself preferred to speak of a 'field' of knowledge:

> What is meant by a field here is in fact simply a collection of knowledge from various forms which has unity solely because this knowledge all relates to some object or interest. There is no inherent logical structure which gives unity to the domain. There are no concepts of a kind peculiar to the field. And the field is not concerned with the validation of distinctive statements according to unique criteria. It follows from this that whereas the advancement of a form of knowledge depends on the development of the relevant conceptual scheme and its wider application according to its canons, the advancement of a field is a far more complex affair. It consists in the development and application of whatever forms of knowledge are considered valuable and relevant in coming to understand the selected topic.[1]

Now the fact that adult education constitutes in the eyes of many of its practitioners a profession, and that it is a subject of study in universities, seems to suggest that it is a body of knowledge distinguishable as theory and distinctively to do with adult learning and teaching. But it is immediately obvious that it is by no means clear whether such a body of knowledge constitutes, in Hirst's terms, a 'form' or a 'field'. On the face of it, in so far as theoretical considerations come into such adult education training and qualification programmes, it constitutes a 'field' of knowledge and is based upon the contributory 'disciplines of education' long familiar in teacher training for school education: philosophy, psychology, sociology, history and so on.

However, it might be more accurate to say that adult education in theoretical terms — and as it is expressed in academic and training courses — is a 'field' of knowledge aspiring to the status of a 'form' of knowledge. For by a 'form' of knowledge Hirst surely meant something much more basic and fundamental:

> The division of modes of experience and knowledge suggested here is thus a fundamental categoreal division, based on the range of such irreducible categories which we at present seem to have ... What we are suggesting is that within the domain of objective experience and knowledge, there are such radical differences of kind that experience and knowledge of one form is neither equatable with, nor reducible to, that of any other form.[2]

In short, the 'adult characteristics' approach to the construction of adult education theory represents an attempt to make out that the principles, theories and practices of adult education are, in an analogous sense, 'neither equatable with, nor reducible to' those of other kinds of education — primarily, of course, those of schooling. This is clearly a useful way of looking at the matter, but it is important to understand that it arises both out of the exigencies of professional practice and a kind of 'academic drift' from a 'field' to a 'form' of knowledge. In fact it is not difficult to demonstrate that a curriculum theory of adult education cannot be derived from such premises, since it fails utterly to account for the problem of the definition, distribution and evaluation of adult knowledge in a context of culture and power. There are doubts, too, as to whether this would constitute an educational theory at all. For it is generally agreed at least that no single academic discipline, no single 'form' of knowledge, could serve alone as the basis of education theory. And yet the three kinds of 'adult characteristics' approaches which will be examined in this chapter do tend to arise rather narrowly within the conceptual framework of such a single discipline: philosophy, psychology, or else somewhere in the historical and social science areas of structure and organisation.

The three approaches to be looked at are: first, that based upon a philosophical or analytic concept of 'adult knowledge'; second, the kind of psychologically-based adult learning theory which has been called 'andragogy', the concepts of which have been mostly of a technical, methodological or procedural kind; and finally, the approach through structure, organisation and strategy, the concepts of which have tended to be prescriptive rather than analytic or procedural. All three levels of discourse, analytic, procedural and prescriptive, are important in education theory but not so much singly as in relation to one another and, above all, in a context of learning and teaching practice. And this is where the difficulty arises in constructing a general theory of adult education, in attempting to move it from a 'field' to a 'form' of knowledge based upon adult learning and teaching practices. Any attempt to challenge or reconstruct the dominant curriculum paradigm of schooling from this perspective raises the issue of education theory as such, and it is important to understand this as a problematic and controversial area but one which is inevitably involved in, for example, an exegesis or critique of andragogy.

Generations of teachers in training have failed to see the point or the relevance of much of the theoretical element in their courses: its concerns have seemed to them far too removed from problems of classroom practice to spend valuable time upon. Sometimes — but not, perhaps, very often — they have correctly identified theory and its more esoteric ramifications with the social status of a profession and its need for a basis in abstract knowledge. One reason for the resurgence of interest in curriculum categories reflects this dissatisfaction with abstract theory: such categories seem much more closely related to classroom practices. But there have been other reasons too for such resistance. For one thing, education theory is itself highly problematic, so much so that teachers in training were confronted with the issue of whether there was such a thing as education theory at all. It seemed that if theorists themselves could not decide this, it was unlikely to be a worthwhile way of spending time in training. Nor is it likely that resistance to theory was simply a manifestation of an unintellectual cultural tradition: theoretical physics has not seemed irrelevant as such to teachers training in the area of science. And it was not difficult, either, to understand the sense in which good teaching practice embodied theoretical principles. The point seemed to be that by 'theory' it was assumed was meant the kind of thing it stands for in science: that scientific theory was a model for all theorising. But theories of education are not scientific theories, and this point has not been lost on education theorists. In the context of adult and lifelong education, however, it seems a point still worth making: that a theory in this context is a theory of *practice*, not one of adult learning, adult needs or adult provision, all of which may, in principle, constitute proper objects of *scientific* investigation and research. The distinction between a scientific and an educational theory has been stressed by Hirst in a way that follows on his analysis of the forms and fields of knowledge, and so may conveniently be described here.

Educational Theory

The forms and the fields of knowledge which Hirst describes constitute the logical patterning of the ways in which we know things, and they function as cognitive maps. But not all knowledge is of this kind:

> We do, however, also have organizations of knowledge which will be called 'practical theories', whose whole *raison d'être* is their practical function. In these it is not a pattern of understanding that is of first importance but the determination of what ought to be done in some range of practical activities.[3]

Educational theory is an example of practical theory and is therefore concerned with (forms of) knowledge only for the purposes of formulating principles for practice. That is to say, the 'disciplines of education' or forms of knowledge as represented in philosophy, psychology, sociology and so on are only of concern in educational theory in so far as they issue in principles for practice: 'The whole point is the use of this knowledge to determine what should be done in educational practice.' This, according to Hirst, places educational theory at a great remove from scientific theory:

> . . . any scientific theory involves distinctive empirical concepts unique in character so that the theory's validity turns on related empirical tests. In educational theory no such concepts exist any more than they do in say geography or any other field. There is nothing logically unique about such educational concepts as, for

example, classroom, teacher, subject, comprehensive school. These simply serve to pick out those particular empirical, moral, philosophical and other elements with which education is concerned. These concepts are used to mark out the area of education and its interests but do not pick out any unique form of awareness or knowledge for, indeed, educational theory has no such function. Because this is so, it follows that there can be no unique form of test for educational principles.[4]

According to Hirst, then, education theory is no kind of autonomous knowledge but consists only in the way we justify educational principles by reference to the distinct forms of knowledge. Such principles stand or fall entirely according to the validity of those forms of knowledge which are judged to be relevant to their formulation. He sums up the basic characteristics of educational theory in these terms:

(i) It is the theory in which principles, stating what ought to be done in a range of practical activities, are formulated and justified.

(ii) The theory is not itself an autonomous 'form' of knowledge or an autonomous discipline. It involves no conceptual structure unique in its logical features and no unique tests for validity. Many of its central questions are in fact moral questions of a particular level of generality, questions focused on educational practice.

(iii) Educational theory is not a purely theoretical field of knowledge because of the formulation of principles for practice in which it issues. It is, however, composite in character in a way similar to such fields.

(iv) Educational principles are justified entirely by direct appeal to knowledge from a variety of forms, scientific, philosophical, historical etc. Beyond these forms of knowledge it requires no theoretical synthesis.[5]

The distinction Hirst makes between scientific theories and practical theories such as that of education has not been universally reflected in the development of curriculum theory itself, and it is sometimes suggested that a scientific curriculum theory, as opposed to a prescriptive one, is possible:

. . . it is also concerned with description and explanation: it describes and explains how curricula *are* designed, how dissemination *is* facilitated, and how time *is* allocated. In this sense curriculum theorizing is 'scientific'.[6]

Many would presumably disagree that description actually *constitutes* theorising, as seems to be claimed here. But in any case there is no doubt that there is much in curriculum theory that seems to lay claim to the status of science, particularly the kind of theory based upon learning objectives, educational taxonomies, etc. Hirst's analysis of scientific and educational theory does, however, cast doubt upon the nature of the claim to derive a science of education from a science of learning, and recent developments in curriculum theory have also, as has been suggested, tended to move the issue of science towards that of ideology.

Hirst's view of educational theory as involving 'no conceptual structure unique in its logical features and no unique tests for validity' would seem to imply that there could be no educational theory based upon 'adult characteristics' kinds of approaches since there is nothing about the nature of such characteristics that does not apply in non-educational adult situations. Nor is there anything about them that could not be explained in terms of the genuinely theoretical insights of psychology, sociology, organisation theory and so on.

On the other hand, as was suggested, curriculum theory based upon assumptions about knowledge different from those of Hirst has become increasingly esoteric and divorced from practical concerns, to the point that theory construction has been superseded by the ideological analysis of educational practices. But in fact, to say that educational theory is a theory of practice, and contrast it with scientific theorising, does lead to problems in the area of theory, ideology and practice which the analytic distinctions of philosophers do not always help us to solve. In this spirit, for example, T.W. Moore has proposed a distinction between theories *about* education and theories *of* education:

> Theories *about* education take education as a datum and make generalisations about it, trying to explain its functions in terms of, say, social or individual needs, or tracing its origins, its history or its social influence. Thus there could be psychological and sociological theories about education as well as historical or political theories about it.[7]

Theories *of* education, by contrast, 'involve a body of prescriptions to guide practice', and Moore does insist upon what Hirst seems to deny, namely, the possibility of valid theories *of* education:

A valid scientific theory gives an adequate explanation of what happens in the world, based on established evidence: a valid educational theory would be one which gave adequate recommendations for practice, once again based on adequate and appropriate evidence.[8]

The kind of theorising described in the first chapter seems quite clearly to fall into the category of theories *about* education rather than *of* it. And the various 'adult characteristics' approaches to adult education which are about to be described also constitute theories *about* adult education rather than *of* it, for the same kind of reasons. But no one who examines these approaches could doubt for long that, in addition to their theoretical bases in psychology, sociology or organisation theory, they are also concerned with the prescription of practice. They are, in short, theories *about* adult education aspiring to the status of theories *of* adult education, in the same way that 'adult education knowledge' is a 'field' of knowledge aspiring to a 'form' of knowledge. But the real problem, it will be suggested, lies not in the philosophical categories of either Hirst or Moore, but in the fact that the prescriptions of 'adult characteristics' theory are not in the curriculum mode but in the mode of psychology, sociology and organisation theory themselves. In other words, they do not contain adequate recommendations for practice at the level of adult teaching and learning in a curriculum context of knowledge, culture and power.

The categories of education theory have tended to be established in rather philosophical terms, so that it has been traditionally left to philosophers to establish the nature of educational theory: indeed it is sometimes quite difficult to see where theorising began and philosophising left off. The result has been a dominance of analytic and conceptual methods which produce the kinds of abstract distinctions, between 'forms' and 'fields' of knowledge, between theories *about* and theories *of* education, between science and prescription and, above all, between theory and practice itself. But while it is important to grasp the complexity of educational ideas in terms of the differing kinds of discourse and the differing logics which they embody, it is equally important to understand that these discourses and logics are actually in relation to one another. Philosophical analysis has failed to uncover adequately the dynamic relations between 'forms' and 'fields', or between theories *about* and theories *of*, or between theory and practice itself, and has taken science and its manifestations as psychology, sociology and so on as received and unproblematic bodies of knowledge. Philosophy has tended to present such a very unsociological construction of reality that it has ceased to convey a sense in which the objects of analysis are related to one another in many problematic ways. Disillusionment about the usefulness or 'relevance' of theory in education has paradoxically been accompanied by a failure on the part of educationalists to see any real difference between philosophy and theory. They have turned, sometimes rather naively, to ideology to perform the functions which theory has seemed incapable of doing, namely, analysing theory in relation to practice and theories *about* education in relation to theories *of* education.

Thus ideology has won a place in curriculum theory as a way of analysing the relations of theory and practice rather than simply setting out their respective internal logics which has been a primary concern of philosophy. This is also part of the appeal of curriculum approaches in education: a practicality at the level of analytic method and not only that of classroom practice. Recent developments in curriculum theory have to a large extent challenged the old basis of theory-practice analysis, and changed the whole conceptualisation of their relation, so that now it is more possible than in the past to think of theory as constituted by the categories of our everyday practices in an area such as education.

We are now in a position to ask whether it is possible to, say, construct a model of the curriculum which is not founded in the practices of schooling and which would have some kind of theoretical status. An approach through 'adult characteristics', it is suggested, will not constitute an adequate basis for any general theory of adult or lifelong education. On the other hand, the same kind of processes which have characterised education theory in its transformation from an analytic and philosophical exercise to one rooted in curriculum analysis and practice may prove a more fruitful approach to the problem of theory in this area.

A curriculum theory of adult education is one which is grounded in the practices of adult teaching and learning. But it is also one which proves resistant to the reduction of substantive theoretical and ideological issues to the level of techniques and organisation. This much at least could be learned from the critique of progressivism in education which much of the recent curriculum approach has achieved through an ideological analysis. To be specific, a curriculum theory of adult education would need to address such questions as the extent to which its provision reproduces (rather than transforms) the curriculum categories of schooling. In order to do this the concern of theory would necessarily be with the content as much as with the aims and methods of adult learning, and with the issue of a distinctively adult knowledge-content of the curriculum. The 'adult characteristics' approaches have tended to concern themselves much more with the methods rather than with the aims or content of adult learning, sometimes exclusively so. In the context of schooling, on the other hand, it would surely be preposterous to try to construct an educational or curriculum theory exclusively around an abstract concept of the 'child' or of the methods of pedagogy, without reference to the problem of 'school-knowledge' in a context of knowledge, culture and power, and the ways in which these are socially defined, distributed and evaluated. In other words, there is no longer any possibility of a valid educational theory (in Moore's terms) *of* schooling grounded exclusively in 'childhood characteristics', however important such characteristics may be for the methods and practices of schooling.

Three 'Adult Characteristics' Approaches to Theory

All such approaches are based on the attempt to establish a view of adult education as a distinctive category by virtue of philosophical, psychological or organisational characteristics of adulthood. The prescriptive element of these approaches varies, as does the directness with which curriculum implications are drawn. They all represent, in different ways, a theoretical potential as yet unrealised for a complete curriculum analysis of adult and lifelong education.

Adult Knowledge

One of the most direct attempts to draw curriculum implications from a philosophical view of knowledge in adult education has recently been made by R.W.K. Paterson.[9] He takes a view of knowledge from the kind of analysis made familiar through the work of Peters and Hirst, according to which education is a process of induction into the public forms and modes of knowledge and experience, the aim of which is intrinsically desirable or worthwhile states of mind. As has been seen in an earlier context, this has served as the philosophical underpinning for a view of 'liberal' education, one in which conceptual and cognitive learning are seen as the most basic kinds of learning as far as education systems are concerned. Paterson therefore poses the curriculum issue of adult education thus:

> Now, in constructing a curriculum for adult education, designed to enlarge the student's awareness and put him in more meaningful touch with reality by building up in him rich and coherent bodies of worthwhile knowledge, on what principles can we decide which items of knowledge ought to be included and which kinds of knowledge ought to be assigned priority?[10]

It follows from such a view that the adult curriculum, in order to count as education at all, must, in Lawton's terms, be the outcome of some kind of selection from among the many possibilities of knowledge and culture. Paterson justifiably reflects upon the difficulties, both in theory and practice, of the view of the Russell Report[11] that, in effect, no such selection process takes place in adult education since no priorities could be established as between one kind of knowledge and another. This is a view of adult education belonging perhaps to an organisational 'adult characteristics' approach and will be reverted to later. Suffice it to say that it is a view of the distinctiveness of adult education based on an assumption that any kind of knowledge is potentially worthwhile, which is not an assumption it would be possible to make in the context of schooling.

It is also clear that exponents of these 'adult characteristics' approaches to the curriculum are not necessarily in agreement as to the nature of the distinctiveness they would claim for adult education. Paterson is quite emphatic that some ordering of priorities, some process of selection, must follow from both the nature of knowledge itself and a cultural idea of liberal education:

> For education to be able to *foster* personal development, that is, deliberately develop a person to a greater degree than he would otherwise attain if left to the fortuitous ministrations of ordinary life, there must obviously be some experiences which are more conducive to this end than others. A man cannot set out to educate others, or to educate himself, without trying to determine, at least tentatively and in general terms, what kinds of knowledge are most worth communicating and most worth acquiring.[12]

The orderings and priorities of which an adult curriculum is the outcome are, for Paterson, centred around the structure of knowledge itself. The object of the process is to determine between the 'elements which together make up the intrinsic value of any piece of knowledge'. But to some extent, the issue is prejudged. For in terms of what he calls 'the supreme worth and cognitive richness' of their distinctive objects Paterson asserts that 'the great forms of knowledge must be considered to enjoy an absolute pre-eminence over all other systems and constellations of human knowledge'. So his answer to the question of what priorities should be reflected in the adult curriculum is that the cognitive value of any piece of knowledge, 'its intrinsic value as knowledge', determines its educational value. These then are the kinds of values that an adult curriculum ought to reflect: the primacy of the forms of knowledge as philosophers such as Hirst have worked out in their analyses:

> A well-constructed curriculum for adult education, then, will be one based on the great forms of knowledge in the sense that the knowledge which it above all seeks to communicate will be our knowledge of those fundamental and architectonic features of reality which are determining or constitutive of the whole of our experience.[13]

Paterson is concerned with the curriculum of liberal adult education, or 'adult *education* properly so called', rather than with vocational or role education for adults. In these areas the distinctiveness of adult education from schooling is established in terms of maturity, but he is concerned to look at the curriculum implications of the 'forms of knowledge' approach for the distinctiveness of liberal adult education as such. This turns out to be much more difficult. Inconveniently, the forms of knowledge do not lend themselves readily to age-specific educational systems:

> And so the liberal education of adults will resemble the liberal education of children in being based on the fundamental forms of knowledge, in the sense that a liberal education will seek above all to develop in the adult, as in the child, a deeper understanding of those ultimate structures of reality — nature, mind, the past, and so on — by which his whole life-experience is shaped and governed.[14]

Unfortunately, having built up a case for a liberal adult education curriculum in terms of the intrinsic, pre-eminently cognitive forms of knowledge, Paterson attempts to identify a distinctive body of 'adult knowledge' based upon quite different criteria, ones which are not so much intrinsic and universal as culturally relative and instrumental:

> . . . there will be items of knowledge or even bodies of knowledge which are characteristically 'adult' and which we judge to be so, not because they are specially easy for adults or difficult for children to grasp (though this may in fact be the case), nor because of some special degree of intrinsic cognitive value (which will not necessarily be any higher or lower than that of other pieces of knowledge claiming a place in the curriculum), but because of their distinctive pertinence to adulthood as an ethical and existential status.[15]

Distinctively adult studies, then, in Paterson's analysis, turn out to be based not really upon the structure of knowledge itself but upon fairly conventional, not to say commonplace, beliefs about what is or is not appropriate for adults to learn. These beliefs concern the degree of maturity or the 'ethical appropriateness' of subjects of study respectively for adults and children. It is hard to resist the conclusion that Paterson is saying that, contingently, the adult curriculum reflects a view of adulthood while the curriculum of schooling reflects a view of childhood. The distinctiveness of the adult curriculum cannot be deduced from an analysis of the forms of knowledge, and Paterson admits as much:

> . . . of the basic forms of knowledge themselves, there is surely none which can be regarded qua form of knowledge, as belonging peculiarly and exclusively to the education of adults.[16]

In view of the foregoing critique of the 'forms of knowledge' as a philosophical basis for curriculum analysis, together with the ideological critique of educational theory as such, it is possible to see how it happened that Paterson failed to account for the adult curriculum as something arising out of the structure of knowledge itself. According to such an abstract analysis there could be no such thing as adult knowledge, and this is established through his own approach to the intrinsic nature of knowledge. And yet, according to conventional and common-sense categories, some kinds of subjects are more appropriate for adults to learn than for children. The fact that he speaks of adulthood as 'an ethical and existential status' adds nothing of substance to received and common-sense views of adulthood.

Paterson's view of knowledge is one of an abstract commodity, capable of division into 'pieces' and 'forms', and it provides no sense in which knowledge is socially defined, distributed and evaluated. Likewise the idea of 'adult' seems to lack much social or cultural dimension. In fact the whole context of Paterson's analysis is liberal adult education, which he associates with the purest form of education and distinguishes from vocational or role education for adults. As a consequence of adopting the conceptual and analytic style of philosophy, he conveys little sense of the way in which these kinds of education are related to one another, only that they are different and that liberal education is closer to education properly so called than the others.

However, Paterson's whole approach to the problem does seem to reinforce the case for curriculum approaches to adult education rather than the routes through a rather traditional theory of education. And nothing illustrates this point better than his treatment of liberal, as contrasted with vocational, adult education. For in fact, there is nothing about the nature of knowledge as such that entails anything about the uses to which it may be put. Nowhere does Paterson justify his contention that only liberal education should count as education properly so-called. The purposes of liberal education are to bring about desirable or worthwhile states of mind for individuals through induction into the great public forms of knowledge or modes of experience. But the purposes of other kinds of education may be instrumental rather than intrinsic, and collective rather than individualistic. Nothing about knowledge *as such* entitles us to describe one kind of education as somehow more 'real' than another, any more than it entitles us to evaluate cognitive learning as a 'higher' form of learning than another. It is not that these distinctions and evaluations are invalid or without meaning and significance, but only that *as* distinctions and evaluations they are not entailed by the nature of knowledge itself. In an important sense they are cultural distinctions and evaluations.

In other words, a philosophical approach such as this gives us little sense of knowledge as, to some degree at least, a social and cultural construction. Nothing illustrates this point better than the concept of a liberal education as compared and contrasted with a vocational one. For whereas Paterson sets out, distinguishes between and relatively evaluates these different concepts of education it cannot be said that he compares and contrasts them very much at the level of curriculum. This surely implies a sense of the social and cultural evaluation of the various uses to which learning may be put — for it is learning as much as knowledge itself that is being evaluated when we express a preference for liberal or vocational or any other kind of education. The Russell

Report, in declaring that 'no academic subject or social or creative activity is superior to another', was not necessarily putting forward a philosophical viewpoint about the nature of knowledge. It was not necessarily expressing some kind of Benthamite calculus whereby 'push-pin was as good as poetry'. What seems much more likely is that the Committee did not see fit to make judgements in the matter of the social uses to which knowledge and learning might be put. In this it may have been mistaken, but if so it was not necessarily in the sense implied by Paterson, namely, in the sense of a mistaken view of the nature of knowledge. It seems much more likely that the committee was concerned with the social uses and the social statuses of knowledge, and unwilling to reassert the primacy of cognitive learning or that of the liberal tradition of education. All of which would have been quite consistent with a view of knowledge itself which was as absolute and intrinsic as that of Paterson or Peters or Hirst.

In constructing an adult curriculum, then, the issue is not one of establishing priorities in terms of forms of knowledge but of establishing them in terms of the purposes of learning – the uses to which knowledge is put. These purposes and uses find social and cultural expression in such concepts as liberal or vocational education. They are not mutually exclusive and they are ranked differently in terms of the social status which they attract and in the degree to which they are connected with power and social control or with individual development and satisfaction. It is in this practical context that priorities are ordered and it was presumably to this context – rather than to the nature of knowledge itself – that the remarks of the Russell Report were addressed.

Finally, this approach is characterised by the fundamental ambiguity of the idea of 'adult knowledge' which, it is agreed, is not entailed by the 'forms' of knowledge but established according to other, perfectly conventional criteria of adulthood. The result is an awkward juxtaposition of conceptual analysis and an uncritical, 'received' concept of adulthood, the distinctive characteristics of which are an 'ethical and existential' status from which can be derived 'adult' items or bodies of knowledge. Adulthood is primarily, however, a social and cultural status from which ethical and existential corollaries tend to be drawn, and drawn in quite different ways from society to society or even from class to class. It is itself as much a prescriptive as a descriptive category for some purposes; it is a status like that of citizen which has a variable association with the capacity for legal and moral rights and duties. It is, in other words, a rather more problematic category than perhaps

Paterson allows for. It is at its clearest precisely in those concepts of education such as vocational or role education which he seems to suggest do not constitute education 'properly so called'.

The 'adult knowledge' approach to a curriculum theory of adult education seems to fail in its own terms. The reasons for this lie in a variety of factors which the recent developments in curriculum theory described in the first chapter have tended to stress. In this case, the problem lay in a view of knowledge which was wholly abstract and provides no sense of the way in which knowledge and the outcomes of learning are socially conditioned. Thus, when a social or cultural dimension impinged — such as a concept of liberal education, or vocational education, or of 'adult' itself — it could only find expression in categories of a most conventional and 'received' kind rather than in a general theory of adult education entailed by a view of adult knowledge. There is no sense, in Paterson's analysis, of the ideological significance of liberal or vocational education and no way in which knowledge could be conceptualised in the framework of curriculum analysis so that we could begin to think of the adult curriculum as a selection from a society's culture, or as a reflection of the complex ways in which a culture functions to define, distribute and evaluate knowledge. The evaluations in this analysis are taken from a cultural tradition, and the view it gives us both of knowledge and adult education are far too bland to enable us to evaluate it in terms of social control, reproduction, transformation, or indeed in terms of power at all.

Andragogy

Paterson stuck successfully to the idea of the content of the adult curriculum, seeing that any attempt to derive such a curriculum from a concept of knowledge itself must have the content of learning as its primary focus. In some ways this is the most difficult approach to the problem. A much more common approach to the distinctiveness of adult education is by way of its methods, which, together with aims and organisation, seems to provide more secure ground upon which to proceed. The idea of andragogy as a name for a science of adult teaching and learning, in contrast to pedagogy as a name for the science of childhood teaching and learning, has been very influential since it was first propounded by Malcolm Knowles.[17] The theory of andragogy is, however, a theory of adult teaching and learning and, following the kind of criteria established by Hirst, it by no means follows that andragogy in itself could possibly constitute a theory of adult education. The scientific element of andragogy is contained almost exclusively in learning psychology, beyond which lie prescriptions for adult teaching which, in themselves, are matters of judgement which have not been uncontroversial. For present purposes, however, the failure of andragogy to function as a theory of adult education has more to do with the way in which it reduces issues to principles of method and technique, and seems incapable of accounting for the substantive issues raised by adult education as are raised by education as such. Andragogy does not address itself to the issues of knowledge, culture and power which have come through curriculum analysis to lie at the heart of any genuine theory of education. Such a theory, it has been argued, is one which issues in principles for practice which are grounded not only in relevant scientific knowledge but also in an appraisal of the ideological content of such principles in terms of knowledge, culture and power.

According to Knowles, then, andragogy is based on 'at least' four main assumptions that distinguish andragogy as a theory of adult learning from pedagogy as a theory of childhood learning. The first of these concerns changes in self-concept:

> This assumption is that as a person grows and matures his self-concept moves from one of total dependency (as is the reality of the infant) to one of increasing self-directedness.[18]

Adulthood is seen therefore as essentially a category of individual development: the point of adulthood, Knowles says, is 'the point at which an individual achieves a self-concept of essential self-direction'. And this is associated with a deep psychological need to be perceived by others in this light. A situation in which an individual is thwarted in his need and desire for self-direction is therefore one of conflict and tension: 'His reaction is bound to be tainted with resentment and resistance.' This reaction will predictably occur if adult learners are placed in situations resembling those of childhood learning and will interfere with the process of learning itself.

The first thing to say about this kind of assumption is that, however scientifically grounded in psychological theory it may be, it does seem to be excessively abstract and excessively culture-bound. 'Adulthood' and maturity itself is a social status in relation to individual development, and as a status it is conferred in very different ways upon individuals. Much depends, in other words, upon factors in the structure and culture of society which will affect, if not determine, the 'point of adulthood'. Neither is it a wholly unambiguous idea from the point of view of morals. It could not be demonstrated scientifically whether 'maturity' finds expression in what are sometimes described as 'adult' books or films. The concept of self-direction which individuals encounter in their own development, both as an aspiration or need and as a desirable social status, depends very much upon how they are culturally or structurally located in society. It would be odd to suggest, for example, that gender is a matter of indifference when it comes to people's expectations about self-direction. In fact, there is a sense in which this basic assumption about andragogy is wholly inconsistent with the outcomes of recent work in theory and ideology, according to which a major function of education systems is precisely the control of the 'self-concept of essential self-direction' on the part of individuals, especially relative to their social class. If the point of adragogy *qua* educational theory is to interfere with events in the formation of an individual's self-concept of adulthood to counter pedagogical and social repression, then much more attention needs to be paid to the content of learning. Sometimes it is the content of adult learning, and not just the methods of adult teaching, that are most relevant to the issue of self-directedness: *what* is being learned will to some extent determine the appropriateness of methods, and not simply a highly abstract concept of 'adulthood'.

Knowles was writing before the full impact was felt of the kind of developments in curriculum theory which were outlined in the first chapter, and it is easy to criticise with the advantage of hindsight. Nevertheless, there is in these kinds of assumptions of andragogy a neglect not only of the social, cultural and political dimensions of adulthood but of the content of adult learning itself, to which curriculum analysis can fruitfully direct our attention.

A second assumption of adragogy concerns the role of experience:

This assumption is that as an individual matures he accumulates an expanding reservoir of experience that causes him to become an increasingly rich resource for learning, and at the same time provides him with a broadening base to which to relate new learnings.[19]

Consequently, says Knowles, andragogy is a method of teaching based much more upon experiential than transmittal techniques, since these are more likely to 'tap the experience of the learners and involve them in analyzing their experience'. Also adults, rather than defining themselves in terms of others as children do, increasingly define themselves in terms of their experience: 'To a child, experience is something that happens to him: to an adult, his experience is *who he is.*' Therefore, a situation in which such experience is devalued or ignored is a situation of personal rejection: 'Andragogues convey their respect for people by making use of their experience as a resource for learning.'

Once some kind of criteria of relevance have been worked out it seems clear that making use of people's experience is *one* way of showing respect for them as learners, and many adult educators would no doubt accept this as a principle of good practice. Again, though, it seems fairly unproblematic in its treatment of experience and the different ways in which an individual's experience is socially located and evaluated. So while at the level of good teaching methods and practice experiential learning is highly suggestive (as well as being morally defensible), at the level of education theory it may fail to account for the different ways in which learner evaluation of experience, rather than experience *as such*, affects the aims of learning itself. Experience such as Knowles presumably has in mind takes place in differentiated social, cultural and political settings and its evaluation is problematic. The acceptance of experiential learning in principle leads perhaps to a more radical kind of learning process than that which Knowles himself is contemplating, unless the danger of imposing evaluation for purposes of method is to be avoided − which he surely thought it should.

The third assumption of andragogy is concerned with the readiness to learn of adults:

> This assumption is that as an individual matures, his readiness to learn is decreasingly the product of his biological development and academic pressure and is increasingly the product of the developmental tasks required for the performance of his evolving social roles.[20]

Unlike children, adults do not learn things because of their relevance to pedagogic assumptions but learn things they need to learn 'because of the developmental phases they are approaching in their roles as workers, spouses, parents, organizational members and leaders, leisure time users, and the like'. The implication of this is 'the importance of timing learning experiences to coincide with the learners' developmental tasks'. What Knowles has to say about this concerns primarily role and vocational education for adults: what has come to be called continuing education primarily in the field of careers.

In this assumption the theory of andragogy has shifted away from a base in psychological theories of individual development or 'self-concept' to one which is much more closely related to the idea of social roles. This is clearly a major change, for while individuals may be said to exercise some degree of choice amongst the roles they play, they cannot be said to define career roles in the way that they can define a self-concept. These are much more given, or even imposed, in terms of what Knowles calls 'developmental tasks'. These tasks are not self-defined or self-imposed but expose the learner to precisely those other-related criteria associated with childhood learning and pedagogy which Knowles contrasted with adult learning and andragogy. The curriculum content of andragogy − in this case, role education − is what really determines principles of good practice in adult education, and not an abstract concept of 'adult', however successfully this is located within scientific learning theory. What can be derived from andragogy are methodological principles for teaching and learning practice. The attempt to derive a general theory of adult education founders upon the narrowness and abstractness of the idea of 'adult' and upon a failure to grasp that, as an idea, it is itself a consequence of the content of learning as much as a principle of good teaching method. As this third assumption suggests, andragogy without curriculum content analysis may simply be tautological: given that the timing of learning experiences is an important principle to observe, as Knowles says, it is not possible to compare and *contrast* it with pedagogy in a context of adult role-learning. As was suggested above, an uncritical comparison simply demonstrates that both pedagogy and role-andragogy involve the learner in the pursuit of 'developmental tasks' set not by the learner but by others: school teachers in one case and professional communities in the other.

The final assumption of andragogy in its 'pure' form is that of orientation to learning: 'This assumption is that children have been conditioned to have a subject-centred orientation to most learning whereas adults tend to have a problem-centred orientation to learning.'[21] Children, in other words, require subject-knowledge not for its own sake but because it is instrumental to passing through the education system itself. Adults, by contrast, come to education because they need knowledge for immediate purposes of solving day-to-day problems of living. This assumption, says Knowles, 'has major implications regarding the organization of the curriculum and its learning experiences'. Subject-centred learning entails a curriculum 'according to the logic of the subject matter and . . . course units should be defined by the logical sequence of content topics'. Adult learning, however, requires a problem-centred orientation in which relevant practical outcomes must determine the aims, content and methods of teaching and learning.

The subject-centred view of the logic of education, associated with the philosophical work of Peters and Hirst in particular has, we have seen, been exposed to a good deal of criticism within the paradigm of the school curriculum, and Knowles does not enter into the question of whether pedagogy is necessarily associated with subject-structured knowledge — much pedagogy nowadays is not predicated on such an assumption. And although he justifiably suggests that important curriculum consequences depend upon a view of knowledge, Knowles has not shown that these consequences are entailed by a view of 'adult knowledge' any more than Paterson did. Indeed, as in the case of the last assumption of andragogy, the context here is exclusively that of vocational, role or professional and continuing education. Now these are precisely the areas of adult education which are susceptible to a 'cognitive-structure' or 'problem-orientation' issue. In other words, in the case of some of the curriculum content of adult learning, it is a substantive issue (as it is in pedagogy) as to whether the best learning is based upon one kind of assumption about knowledge and teaching practices or another. The example of social work education which Knowles mentions, as with teacher education itself, has traditionally lent itself to a substantive issue of how relevant academic disciplines are to be represented in the learning experience. But large parts — perhaps predominant parts — of the adult curriculum, such as the affective, recreational and cultural, as well as the manifestly cognitive and academic areas, simply do not lend themselves to such an issue of subject-structure/problem-orientation dichotomy: it is irrelevant. Of course, the best teaching strategies to adopt are always a matter for continuous review, and the ways in which to arrange cognitive, expressive or problem-solving elements in the learning are always a potential issue. But the capacity of the many different areas of adult and continuing education to find expression in such simple dichotomies must vary greatly.

The theory of andragogy associated with Knowles has been reviewed and criticised here in its simplest and quite unrevised form. The reasons for this are that these kinds of assumptions are not the exclusive preserve of a particular theory of adult learning but have tended to be a common property of adult educators. This is hardly surprising. For not only does andragogy promise something of the esoteric knowledge which is the exclusive possession of an aspiring profession, it also contains some common-sense prescriptions for good teaching and learning practices which can be substantiated by reference to scientific, that is to say psychological, evidence. So in terms of some at least of Hirst's criteria it is suggestive of education theory which is scientifically grounded in relevant disciplines and which is concerned to issue in principles for good teaching practice.

But Knowles's approach — in the simplest possible form in which it has been presented here — could not possibly constitute a theory of adult education as such. It is a learning theory, based upon extremely simplified and abstract dichotomies of pedagogy and andragogy. Many of the curriculum implications turn out to be indifferent as between these polarities, and those that have a strictly adult reference are vitiated by a general absence of curriculum content analysis. It is essentially a prescription for adult teaching methods derived from learning theory, and as such provides little insight into the idea of adulthood as a social status and adult knowledge as something that is socially defined, distributed and evaluated in a context of power and ideology. After all, if, as Knowles says, children have been 'conditioned' into thinking of knowledge as essentially subject-structured, then it is the transforming curriculum content of adult education and not just its teaching methods that are at issue. It seems highly unlikely — since people are similarly 'conditioned' into views of adulthood and knowledge too — that a curriculum transformation could be effected from a basis of individual self-concept formation.

Knowles's theory of andragogy is therefore one of the characteristics of adult learning rather than one of adult education as such, which would be concerned with far wider issues than those of adult teaching and learning methods. In particular, it is being argued here, there is such a neglect of the content of learning that there is no sense of the social significance of knowledge at all, let alone any sense of the political dimensions of adult learning. There is nothing about the dynamic relations of andragogy and pedagogy: is pedagogy necessary to stimulate andragogy, or do they simply co-exist? As it stands, the theory seems to suggest that pedgagogy stands for the powerlessness of the learner and andragogy for the learner's autonomy, but power and autonomy are social dimensions of situations which require elucidation in the context of knowledge, culture and politics. No doubt it was never claimed that andragogy addressed these issues and was not intended to do so. But since it might be easy to suppose that andragogy could function as a theory of adult education, it seems important to suggest why this is not possible.

Andragogy shares in this respect similar features with another important and influential 'characteristics of adult learning' approach, that of Allen Tough, whose research has been concerned with the vast amount of self-directed independent learning which goes on quite outside the formal organisations of adult education.[22] Such research is of great methodological importance and very suggestive for the provision of adult learning opportunities at the level of social policy and professional strategy. As with andragogy, however, it conveys an inadequate sense of the significance of the content of adult learning in terms, say, of the de-institutionalisation of knowledge in society. And again, there is little about it to connect the content of adult knowledge with dimensions of power and control in society. Indeed, neither Knowles nor Tough seem to account for the social distribution and evaluation of knowledge and of the crucial distinction between the individual purposes and social consequences of learning.

The dominant methodological paradigm of the 'adult learning characteristics' approach seems to be one of extreme individualism which narrowly reflects perhaps the predominance of scientific evidence from psychology in theory construction. This means, however, that the central theoretical issue of the curriculum approach – that of the social construction of the curriculum – is begged. In effect, the social functions of adult education are reduced to the sum of the purposes of individual learners.

Not all approaches to theory in adult education are based upon methodological individualism, and 'adult characteristics' approaches may be grounded in other scientific theories than those of psychology and other conceptualisations of aims than those of philosophy. As adult and continuing education have developed so has the professionalisation of the field. A third and very important 'adult characteristics' approach has arisen out of the process of professionalisation itself, and this is a view of adult education as a structure of provision for meeting adult learning needs as a professional strategy. The theoretical underpinning of this approach has tended to be found in organisation theory.

Structures of Provision

In its simplest form the approach constitutes a view of adult learning needs as a function of professional response and its prescriptions take the form of strategies to maximise both the flexibility of response and, indeed, the case for adult learning needs. It is not entirely clear whether such an approach could be contained within the view of adult learning projected by Tough: the nature of institutional provision becomes a crucial issue. However, it does seem clear that this is an issue of professionalism, institutionalisation and organisation, and not an issue of knowledge, culture and power as far as those involved are concerned.

Like the other 'adult characteristics' approaches, this one fails to raise
— let alone problematise — the issue of the curriculum of adult and lifelong education: the aims, content and methods of adult learning (in
the context of knowledge, culture and power) are reduced, in this
view, to received categories. Professionalism itself moves to the centre
of the stage, and the concept of adult learning need and possible
structures of provision for it become objects of organisational strategy,
no more and no less. It is also an approach where professional rhetoric
tends to outweigh the theoretical content which is sometimes claimed
for it — an outcome, perhaps, of a determination to eschew all 'philosophising'.

This kind of view — strategic prescriptions in a context of organisation theory — has been advanced by Graham Mee in his recent book on
adult education organisation:

> What is needed is a service for *adult persons, not for childern or
> adolescents*. Its environment must be adult, both physically and
> psychologically; its methodology and content must be appropriate
> to adults.[23]

Immediately we are presented with a confusion of categories: are
the methodology and content those of the professional service itself,
or are they those of adult learning (which would constitute a dimension
of the curriculum)? The general impression conveyed by Mee's whole
approach is that he is concerned with the system of provision itself and
with its openness, accessibility and relevance to adult learners. The
system as an object of professional design calls not upon a view of
knowledge, culture and power but upon 'theory generated in such disciplines as psychology, organisation theory and management theory'.[24]
So despite an apparent rejection of abstract philosophising, Mee is
inclined to look for an answer to the question of 'what are the characteristics of the adult person and are they consonant with the demands
of organisational life?' and to find it within the terms of such disciplines. The concept of adult, in the end, is defined therefore through the
findings of research in industrial psychology, which has stressed the
adult's need for 'autonomy, challenge and a chance to go on learning,
variety, mutual support and respect, meaningfulness and a desirable
future'. It is a bland and not very satisfactory account of adulthood,
not merely because it is culturally and politically contingent nor
because it does not sufficiently distinguish these needs from those of
children, but because the need for a professionally organised system

comes to stand over and against the adult learner's need for autonomy. Rather contrary to Allen Tough's findings, Mee asserts that 'learning adults need to work in a learning system',[25] and there is no doubt that by system he means a system of institutional structures. But he is talking about 'learning systems', which, according to Schon, are 'systems capable of bringing about their own continuing transformation'. Mee goes on to recommend as design principles for adult education systems a shift from centre-periphery to network-structure models according to the organisational concepts developed by Schon in *Beyond the Stable State:*[26]

> An ideal system would create roles for people which took full account of their adult status. Existing organisations tend to frustrate adult needs for autonomy, challenge and the opportunity to learn, variety, etc. An ideal system would also be a learning system capable of continuing transformation.[27]

The organisational characteristics of the adult learning systems approach adopted by Mee are based upon a profound ambiguity in the idea of learning. Obviously there are senses in which institutional systems could be described as 'learning systems', just as some adult situations could be described as adult learning situations. But the relation is by no means as simple as Mee seems to assume. And the reason for this is that there is simply no sense of the social, cultural and political content of learning itself. There is, as it were, a curriculum vacuum consequent upon a highly abstract model of both a 'learning system' and an adult learner, and no sense of *what* the system or the adult learns as a social, cultural and political construct. Nevertheless, the 'structures and strategies of provision' approach, based as it is upon received categories of both 'adult' and 'education' and which treats the curriculum content of learning as unproblematic and unconstructed in social, cultural and political terms, has been very influential, not least in comparative studies of adult education[28] where some sense of these 'curriculum significances' of adult education would be particularly interesting. For above all, the ideological significance of the curriculum is what really indicates the ways in which adult education relates to the social and political structures of society. And, as we have seen, knowledge itself is to some extent at least a cultural construction.

Summary

The developments in curriculum theory which were outlined in the first chapter have not found reflection in recent theoretical work in adult education. In the effort to 'distance' adult education from schooling, writers have fallen under other influences; there has been a tendency for 'guru' figures such as Illich, Freire, Maslow or Schon to leave a mark greater perhaps upon adult education than elsewhere. What is lost, especially if such influences are not thoroughly and critically digested, is the sense that adult learning raises problematic and ideological issues of knowledge, culture and power as important as those of schooling and possibly more so. For what adults learn is as ideologically significant as what schools teach.

Adult education shares with schooling some central problems of theory construction, and some reasons for the present undeveloped state of adult education theory undoubtedly lie in this area of the 'forms' and the 'fields' of knowledge, the possibility of 'theories of practice' and the contribution of analytic concepts and scientific evidence from relevant disciplines. The situation is no different as between adult education and schooling in these respects.

But this chapter has attempted to demonstrate that there is no possibility of an adult education theory constructed from a basis of 'adult characteristics' which either fails in its own terms or else fails to give any adequate account of the curriculum issues which are inherent in learning *as such*. To concentrate upon 'adult' is, indeed, necessary. In the end, however, a philosophical, scientific or cultural concept of adult is only a prerequisite of theory and not a theory of adult education as such: it is a necessary but not sufficient condition of one. And in the case of some ideas of lifelong education it may not even be a prerequisite.

A theory of adult education *as* a theory of learning must inevitably give expression to the concern of curriculum studies with the educational centrality of knowledge, culture and power, together with the roles of philosophy, sociology and politics as they contribute to the formulation of any education theory. However, the concern of adult education theorists so far has been with defining adult characteristics and with designing systems, strategies and structures for adult learning. More specifically, their concern has been with needs, access and provision, and to these ideas it is now necessary to turn.

Notes and References

1. Paul H. Hirst, 'Educational Theory', *The Study of Education*, ed. J.W. Tibble (London: Routledge and Kegan Paul, 1966), p. 47.

2. P.H. Hirst and R.S. Peters, *The Logic of Education*, pp. 64-5.

3. Paul H. Hirst, 'Educational Theory', p. 48.

4. Ibid., p. 49.

5. Ibid., p. 55.

6. Philip H. Taylor and Colin Richards, *An Introduction to Curriculum Studies*, p. 143.

7. T.W. Moore, *Educational Theory: An Introduction* (London: Routledge and Kegan Paul, 1974), pp. 9-10.

8. Ibid., p. 11.

9. R.W.K. Paterson, *Values, Education and the Adult* (London: Routledge and Kegan Paul, 1979).

10. Ibid., p. 85.

11. Department of Education and Science, *Adult Education: A Plan for Development* (London: HMSO, 1973).

12. Paterson, *Values, Education and the Adult*, p. 85.

13. Ibid., pp. 94-5.

14. Ibid., p. 97.

15. Ibid.

16. Ibid., p. 99.

17. Malcolm Knowles, *The Adult Learner: A Neglected Scpecies*, 2nd edn (Houston: Gulf Publishing Co., 1978).

18. Ibid., p. 55.

19. Ibid., p. 56.

20. Ibid., p. 57.

21. Ibid., p. 58.

22. Allen Tough, 'Major Learning Efforts:Recent Research and Future Directions', *Adult Education* (USA), vol. 28., no. 4. (Summer 1978).

23. Graham Mee., *Organisation for Adult Education* (London: Longman, 1980), p. 22.

24. Ibid., p. 24.

25. Ibid., p. 26.

26. Donald Schon, *Beyond the Stable State* (Harmondsworth: Penguin Books, 1971).

27. Mee, *Organisation for Adult Education*, p. 29.

28. See, for example, W.J.A. Harris, *Comparative Adult Education: Practice, Purpose and Theory* (London: Longman, 1980). On the other hand, some sense of the social, cultural and knowledge contexts of comparative provision is conveyed in another recent study: Colin Titmus, *Strategies for Adult Education: Practices in Western Europe* (Milton Keynes: Open University Press, 1981).

3 AN IDEOLOGY OF NEEDS, ACCESS AND PROVISION

Introduction

One of the most obvious 'adult characteristics' approaches to theory in this area is one based upon the distinctive ideology of adult education as compared with that of schooling. As an approach, however, it is of very limited potential if the curriculum dimension is missing. For example, it is only too easy to confuse the aims of adult education as an object of philosophical analysis with adult education itself as an object of ideological analysis. A major problem of philosophical analysis was that it provided little sense of the degree to which knowledge is itself a social construction, and its conclusions tended towards a somewhat individualistic and abstract view of the aims of education. Typically, it concluded with a concept of education 'properly so called' which largely corresponded with the idea of a liberal education, based upon received and fairly traditional categories of knowledge, teaching and learning. In other words, the content of learning was of educational significance only in terms of some such concept as 'worthwhileness' or the desirable states of mind consequent upon induction into public forms of knowledge, experience or meaning, and so on. A curriculum approach, on the other hand, was based upon an assumption that the learning content was of direct educational significance, whereas 'worthwhile' and 'desirable' states of mind constituted some kind of ideological intrusion into the real logic of education. This approach, in other words, is based much more upon an assumption that the aims of education are not intrinsic but are, like knowledge itself, to some degree at least a social construction. Their construction is, to a large extent, a function of professionalism, whether we are talking of adult education or of schooling. And this is a dimension which seems to lie outside the scope of the philosophical analysis of aims but well within that of an ideological analysis of the social construction of values.

This is the kind of divide which recent developments in curriculum theory have opened up between traditional philosophising about the aims of education on the one hand, and a view of the social and political contexts in which knowledge is defined, distributed and evaluated, on the other. So it is very important to distinguish between aims and ideology, especially for such purposes as identifying the distinctiveness of adult education.

However, this distinction is not always achieved, and what may begin in a discussion of the intrinsic aims of adult education can only too easily end as a discussion of its ideology. John Hostler, for example, in a recent monograph on *The Aims of Adult Education*,[1] concludes by identifying three of the most fundamental aims of adult education which distinguish it from schooling:

> Whether the tutor's immediate aim is primarily liberal or instrumental, however, it should ultimately harmonise with the long-term goals of adult education. We have seen in the course of this survey that these are many and various, but three of them are especially notable. The most fundamental of them all is *autonomy*, which prescribes the student's right to choose the classes he will attend and to evaluate their success. Autonomy in turn implies *individuality*, which enjoins that he should develop in a unique way and that he should be able to select from a very broad curriculum. And it entails also *equality* in his relationship with the tutor, whereby both of them develop through the process of learning together.[2]

These aims, or long-term goals, says Hostler, constitute the distinctive ideology of adult education which sharply contrast with the ideology of schooling:

> These three values deserve special emphasis in this final section because they are the ones which make adult education a distinctive enterprise. They constitute the basis of its whole ideology, and thus they ultimately account for most of the characteristic features of its procedure and organisation. And they contradict absolutely the current theory and practice of most English education. For example, Illich shows how most established approaches to schooling totally deny the pupil's autonomy. Postman and Weingartner likewise argue that they restrict his individuality, while Freire contends that they keep him subordinate and oppressed, precluding equality with the teacher. Obviously adult education is the complete antithesis of them. Its whole ethos is opposed to such attitudes to education, and in fact, as Paterson remarks, it embodies the very principles which are being proposed by supposedly 'radical' education today.[3]

There are several difficulties about this argument. For one thing, it begins in aims and ends in ideology without really accounting for the relation of two quite distinct kinds of analysis. And for another, the basis of the comparison between adult education and schooling seems a very doubtful one in the terms in which it is cast. Is it valid, in other words, to compare a compulsory with a voluntary system *in terms of* autonomy, individuality and equality, or are there better grounds for establishing the ideological distinctiveness of adult education?

Hostler's comparison seems to be made in terms of abstract philosophical ideas, whereas the *ideology* of schooling — at least in a liberal democratic society — could hardly be based upon contrary ideas of repression, collectivism and inequality. The manifest aims of schooling in liberal democratic societies, such as the development of individuality and of competitive individualism in conditions of equal opportunity may, as some would argue, be defeated by the institutions of bourgeois society. But they are not defeated by the compulsoriness of schooling as such, and repression, collectivism and inequality are not intrinsic to education but rather, as Illich and Freire were arguing, to the conditions of institutionalisation in certain kinds of societies. Compulsion itself is an element of ideology rather than of the aims of education: it could not constitute an aim of education although it could clearly represent an ideological view of schooling, as it has done historically in this country and as it may do under conditions of social development. Also, if professionalism constitutes a major source of ideology in institutionalised education, then this comparison of Hostler's again seems overdrawn. The majority of adult educators as professionals, unlike the majority of schoolteachers as professionals, do not directly face the issues of learner autonomy, individuality or equality. The ideology of adult education is much more likely to reflect the organisation and administrative concerns of full-time professional workers rather than the philosophical aims of the kind that schoolteachers may or may not profess.

Now the aims of adult education may well be, as Hostler claims, those of autonomy, individuality and equality. The point is that these do not really distinguish it from schooling (since such aims are not logically precluded by compulsoriness) nor, if we make the proper distinctions, do they constitute its ideology. Aims and ideology are quite different things, as Hostler himself implicitly acknowledges when he interestingly points out the way in which adult education functions as a 'hidden curriculum' of political control in spite of its manifest aims of autonomy, individuality and equality.[4] In terms of the analysis of such writers as Illich and Freire we should expect the real ideology of adult education to reflect the concerns of its institutionalised professionals, which are much more likely to be with needs, access and provision than with the kind of philosophical aims which could be logically associated with schooling. As an ideology this gives better grounds for the distinctiveness of adult education, and it is the subject of the present chapter. It only remains to review the theoretical implications of the ideological version of the 'adult characteristics' approach which is embodied in the kind of view expressed by John Hostler.

It is a view which, if anything, demonstrates the degree to which the dominant school curriculum paradigm determines the categories according to which adult learning is conceptualised. As aims of education, autonomy, individuality and equality are very recognisable, and the failure of education systems to achieve them in practice is extremely well documented. So paradoxically, as aims of adult education they do little to establish its distinctiveness. Whether adult education could be more successful than schooling in the same social conditions is by no means guaranteed. And this leads to a final point. If, as it is claimed, 'the whole ethos' of adult education 'embodies the very principles which are being proposed by supposedly "radical" educators today' then it needs to be pointed out that it is precisely these forms of educational progressivism which have come under attack from radical curriculum theorists, concerned as they have been with the ideological conditions and consequences of knowledge, to the extent that progressivism itself may stand in the way of radical educational change. In this way the oversimple dichotomies of the 'adult characteristics' approach have tended to obscure developments in the general field of curriculum theory which may be of considerable importance and relevance to a theory of adult and lifelong education itself.

One of the difficulties of constructing such a theory arises to some extent out of the problems of constructing *any* education theory, and they are compounded by what has been described as the dominant school curriculum paradigm, from the categories of which it is extremely difficult to escape, as the above discussion about aims has suggested. In fact all of the 'adult characteristics' approaches, whether they are based on views of knowledge, learning, organisation or ideology, run into difficulties of this kind: they all postulate the kind of dichotomy between schooling and adult learning which proves too simple to bear the weight of a curriculum theory of adult education; one which is primarily concerned with the social and political definition, distribution and evaluation of knowledge. One solution to this kind of problem would be to think of adult education not so much in terms of a theory of knowledge and education as one of social policy in the area of education. Indeed, there may be no need to use the term education in a strict sense but to think of the provision of welfare and social services as the kind of thing that adult educators are primarily concerned with. It seems reasonable to suppose that a practitioner's ideology will reflect a 'public service' ethos at least as much, if not more so, as a 'radical education' one. Perhaps this is where ideological distinctiveness should be sought, along the lines of a professional service concerned in a traditional way with entrepreneurial marketing and with organising provision, responding to adult learning-related needs, and with facilitating access to adult learning opportunities.

The problem of access, for example, does suggest a useful basis for real ideological distinctiveness from schooling where compulsory attendance is the norm. Even here, of course, it should not be supposed that the concept of access is unproblematic in the context of schooling, for the kinds of schools and schooling to which children have access is clearly very controversial. Nevertheless, there are in these issues of needs, access and provision both a professional concern and a possible basis for distinctive theory. In which case, the analogy shifts rather from education to social theory, and in particular to theories of social welfare. In examining adult education ideology, therefore, it seems important to look at the social welfare analogy in general terms before considering one or two specific issues in the area of needs, access and provision. In fact it is quite useful to compare problems of developing a theory of adult education with problems in the area of social policy and administration.

Adult Education and Social Policy Theory

If, despite a view of the aims of adult education as autonomy, individuality and equality, we postulate a professional ideology as one of needs, access and provision, then the comparison with theories of social policy and administration seems quite close. After all, a social administration approach is based on exactly such elements, as recent writers on the subject point out: 'Social administration is traditionally defined as the study of social arrangements for meeting need.'[5] And in welfare societies meeting needs is largely carried out by agencies of the state. But the authors of this particular study are concerned to do — more or less — what the radical curriculum theorists have been concerned to do in the case of the traditional language of education and knowledge, namely, to problematise the issue in terms of social, cultural and political determinants of need:

> To escape the assumptions built into the traditional language of 'social arrangements for meeting need', our starting point in contemporary social administration studies must be the political process of the regulation of need. This stresses the political concern of the subject and avoids a facile equation of need with the goal of social policy.[6]

A curriculum theory of adult education (stressing the political concern of the subject with knowledge) would therefore avoid this facile equation which, it will be suggested, is inherent in the professional ideology, at least in so far as it relates to need. There are some suggestive parallels, too, for issues of theory construction as between adult education and social administration, where these writers argue that 'an uncritical empiricism tends to take existing arrangements for granted'.

So the kind of question which would take us to a theoretical level of analysis of adult education ideology concerns the extent to which needs, access and provision are taken-for-granted elements in the situation to which it is addressed. How close is the field of adult education to that of social administration in terms of problems of theory?

> The dominant perspective in this field has emphasized practical solutions to practical problems . . . Since theory remains implicit it is hard to identify this perspective by overt allegiance to theoretical tenets.[7]

In this study the authors, Peter Taylor-Gooby and Jennifer Dale, draw attention to the uncritical empiricism of social administration which restricts the possibility of theoretical discussion of its object — social arrangements to meet need. One purpose of this chapter is to consider the hypothesis that central concepts of adult education ideology rest upon an analogous 'uncritical empiricism' which restricts the possibility of theoretical discussion of *its* object — the social, cultural and political distribution of knowledge and skills.

The concept of need in social administration, argue Taylor-Gooby and Dale, is managed in such a way as to 'reify' it or relate it to 'society' as such, rather than to see it as an outcome of social groups and values in conflict. At this level all needs are equally to be met. At the level of practice and in conditions of scarce resources, social policy becomes an exercise in rationing and in ordering needs according to a view of priorities among them. Responding to need, in other words, becomes a technical matter rather than, say, a political response among a variety of conflicting and possibly irreconcilable interests:

> The discussion of need as the prioritizing of competing claims in the face of restricted resources reduces the issue to a question of administrative rationing, which is precisely what it becomes for a consensual welfare state. The concept is robbed of all subversive content — the possibility that human needs may be such that this form of society cannot meet them becomes unthinkable, as does the possibility that values dominant under democratic welfare capitalism may produce unsatisfiable needs.[8]

A theoretical view, therefore, as opposed to an abstract or conceptual view of needs, or one based upon an 'uncritical empiricism' of practice, is one which locates them in the contradictions of social life. In other words, the whole concept of need is problematic with regard to consensus and conflict, and, by implication, the role of a professional needs-meeter is to allocate priorities in conditions of seeming ideological neutrality — the uncritical empiricism of practice. In the case of the analysis under discussion, a Marxist critique of the concept of needs in capitalist society later follows,[9] but the argument here is only that a theoretical account of the concept of need must be critical in this way and transcend the social conditions in which it arises. But the ideology of adult education rarely moves beyond the abstractions of philosophical analysis on the one hand or the prescriptions of uncritical empiricism on the other, and the position of theory in this respect is quite similar to that of social policy and administration when viewed in a critical light. So how problematic is the concept of adult learning needs as an element of ideology?

Needs

On the one hand, the tradition of education theory includes the philosophical or conceptual analysis of the concept. And according to one view at least, the idea of need, together with other members of the family of ideas, such as wants and interests, is not necessarily of the utmost significance for understanding curriculum matters but has a significance which is more rhetorical and to do with the formation of professional ideologies. If this is the case with schooling then we may look for an analogous significance for adult and lifelong education. This is the logic of the idea, since here we are pursuing the philosophical approach: it is important to understand that to establish a distinctive category of adult learning needs (as opposed to the learning needs of children) does not invalidate this kind of analysis, which is of the general curriculum significance of needs rather than of the specific (andragogic) implications of needs for teaching methods. Of course, from the analytic point of view such a topic could be expanded to fill volumes, but Hirst and Peters put the matter quite succinctly:

> A major book could be written solely around the problems raised by this emphasis on needs and interests. Our treatment, however, will be very brief, selective, and tailored to the general theme of this book. We shall try to show that this approach in fact contributes little to determining the content of education, though it may have more relevance to methods. Its psychological trappings too are deceptive; for they conceal valuative assumptions. In so far as it is informative about tackling the problems of classroom motivation in a positive way, it brings us inexorably back to motivational aspects of modes of experience . . . [10]

So now there are two utterly different perspectives, radical social administration theory and traditional educational philosophy, which both suggest the essentially problematic nature of the idea of needs and the way in which it is inevitably impregnated with values of a moral, cultural or political kind. Not only is the idea of need strictly incapable of neutrality in these senses, but as Hirst and Peters argue in their traditionally-minded critique of learner-centred education, it is a very limited idea when it comes to determining the content of learning. The same kind of conclusion is reached from the point of view of critical social policy theory by Taylor-Gooby and Dale, who argue that an ideology of needs-meeting in social policy provides a very limited insight into the content of policy in capitalist society. We need to look more closely at the function of 'needs-ideology' in all the contexts where it becomes prominent.

Hirst and Peters elaborate their point thus: needs are always evaluative conceptions (they 'ought' to be met) and they are not always motivational in character (needs do not necessarily correspond with 'wants'). To attribute a need to someone is to diagnose a lack of something on various grounds of desirability. On different grounds, therefore, we may diagnose needs as biological, psychological, basic cultural needs and functional needs. So what kinds of needs are reflected in the content of schooling?:

> Most of what is taught in school could only in fact be related to the last two types of needs. Autonomy, for instance, could be described as the need to resist influence or coercion. What is lacking in the case of needs such as these is a way of behaving which is approved of in certain societies. For children are not necessarily mentally ill if they lack these dispositions. To talk about a 'hierarchy of needs' at least draws attention to the different status of needs, though insufficient attention is paid to the differences in the norms with which they are connected.[11]

Hirst and Peters are stressing the cultural relativity, that is, the normative relativity of the idea of needs and perhaps, by implication, criticising influential psychologcial theories about 'hierarchies of need' which have little or no cultural reference. Interestingly enough they see the need for autonomy in cultural rather than psychological terms and, *pace* Hostler, they see it as an ideological constituent of schooling in certain kinds of societies whose value-systems reflect the bourgeois individualism of capitalism itself.

Children have functional learning needs too, and these are also what schools are intended to meet. In the end, however, what is the real significance of the 'needs-ideology'?:

> . . . the nearer we come to the class-room the nearer we come to the starting point of this chapter. For how do 'needs of the child' of this sort differ from aims of education? 'Education', in its specific sense, consists in passing on desirable states of mind involving knowledge and skill. These have to be interpreted in terms of aims such as literacy, numeracy, autonomy, co-operation and so on. So how does the reference to 'needs of the child' help? For the same sorts of thing appear as 'needs of the child', when we enter the class-room, as we already have formulated as being amongst our aims of education.[12]

The concept of need, say Hirst and Peters, is 'otiose in the case of the content of education'. In fact, they are saying, there is no substantive difference between the way in which we talk of the content of education as realising the 'aims' of education and the way in which we talk of it as being addressed to the 'needs' of learners. One is a philosophical discourse which rests upon the analysis and the logic of ideas and the other enters as an ideological account of practice. It should be abundantly evident by now that the aims and the ideology of education must have distinct and different reference. 'Needs' has emerged from quite opposed analyses — of radical social policy theory and traditional philosophy of education — as an idea rooted in ideology and standing for a conception of the aims, in this case, of education, and which functions to *justify* practice, not to criticise it. Whereas philosophical discussions of aims are concerned with the abstract and the conceptual, the ideology of needs directs our attention to the way in which they are formulated in social, cultural and political terms. The role of professional workers is crucial in such processes and it would be necessary to study it in some depth to understand the role of 'needology' (paraphrasing Taylor-Gooby and Dale) in the practices of adult and lifelong education. Almost certainly, as Hirst and Peters imply, the perception of aims and needs, of philosophy and ideology, will vary proportionately 'the nearer we come to the class-room'.

'Statements of "need" abound in educational writing', as R.F. Dearden says in another philosophical discussion of the idea.[13] As far as schooling is concerned he is saying some things similar to the analysis of Hirst and Peters. One function of 'needology' is to by-pass a discussion of aims.

The apparent reason for doing this is that it is supposed that, unlike aims, needs are empirically verifiable. Again, however, it is important to acknowledge that needs are not absolute but relative to moral values and cultural beliefs, and therefore that we must recognise 'the *valuational* basis of needs-statements, and the necessary subservience of the empirical data to such values'. Dearden is concerned, too, with the relevance of these concepts to motivation and with attacking some aspects of progressivism in schooling: 'Child-centred theorists, however, are sometimes apt to take wanting as a *criterion* of needing.' Clearly the ideas of wanting and needing are different, and in practice sometimes actually opposed to each other. Childhood learning, at least in terms of its content, is imposed according to philosophical criteria of aims or ideological criteria of needs, and this ideology reflects the dependency of childhood. But in the case of adult learners, although the conceptual relationship of wanting and needing is identical with that in the case of children, the ideology is still cast in terms of needs rather than wants — still imputing dependency to the learner. The question arises therefore whether in the context of adult learning the relationship of wanting and needing could be radically transformed, or whether the logical primacy of needs-statements is entailed by *any* educational ideology, whether it is concerned with the learning of either children or adults. If the concern is with the content of learning, however, one thing is clear: it remains a matter of judgement — moral, cultural and political judgement. Curriculum approaches postulate the content of learning as fundamental to the educational process, upon which philosophical views of aims or ideological views of needs are only a gloss. In the end, whether we are talking of schooling or of adult learning, the content is an object of decision-making processes in which some priorities come to prevail over others, and substituting an ideology of needs for a philosophy of aims does not fundamentally change this reality. As Dearden puts it: ' . . . the heart of the matter lies in the prior notions of what is valuable or desirable. It is here that a criterion of choice must be found.'

Bearing in mind these analyses borrowed from theories of social policy and philosophies of schooling, would it be true to say that adult education consists in providing adult learners with what they want, conflating their wants to needs for ideological purposes? Or do adult learners themselves learn to want what adult education can provide? The ideological primacy of needs-statements is widely acknowledged. Kenneth Lawson has analysed the logic of needs and wants in the context of adult education and points out, to start with, that the concept of need is as pervasive in this sector of education as it is in that of primary education with which Dearden was concerned:

At the level of programme planning in adult education the concept of 'need' plays a very distinctive role; and as Wiltshire has pointed out, this concept along with that of 'learning', has emerged as a dominant one in the vocabulary of the adult educator.[14]

The task of the adult educator is often conceptualised in terms of meeting the needs of individuals or communities. Although Lawson does not, as someone concerned primarily with philosophical analysis, express this as a problem of ideology, he does suggest that the stress on needs, as compared with wants, indicates its significance in terms of professionalisation and the nature of all educational provision in terms of worthwhileness:

This emphasis upon meeting needs can be seen as a refinement of the 'service' orientation which was discussed in chapter 2 and it represents a shift from the recognition of what the students want, which is a psychologically based concept.[15]

By the 'service' orientation of adult education, Lawson referred to the consumption-model of education associated with market-economy societies: 'Programmes and curricula are devised in response to the demands of potential users of a "service" which recognises them as consumers.' The consumer model or 'service' orientation of adult education, it should be pointed out, constitutes in itself a political model of provision rooted in economic structures and ideological practices. In terms of social policy analysis, in other words, this state of affairs does not preclude what Taylor-Gooby and Dale called 'the political process of the regulation of need'. The service orientation of adult education is of considerable ideological consequence although, of course, the political system from which it springs remains 'given' and unanalysed. Lawson, however, pursues an analysis somewhere between critical ideology and uncritical empiricism in his distinction between wants and needs. He points out that wants are of the nature of statements of personal taste which express no rationally defensible value judgements. Needs, however, are capable of reference to a framework of relevant standards and criteria. And although, as he argues,[16] some adult educators avoid the ethical issue, Lawson is suggesting that an ideology of needs-meeting cannot really absolve practitioners from making value judgements:

> The programme planner in moving away from simple considerations of what the market wants is taking a significant step. He is moving into a frame of reference in which value judgments are appropriate so that it does make sense to ask whether a given expression of want is justifiable on any grounds. He begins to ask the question 'given that x is asked for (wanted) ought I to provide it?' or 'are there any grounds for supposing that the students ought to have it?'[17]

So Lawson sees a clear connection between needs-meeting and professionalism, which is a status conditional upon some clearly demarcated area of decision-making, priority-ordering and the disposal of scarce educational resources. Precisely as in the case of other educational contexts (of schooling) the concept of need serves to divert attention from a more problematic concept of aims and constitutes an empirical basis for the justification of practices. It is used, says Lawson, 'to extricate the organiser from his dilemma by apparently providing an objective basis on which to make judgments'. It is used, he continues, 'as a logical stop beyond which there is nothing to be said, nothing to argue about'.

If we consider the function of the needs-meeting ideology, therefore, there are some remarkable similarities between schooling and adult education: professional practitioners, especially those committed to a progressive approach, both move towards the needs of the children and the adult learners. But in both cases, the social formulation of 'need' is much more problematic than is accounted for in its ideological function. That the concept of need is an element of professional ideology is made quite clear in several contexts and from several different points of view: in schooling and in adult education, from the point of view both of conceptual analysis and critical theory. Paradoxically, the centrality of need and the capacity of professional workers to define it and order its priorities would seem to cast the adult learner into the same kind of dependency as that inherent in schooling. The issue of autonomy is sharply raised by the analysis of need, and the crude equation of childhood with dependence and adulthood with autonomy does not really stand up to the kind of analysis which postulates social policy under capitalism as the creation of needs together with an inability to satisfy them.[18] Whatever kind of society is in question it is clear that the idea of need does not exist in a social vacuum but is relative to prevailing cultural and political conditions. It is a weakness of the uncritical account of need to neglect the social conditions in which they are, quite literally, created, and the role of professional workers in the creation of, as well as response to, need.

From the point of view of curriculum theory, as Dearden suggested in the context of schooling, the idea of needs is of very limited relevance. Its significance is not so much for teaching and learning (where it is assimilable to the idea of aims) as for justifying practice. Indeed, the theoretical emptiness of 'needs' can be illustrated in a variety of ways by the issues which the concept fails to raise. In the first place, what kind of realistic alternative to a needs-meeting rhetoric exists in a market-oriented society, one in which 'education' is 'consumed' as a commodity along with other goods and services? The rhetoric of needs arises inevitably from the general conditions of society and professional practice. As a result, the problem of the content of learning tends to be resolved through market forces, and the curriculum of adult education in terms of knowledge seems of less consequence than it has done in the case of schooling. The needs-meeting ideology, in the kind of analysis provided by Dearden and Lawson, makes it possible to by-pass issues of aims, or to avoid the ethical issues. In terms of the analysis of needs from the point of view of radical social policy theory, an ideology of needs-meeting effectively depoliticises adult education by avoiding the issue of aims, on grounds of philosophical scepticism or professional neutrality, and thereby reducing decision-making to a straightforwardly technical exercise in which market forces themselves constitute, in Lawson's apt phrase, the logical stop. The 'hidden curriculum' of adult education which Hostler identified is, in fact, hidden behind an ideology of needs-meeting.

A good example of how this ideology works through the practice of curriculum development in adult education was recently provided by D. Barry Lumsden.[19] In this article the author sought to define curriculum development in the context of adult education, and to provide an associated conceptual scheme with evaluative criteria for each phase of the process. He offers six important phases or stages of the curriculum process and, more important still for present purposes, a classical example of the needs-meeting ideology of the adult education curriculum process:

> In essence and substance, curriculum development is a process involving numerous aspects and phases, the most important of which are the analyses of situations, identification of needs, establishment of objectives, assignment of priorities, action implementation, and curriculum evaluation.[20]

It is important to understand that this is an essentially administrative conception of curriculum development, rather than one in the conventional educational sense of being concerned with knowledge. Administration, institutions and programmes, not knowledge, are the objects of the process:

> Adult education administrators must at some time come to grips with the issues involved in the questions raised . . . The institution must be aware of the 'urgent wants' requisite for individual self-actualisation and social progress if the organisation's existence is to be justified and its purposes realised.[21]

Lumsden tends to define needs, upon which the whole of the process of curriculum development in adult education turns, as 'urgent wants' which are requisite to some desirable condition or state of affairs. The problems inherent in this kind of reductionism have by now been sufficiently reviewed. The important point is that, according to this kind of argument, curriculum development in adult education becomes synonymous with the process of ascertaining need: 'The question of how these needs were, or are, ascertained becomes the very fulcrum upon which all curriculum development rests.' There is, he says, a case for as wide an involvement as possible in the process of ascertaining needs. In the end, however, an administrator's task is to define the kind of need which adult education can properly meet:

> By involving individuals in the various social systems and subsystems outside the institution, administrators can ferret out irrelevant factors affecting needs and better define the problem of need satisfaction.[22]

When it comes to deciding between priorities, however, here is a good example of how, from the standpoint of the professional administrative ideology, substantive issues seem to resolve themselves in the light of experience, without the necessity for decision-making:

> At this point it must be asked how one differentiates between relevant and irrelevant systems within a given community. In other words, what criteria are employed in this differentiation process? The answer is that only experience will reveal which systems, subsystems and extrasystems are relevant in relation to the change being promoted.[23]

These ideas are not dissimilar from that of the 'learning system' discussed in the previous chapter: a 'reified' and self-regulating concept of social relations, functioning always in the direction of harmony and requiring only the minimum of human intervention or − at least − the most sensitive professional regulation. Accepting that needs may not always present themselves 'in distinct hues of black and white', Lumsden suggests that administrators must 'rely upon experience, good common sense, and even, at times, intuition'. There are, of course, ways of discovering areas of need and contributing towards the solution of social problems on an informed basis, and Lumsden's view is that the role of adult education institutions is potentially important:

> The adult education institution presumably has the expertise and means needed to solve community problems, but the community has the problems needed to make practical and beneficial the institu-

tion's expertise and means.[24]

It is an organic relation of adult education institutions and local community structures. Indeed the function of such institutions in relation to dominant community power structures is made manifest:

> Once the power structures within a client system have been identified, those planning a curriculum, or programme, will certainly desire association with them in order to gain approval for action.[25]

Lumsden's context is that of adult education in the USA but there can be little doubt that much of his argument would find reflection in the ideology of adult education in Britain — to some extent, it is suggested, this is rendered inevitable in prevailing social and political conditions of both countries. As a case study of 'needology' in practice it does seem to bear out the kind of analysis which constituted the first half of the present chapter: by-passing the issue of aims, avoiding the ethical issue, depoliticising adult education whilst at the same time claiming a significant role in the solution of community problems; an 'uncritical empiricism' in the methodology of needs; association with dominant power structures in conditions of professionalism; even, perhaps, manifestly substantiating the idea of adult education's 'hidden curriculum' of political control.

The most important theoretical consequence of this kind of approach, however, is that the concept of curriculum as a definition, distribution and evaluation of knowledge in social, cultural and political conditions is entirely missing. Any concept of curriculum development, it will be argued, must be organised around the problems of redefining, redistributing and re-evaluating knowledge in these conditions, and this is the case both with schooling and adult education. Anything less than this, anything, that is, that reflects an ideology of needs-meeting in prevailing social and political conditions, will function overwhelmingly to reinforce prevailing definitions, distributions and evaluations of knowledge. Lumsden's view of the curriculum and of curriculum development is one in which the social, cultural and political construction of knowledge has no part, and in his rather bland social context the curriculum development process in adult education is transformed and reduced to the administration of needs.

From a variety of perspectives, then, the idea of needs and needs-meeting has been found to be of limited theoretical but of considerable ideological significance. Its consequences for the curriculum content of education are primarily to subvert substantive philosophical, moral and political issues and to reduce them to technical and administrative issues resolved at a level of professional ideology. And this is a critique of needs which can apply in the context of progressive schooling or of adult education in its socially progressive function as described by D. Barry Lumsden.

So the idea of 'needs' as an element of a distinctive adult education ideology fails: it fails both as a theoretical contribution to our understanding of the curriculum (being an uncritical reflection upon received ideas and practices) and it also fails to establish the distinctiveness of adult education ideology from that of schooling itself. However, there is an idea which does seem to constitute an element of a distinctive adult education ideology, and it is that of access.

Access

It should be pointed out to begin with that whereas access does function as a distinctive ideological concept for adult education it does not constitute a logical distinction between adult education and schooling. For it makes perfectly good sense to speak of the access of children to schooling as it does to speak of the access of adults to education or learning opportunities. It makes sense to speak of the access of children to schooling in a social developmental context or one of differentiated education systems as a problem or an issue, and indeed it is often regarded as such.

But there is another level of analysis here, and one which is directly of concern to our present purposes. For clearly there is a sense in which when we speak of access we do not only have in mind access to a particular kind of institution or system but rather to a particular configuration of knowledge itself. In other words, the theoretical potential of the idea of access (as contrasted with its ideological function) is in the area of the curriculum content of education. When we are talking about access, however, is it to knowledge or to institutional systems that it is sought, especially in the case of adult learners? Access, therefore, has a range of significances, and in theoretical terms its curricular significance is the most important of them all. It is easy, of course, to conflate the institutional and curricular significances of access but it should be remembered that to do this is to conflate schooling and learning. The dominance of the institutional significance of access is a measure, therefore, of the dominance of the school curriculum paradigm itself. So in examining the part played by the idea of access in the ideology of adult education it is important to bear in mind the range of significances which it can convey, and to try to evaluate the curricular as opposed to the ideological aspects of its use and meaning.

The true distinctiveness of access in the contexts of schooling and adult education is constituted by the different ways in which the issue is problematised. In both contexts, of course, the same range of significances enters into the problem, but the compulsoriness of schooling and the voluntariness of adult education mean that the problem as such is quite distinct.

These different dimensions of accessibility can easily be confused, however, and it is possible to achieve a greater degree of openness, flexibility and accessibility in the educational system without necessarily achieving (or desiring to achieve, of course) the kind of curricular change which is entailed by a redefinition, redistribution and re-evaluation of the knowledge-content of education. Adult educators, working in market conditions, must perforce think of access in institutional rather than curricular terms, arguing, not unplausibly, that these two aspects of access mutually influence each other.

Nevertheless, access is a distinctive ideological element of adult education which has stimulated important technical and methodological innovations in areas such as distance learning and the rationalising of provision and the transferability of academic credit and so on. But of course it is possible to achieve all this without radically affecting the curriculum content of a traditional educational system. The Open University, for example, has been instrumental in revolutionising educational technology without abandoning a fairly traditional knowledge-structure of subjects and faculties. Indeed, it was important for the success of the university that it should establish traditional standards of academic respectability. Relatively open and flexible access to a fairly traditional knowledge-content must be weighed against the possibility of a transforming curriculum development process in adult education. In other words, access and openness must remain conditioned by curricular as well as technical, economic and institutional considerations. Curriculum approaches to the idea of access invoke the additional barriers constituted by the 'social construction' of knowledge. It is not only the material conditions of working-class people which account for their proportional underrepresentation among Open University students but the barriers constituted by the conceptions of knowledge embodied in its curriculum. It would be surprising if they were proportionately represented: paradoxically their underrepresentation may be as much evidence that the Open University is a *bona fide* institution of higher education as are the high academic standards which it has achieved. The same kind of reasons, to do with the 'social construction' of knowledge, must also have to do with the failure so far of the university to move into certain fields of knowledge such as law and medicine, in addition to technical and economic reasons; quite simply, there are cultural restrictions upon access to high-status knowledge.

The idea of access, therefore, although it constitutes a distinctive element in the ideology of adult education, can only be conceived in simplistic and material terms unless some kind of curricular dimension is attributed to it. The problem of access in adult education is often expressed in terms of the proportional underrepresentation of working-class people among its participants, together with the corollary that those who are relatively well educated are proportionally overrepresented. If we think of access in curriculum terms, or of the social and cultural determination of knowledge, this becomes no more surprising than the fact that the relatively better off benefit most from the existence of a welfare state. The efforts that are made to make adult education accessible to working-class people, either through (de-) institutional change or associated criteria of 'relevance', whilst being intrinsically worthwhile, are necessarily conditioned by the culturally complex idea of access itself. The idea of access is distinctive in adult education ideology when the comparison is with compulsory schooling, in that it can be 'problematised' in a different way — in a way, that is, exemplified by the Open University and by cultural barriers which limit universal access to knowledge in societies where knowledge itself is stratified.

But when the comparison is not with compulsory schooling the idea of access may take on different meanings whereby it cannot be so clearly differentiated as an element in the ideology of adult education. It may, either for intrinsic educational reasons or in temporary and local conditions, be adopted as a strategy of other educational institutions and ideologies. It is, for example, adopted as an important strategy of recurrent education, especially as this constitutes a view of a comprehensive education system:

> Diversity, accessibility, transferability and accountability are the essential ingredients of a truly comprehensive system of education. It is impossible to conceive of comprehensive education in Britain until adults are included naturally, and as of right.[26]

Although the authors of this study, Ray Flude and Allen Parrott, propose 'local, comprehensive, all-age institutions' as the 'front line' of a recurrent system, it remains a view of access curiously devoid of curriculum significance. Institutional resistances to change, rather than the social dynamics of change and cultural resistances, are the objects of the authors' strategy. Without a dimension of the social construction of knowledge, together with its cultural and political significances, the overall impression of this kind of strategy of recurrent education is one of educational innovation in conditions of social conservatism. A mass system of education in the absence of a common culture of knowledge raises the issue of access in a far more difficult way than many educational progressives seem to allow for. In this way, the idea of access itself becomes a strategy of adult, continuing or recurrent education related to, or directed at, the institutions of an education system rather than the structures of knowledge to which they give expression:

> Accessibility is . . . vital in order to ensure a mass system. The opportunities for adults to learn must be genuinely open to every member of society, without any financial strings or other disincentives.[27]

The strategies associated with such a conception of access are those of positive discrimination and paid educational leave, together with counselling, information and advice services, and the kind of distance-learning technology associated especially with the Open University and other open learning systems:

> Accessibility to adult education means that people will be enabled to take courses of their choice at recurring intervals. This implies that these courses will be available when and where the student can use them. A considerable increase in the use of distance learning methods can be envisaged, therefore, in a system of recurrent education.[28]

The authors go on to commend the Open University as an example of the ways in which education may be made more accessible:

> The Open University has shown that a mixture of well-designed individual study, occasional and intensive group work and long-term counselling can function very satisfactorily at degree level. All types of education could benefit from this mixture.[29]

The success of the Open University has, however, been constituted more by its contribution to the accessibility of higher education rather than by its potentiality as a system of mass education. As Flude and Parrott say, its educational methods have major implications for education as such. But the curriculum implications of this concept of access, as they stand, are much greater in the context of educational methods than they are for the knowledge-content of the curriculum itself, and the kind of radical change implied by the idea of a 'mass' education system would surely entail a correspondingly radical change in the way in which, in society and culture, knowledge is defined, distributed and evaluated.

The Report of the Open University's Committee on Continuing Education raised the issue of access along with those of information and advice, provision, and learning resources and facilities.[30] And here too we may explore the ideological significance of the concept of access, and the paradox that lies at the heart of the matter in curricular terms. For the problem of access is seen primarily in terms of the access of individuals (either as such or else as members of particular groups) to learning opportunities, the barriers to which are constituted in wholly material terms. In fact barriers to access are collectively as much as individually experienced and culturally as well as materially constructed, and the paradox lies in confronting the individual learner with the problem of the socially and culturally constructed contents of learning. All the barriers likely to be experienced in these circumstances are equally real, but access does seem to be conceptualised in terms which ignore the cultural barriers to learning, which isolate and abstract the individual learner, and which tend to reduce the issue to one wholly resolvable in technical and institutional terms. There is little sense here that access to education might be a collective and political issue of knowledge and power in society. Indeed an equivalent concept of access has been more thoroughly explored in the context of the politics and ideology of schooling, because, as was outlined in the first chapter of this book, the curriculum itself is seen there in terms of knowledge, culture and power.

In a way, too, the ideological content of access is constructed by the professional need to impute learning needs to greater numbers of people. Access is a need of the system itself, in other words, and in this respect it is similarly conceptualised in higher and further education. Despite the fact that the openness of adult education really is more intrinsic and inherent than it is in other sectors of education systems, it needs to be remembered that, in the last resort, access is a function of provision, as well as a response to learning needs. For although attitudes to access in further and higher education may be opportunistic in certain conditions, there are no logical barriers to open learning systems but rather material and cultural ones. As far as adult education is concerned, it seems of ideological importance to impute theoretically limitless learning needs, however, and in this way needs, access and provision are functionally related to one another.

Access, is is being argued, can be justified on a whole range of criteria: moral, social and political. In the case of adult education, however, it is sometimes justified on extraordinarily narrow grounds which provide little sense of the meaning of access for knowledge, culture and power. In its most extreme form access may come to seem simply the projection of a professional ideology of provision — a direct function of provision itself, since if the learning opportunities are provided, ought not people to have access to them? Something of this ideological sense comes across in the Open University Committee's Report:

> In considering the evidence, the Committee was brought back repeatedly to an acknowledgement of the fact that any proposals made for increased scope in continuing education are substantially reduced in value if significant numbers of students do not have access to what is provided.[31]

The object of access is provision, and barriers are constituted by working conditions for those who work long hours or 'unsocial' hours and for whom the Open University Committee propose the strategy of paid educational leave. Barriers to access to provision are also constituted by the lack of financial support for part-time learning: ' . . . the Committee is clear that to be effective, plans for educational provision must be accompanied by financial plans to ensure ready access to those who need it'.[32]

Access is to educational provision, therefore, rather than to a more problematic knowledge-content of learning (who learns what?), and barriers to access are conceived in material rather than cultural terms. The analogy with the problem of schooling is interesting and worth pursuing in a context of critical theory. Universal and compulsory provision can hardly be said to pre-empt a problem of access to schooling and, as was suggested earlier, despite the distinctiveness of a compulsory and a voluntary system, the idea of access itself — unless conceptualised in the crudest possible terms — raises issues as much for schooling as for adult education voluntarily engaged in. Indeed, a major theme of the sociology of education, in so far as it is concerned with children's experiences and achievements in school, has been precisely one of access, and one in which it is the interplay of material and cultural factors which constitutes barriers to learning. Adult education theory, as it became assimilated to curriculum theory, would perhaps move along a similar line to that of curriculum theory of schooling and conceptualise access in terms of knowledge, culture and power as much as in terms of material conditions. And then doubtless what is truly distinctive about access in adult and lifelong education, as opposed to schooling, would emerge. That would be the point at which the idea would be of theoretical and not only ideological significance.

Ideologically, it was argued, access is seen as having provision as its object. And here again, the analogy with theories and ideologies of schooling might prove suggestive in the context of adult and lifelong education. For in the case of schooling, as was briefly described in the first chapter, the nature of 'provision' has been increasingly called into question, together with other hitherto apparently unproblematic categories concerned with educational achievement: the 'hidden' or uncritically received social, cultural and political aspects of educational provision have been subjected to an increasingly ideologically-oriented analysis. The status of 'provision' as an element in the ideology of adult education, however, remains relatively unexamined. Relative especially, that is, to the amount of description of provision which features in the literature, for provision is not only an object of access but an object of strategy and policy in the field.

Provision

It is hardly surprising that descriptions of provision should feature so prominently in adult education. For one thing, provision in this area is so diverse, complex and ambiguous that it is invariably necessary in a policy or strategy context to review existing institutions and practices. It is not normally a critical analysis of provision so much as a description of it which serves as a basis for developing strategies and policies of expansion and rationalisation on the functionally-related grounds of needs and access which have been mentioned. Another reason why descriptions of provision abound is perhaps that provision itself constitutes unambiguously a distinctive characteristic of adult education as opposed to schooling.

Provision, it was said, is an object of strategy and policy, and therefor descriptions in these terms (as opposed, say, to descriptions in terms of comparative adult education) tend to incorporate a view of the adequacy or inadequacy of provision. Strategic and policy priorities are in turn deduced from such a view of provision. Substantial proportions of key policy documents are devoted to provision in this sense. In Britain the most important recent report under the auspices of the Department of Education and Science[33] devoted a major section to a review of existing provision for non-vocational adult education, as specified by the terms of reference of the committee appointed to produce it. This part of the report, following the first part which was concerned with the assessment of need, describes the diverse agencies of provision of adult education before dealing in Part III with the future of adult education. In England and Wales, too, the National Institute of Adult Education constitutes a major source of our knowledge of provision[34] in the context of policy, while the Advisory Council for Adult and Continuing Education also keeps provision under review in the same context.

One of the Advisory Council's most recent reports devotes a major section to the use of resources in the provision of adult general education, concentrating upon the same kind of education as that dealt with by the Russell Report but focusing rather more upon the provision made by the local education authorities.[35] The point of describing provision is more or less the same as it was for the Russell Committee:

> The following sections of the report discuss the main resource elements and make suggestions about their deployment which, it is hoped, will be considered by the local education authorities and their partners in the provision of adult general education. Many of the examples quoted derive from existing practice; much of what is said is not new, but it is important at the present time that good practice, whenever identified, should be as widely known as possible.[36]

One of the functions of descriptions of provision is clearly the communication of information about good practice among adult educators; the publication of the Russell Report also stimulated and fostered a sense of professional identity, and this is clearly an important ideological characteristic of the concept of provision itself. In summarising their own review of provision, the Russell Committee said:

> In this section we have been endeavouring to draw out from the great wealth of evidence submitted to us the broad features of the present situation which may be taken as the starting points for

further development.[37]

Forging a sense of professional identity and solidarity is therefore at least a latent ideological function of the concept of provision. That is not to say, of course, that descriptions of provision have no comparative significance or no significance for theoretical analysis, and indeed there is no absence of comparative and theoretical analysis of provision.[38] The point made here has been that provision as a concept of adult education has functioned in ideological terms, and that its theoretical formulation has consisted so far of the reproduction of fairly uncritical curriculum categories. Accordingly, adult education ideologies stand in the same relation to critical theory as do those of schooling or social policy itself.

Summary

It has been argued in this chapter that an ideology of adult education is constituted by ideas of needs, access and provision. This is not the same thing as an ideology of autonomy, individuality and equality, because these are philosophical conceptions of the aims of education, and aims which are not logically distinctive to adult education in so far as their attainment is not precluded by schooling (whether or not in practice schooling defeats them).

If the literature of adult and continuing education is anything to go on, professional workers in this field rarely philosophise about their activities in this way, although they may believe strongly in such aims: the actual distribution of professional roles in adult education makes it much more likely that their concern is with needs, access and provision. In other words, the relevant ideological criteria are of an administrative and organisational kind rather than an abstract and philosophical one. In distinguishing between aims and ideologies it is important to understand the role played by professionalism in such a distinction and the way in which, for example, needs, access and provision are functionally related to one another.

The ideological significance of these ideas is that of the description and justification of practice. Indeed, as Lawson's analysis suggested, the function of 'needs' may be precisely to pre-empt by an uncritical empiricism a problematic view of the matter — one which raises philosophical, social and political issues. For it is a function of the ideology to reduce such issues to the level of technique, methodology and administration, and generally, as far as possible, to 'depoliticise' what have been described as the curriculum issues of adult education, those constituted by a view of the content of education as socially defined, distributed and evaluated knowledge.

The distinctiveness of the ideology raises the same kind of question as did the last chapter about the extent to which 'adult' could constitute a genuine curriculum category. The idea of needs seems quite undistinguishable in curriculum terms from its use in the context of schooling, where it is of little significance for the content of learning. Those of access and provision are of much more distinctive ideological significance for adult education, although each in its way can be shown to rest upon fairly uncritical and received curriculum categories.

Notes and References

1. John Hostler, *The Aims of Adult Education*, Manchester Mongraphs, 17 (Manchester: Manchester University Department of Adult and Higher Education, 1981).

2. Ibid., p. 56.

3. Ibid., pp. 56-7.

4. Ibid., p. 21.

5. Peter Taylor-Gooby and Jennifer Dale, *Social Theory and Social Welfare* (London: Edward Arnold, 1981), p. 3.

6. Ibid., p. 4.

7. Ibid., p. 9.

8. Ibid., p. 23.

9. Ibid., Chapter 8.

10. P.H. Hirst and R.S. Peters, *The Logic of Education*, p. 33.

11. Ibid., p. 34.

12. Ibid.

13. R.F. Dearden, *The Philosophy of Primary Education: An Introduction* (London: Routledge and Kegan Paul, 1968), pp. 14-18.

14. K.H. Lawson, *Philosophical Concepts and Values in Adult Education*, revised edn (Milton Keynes: Open University Press, 1979), p. 35.

15. Ibid.

16. Ibid., Chapter 2.

17. Ibid., pp. 35-6.

18. See above (8).

19. D. Barry Lumsden, 'The Curriculum Development Process in Adult Education', *Adult Education*, vol. 49, no. 5 (January 1977).

20. Ibid., p. 279.

21. Ibid., pp. 279-80.

22. Ibid., p. 281.

23. Ibid.

24. Ibid., p. 282

25. Ibid., p. 283.

26. Ray Flude and Allen Parrott, *Education and the Challenge of Change: A Recurrent Education Strategy for Britain* (Milton Keynes: Open University Press,

1979), p. 120.

27. Ibid., p. 121.

28. Ibid., pp. 121-2.

29. Ibid., p. 122.

30. Open University, *Report of the Committee on Continuing Education* (Milton Keynes: Open University, 1976), Section 3.

31. Ibid., p. 27.

32. Ibid.

33. Department of Education and Science, *Adult Education: A Plan for Development*, Part II.

34. National Institute of Adult Education, *Adult Education: Adequacy of Provision* (London: The Institute, 1970). See also the *Year Book of Adult Education*.

35. Advisory Council for Adult and Continuing Education, Reports: *Protecting the Future for Adult Education* (Leicester: The Council, 1981), Section V; *Continuing Education: From Policies to Practice* (Leicester: The Council, 1982).

36. Advisory Council for Adult and Continuing Education, *Protecting the Future for Adult Education*, p. 20.

37. Department of Education and Science, *Adult Education*, p. 48.

38. See, for example, Graham Mee and Harold Wiltshire, *Structure and Performance in Adult Education* (London: Longman, 1978).

4 ADULT EDUCATION AND SOCIAL POLICY

Introduction

It is possible to think of adult education in a variety of ways. In the last chapter it was suggested that one of the most useful was to think of it as the way in which it is reflected in the preoccupations of professional strategy, which are primarily with needs, access and structures of provision. It was further suggested that it is important to distinguish between these ideas and the ways in which it is possible to conceptualise the aims of adult education. In the case of adult education, as in that of schooling, these aims reflect evaluative priorities which are both rationally defensible (which is a task of philosophical analysis) and taken for granted (which is an objective of ideological analysis). It seems significant that, from a philosophical point of view, adult education 'properly so called' turns out to be concerned primarily with the self-development of the individual, a prescription heavily reinforced by the scientific contribution of psychological learning theory, which is itself so much concerned with concepts of the self.

So there is a philosophical or aims-oriented approach to theory in which as much intellectual effort is expended in distancing adult education 'properly so called' from other kinds of adult learning as it is in distancing the whole thing from schooling. There is also an administrative, institutionally-based distinction between this kind of 'liberal' or 'general' adult education and other kinds of adult learning, which is based not so much on philosophical principles as the sheer convenience of functional differentiation in administration, and which continues to be reflected in the reports and documents of policy agencies. And at what is possibly the deepest level of analysis there are the ideological evaluations which are unthinkingly embodied in day-to-day practice, at which level it is possible to discover the ideology of individualism which brings philosophy, administration and practice into relation.[1] At least, these are the kinds of elements necessary to analyse adult education in ideological terms.

However, the philosophy, administration and practices of adult education do not exist in a social and political vacuum, and as an ideology of 'individualism' or of 'needs, access and provision', adult education must be located in a wider social environment. In other words, the distinctions between 'liberal' and 'non-liberal' education, or between individual and collective purposes or aims and practice or whatever, must make sense in a wider ideological context where corresponding distinctions occur in other and related contexts. For a variety of reasons to do with history, culture and politics an ideology of adult education will obviously be relative to social conditions, where ideology will equally find reflection in administration and practice. The 'individualism' of adult education only arises in societies relative to a socially-determined notion of 'individualism' itself. In Western industrialised societies individualism has a cultural distinctiveness, as does voluntarism and market-entrepreneurialism and other ideological constituents of adult education, and the cultural significances of other constituents of, say, non-liberal education or community and social development, have been a source of controversy and debate. The issue, for example, of whether and to what degree adult education could or should constitute a form of social intervention,[2] or the issue of whether or not it could or should constitue a form of social control are issues which presuppose an ideological context in which they are meaningful issues which it is worthwhile to argue about. These are issues, whether adult education is in essence a 'liberal' or 'liberating' enterprise, or whether or not it is distinguishable from vocational or community and social developmental education, which can only in fact arise in a historical, cultural and political context which makes them possible: they are basically ideological issues and could not be resolved, only classified, by way of conceptual or philosophical analysis. What are often taken to be 'competing philosophies' of adult education are therefore more usefully regarded as issues of ideology, reflecting not so much timeless verities as local and relative conditions of culture and politics.

To pursue this argument further, whatever conditions make possible an ideological issue of 'liberal' or 'vocational' education or individual or collective purpose, there can be little doubt that adult education is an object of social policy. The purpose of the present chapter is to consider adult education as an object of social policy particularly in relation to curriculum analysis and curriculum development. As an object of policy, the question now runs, does adult education function to transform or merely to reproduce existing definitions, distributions and evaluations of knowledge? This is the kind of question, posed in relative historical, social, cultural and political conditions, which the curriculum approach demands of comparative social policy analysis. There seems reason to suppose that, in so far as adult education *is* an object of social policy, its categories are transformed sometimes to the point where that of 'adult' itself ceases to be of the same significance for the development of theory as it has been thought to be in the past: the primacy of curriculum categories of learning and knowledge in their cultural and political setting is established over administrative and institutional categories both of schooling and adult education.

Before social policy theories of adult education can be thought of as transforming or reproducing curriculum categories, however, it is important to distinguish methodologically between social policy and legislation. As an object of legislation adult education is constituted by an ideology of needs, access, provision (its institutionalisation in conditions of capitalism, socialism, development and so on). This may not, however, exhaust the significance of the process: a shift in the cultural significance of knowledge may or may not be an intended outcome of legislation, and it is not always possible to assume that legislation is directed towards curriculum transformation. The existence of apparently 'progressive' education in 'conservative' societies and 'traditional' education in 'progressive' societies indicates the cultural relativity and autonomy of education as an object of social policy. So we may not reduce adult education as an object of social policy to adult education as an object of national legislation, since to do so would be to lose the sense in which legislation is itself conditioned by historical, cultural and ideological factors.

There can be no doubt, however, that legislation for adult education remains the best evidence we have for the growing importance of it as an object of social policy. The increase in such legislation, at least in some European countries, has recently been documented in a context of comparative adult education by Colin Titmus and Alan Pardoen:

> The conscious and deliberate involvement of government in the field, the rapid and significant increase of this involvement in the last two decades, the forms it takes, and the purpose it is intended to serve reveal the growing interest and involvement of the government.[3]

This spate of legislation has been associated with recent concepts of lifelong education and, as the authors point out, there is no necessary connection between the development of theory and the rate of legislation, because despite common pressures 'a causal relationship between the concept of lifelong education and the quantity of adult education legislation cannot be generally established'.[4] In other words, legislation does not depend upon the theoretical elucidation of lifelong education, it may not involve a transformation of the knowledge-content of learning, and indeed as a piecemeal response to social problems it may function to reproduce traditional curriculum categories and reinforce a view of the education system as such as a form of social control. And Titmus and Pardoen are well aware of the methodological limitations of comparative education legislation:

> Laws prescribe what may or shall be done; they are evidence of intention, not proof of realization. The student of comparative adult education who takes the word for the deed may be sorely led astray. Between the enactment and implementation may be a broad gap, which is an important subject for comparative studies.[5]

This gap, it is argued, may be filled to some extent at least by a concept of social policy much broader and more problematic than that of legislation. Social policy, a process in which social, cultural and political forces contend, may elucidate the theoretical issues of adult education change better than legislation because these forces are the same ones as those which are brought to bear upon the curriculum itself.

The tradition of social policy analysis is well established in those liberal-democratic societies in which such issues in adult education as have been mentioned arise. It may therefore be useful to look briefly at such theories and models which have had as their object the kind of public policy and social welfare and which may help us to understand such categories as 'reproduction' and 'transformation' not only in terms of social and cultural relations but in terms of the adult education curriculum.

Social Policy Theory

With social policy as with the idea of 'needs' itself, it is of central importance to identify the problem of value judgements and this is generally agreed to be expressed in terms of normative rather than non-normative theory which aspires to the status of science. It is important to hold them conceptually distinct, for as Robert Pinker put it:

> The danger in all forms of theorizing and model-building in social policy is that sociologists may confuse their own constructs with the subjective reality of ordinary users. This danger is especially strong when the models in question contain strongly prescriptive and moral elements.[6]

This is a methodological problem common, of course, to all social science theorising: in the context of philosophical and psychological theories of 'adulthood', for example, it could be argued that they contain 'strongly prescriptive and moral elements' notwithstanding the analytic categories and experimental evidence upon which they claim to be based. But in this context of normative theory Pinker distinguishes between two models of social welfare policy, which he calls respectively the 'residual' and 'institutional' models, and these models may help us to conceptualise the adult curriculum as an object of social policy rather better than could legislation, at least if such an analogy truly holds good. Pinker describes the first model in these terms:

> The residual model of social welfare is closely linked to 'optimistic' theories of economic growth, of 'embourgeoisement' and 'convergence'. It is argued that with increasing and more diversified prosperity, the incidence of such problems as poverty is declining. The aim of social welfare under these circumstances should be to focus selectively upon a residual and declining minority of needy groups.[7]

This model adopts selectivism according to criteria of need as a dominant normative principle, whilst its opposite is based upon a 'universal provision' strategy:

> The 'institutional' model of social welfare is closely related to differing interpretations of the effects of economic growth, and the extent to which either 'convergence' or 'embourgeoisement' have occurred. The evidence of a persisting and increasing incidence of poverty is stressed rather than the growth of affluence . . . The inability of the market to achieve anything remotely akin to a 'just' allocation of goods and services renders it necessary for social services to be established as major institutions rather than residual agencies in industrial societies.[8]

In these simple terms Pinker expresses an ideological issue of social welfare policy over the primacy of selective or universal provision; it is also an issue about whether provision should be decided along lines influenced, if not decided, by the play of market forces.

The analogy with adult education provision can be crudely sketched, but usefully so perhaps, before other social policy theories and models are briefly described. According to the 'residual' policy model, in terms of an ideology of 'educational need', market forces adequately cater for it:

those better off in both material and cultural circumstances are able to afford their recreational or personal-developmental education or to improve their own market position as far as occupations are concerned. The 'social welfare' element of provision is addressed to 'disadvantaged groups' in material, cultural or social terms, and the curriculum of this kind of provision is variously described as 'remedial', 'compensatory' and so forth – at least it is distinguishable from the market provision as far as the knowledge-content of the curriculum is concerned. The 'residual' policy model illuminates perhaps the traditional adult provision and throws into relief the often unacknowledged contradiction between the market principle, whereby those better off both materially and culturally traditionally have greater proportional access, and the residual need principle whereby certain groups gain selective access to provision for as long as their need persists (during unemployment, for example, or in conditions of discrimination or inequality). The 'institutional' policy model proposes universal provision in the light of the failure of market forces to eliminate need and in the light also of a view of social problems, such as those of change or unemployment or inequality, which makes them more intractable and permanent. Such problems, and the needs associated with them, seem to be inherent in the institutions of modern societies and institutionalisation of provision seems a more rational response to this kind of need than do the workings of the market. The 'institutional' model would appear to describe adult education in different terms – its object is not to respond to educational needs which are residual consequences of market forces and inequalities, but rather to constitute an institutionalised and permanent educational function in society, integrated much more completely into the general educational provision on the grounds that the needs which are its object are permanent – not temporary – conditions of society.

In curriculum terms, therefore, such policy models as these may contribute to the construction of a theoretical view of lifelong education which, as was suggested, is not necessarily entailed by the spate of legislation on adult education provision. There are elements of the adult curriculum which represent functionally a failure of schooling: basic education, literacy and numeracy which have achieved the status of priorities for adult education in certain conditions are, in terms of our 'institutional' model, priorities of an education system *as such* rather than of any specific sector. These key elements of an adult curriculum, when they achieve a certain scale, are a function of the failure of schooling rather than of intrinsic adult learning needs. These are permanent needs inherent in the conditions of society itself — its patterns of change and associated degrees of alienation and anomie, its inequalities, divisions and repressions, all of which have an ideological significance relative to the society in question. Some such institutionalised learning needs will be of consequence for the cultural and political significance of knowledge itself, and if they are met then perhaps it could only be by the means of a 'transforming' curriculum rather than a 'reproducing' one which would reproduce, among other things, precisely the same conditions which give rise to the 'residual' needs of the existing system.

'Residual' and 'institutional' models of social welfare policy suggest, therefore, ways of conceptualising the adult curriculum. This will reflect both residual and institutional needs: traditional adult liberal or general provision along 'market' lines as well as selective 'remedial' or 'compensatory' provision for specific groups or classes of people. Both of these constitute 'residual' provision in that they respond to needs generated in the education system itself — respectively, perhaps, to needs generated by its successes and failures. But this kind of analysis also suggests a way of thinking about adult learning needs which are intrinsic, that is to say, which are not a function of schooling but which are inherent or 'institutionalised' in social change as such. Responding to these kinds of adult learning needs — and thereby shifting the emphasis in the direction of curriculum analysis from educational provision towards the content of learning — seems a much more promising starting-point for adult education theory than the various 'adult characteristics' approaches which have been mentioned and which all too often collapse into descriptive and methodological categories in reaction to the dominant paradigm of the school curriculum. In other words, the distinctiveness of adult education has been sought for on the wrong grounds and, by neglecting the educational centrality of the content of learning, has tended if anything to reproduce rather than transform the categories of the dominant paradigm. But it is only possible to achieve real distinctiveness if the kind of distinction with which we are presently concerned, that is adult education as an object of legislation and as an object of social policy, comes to the fore at the expense of the traditional and rather unfruitful distinctions between adult education and schooling. Above all, the focus of any really useful analytic distinctions for education theory must be upon the ways in which the knowledge-content of *any* learning is socially, culturally and politically constructed. Learning which is voluntarily and individually undertaken does not of course re-create or transform its content any more than that undertaken compulsorily and collectively under schooling. It may or may not have some trans-forming potential — many would argue on the contrary that learning collectively engaged in has a greater potential for transforming its content. It is an issue which cannot be pursued here. The point is, its pursuit would have to be conducted in terms of critical curriculum theory, where the construction of knowledge is the process to explain.

Social policy theories and models — because they are fundamentally concerned with the social construction of public policy (and distin-guishable from theories and models of social administration) — may serve as useful analogies for thinking about the social construction of the adult curriculum. But before looking at other examples in this field it may be useful to restate the grounds of the analogy.

If we think of the content of adult learning as determined by a range of social factors both material and cultural, such as family, com-munity and work experience, together with demographic, class and status experience, the influence of media cultures and so forth, then the provision of formal learning opportunity could only play a limited role in the construction of the adult curriculum. This is why it is useful to think of this curriculum more as an object of social policy (the social construction of public policy) in analogous terms rather than as an object of legislation. The object of legislation as such is the institutional system of education. Legislation, in other words, is for provision and could not be, in voluntary conditions, for a curriculum as such. Legis-lation, from the point of view of learning, is 'enabling': its ideological focus is upon access to provision. There is no necessary connection between legislation which secures the condition of access to provision on the one hand and changes in the curriculum content of learning on the other. On the contrary, it is possible that securing more universal access to a traditional system of provision reinforces and reproduces traditional curriculum categories. Put simply, a spate of adult education legislation may not be of any theoretical significance for the content of adult learning: its potential is either to reproduce or transform the curriculum of schooling, and whether it does one thing or the other is a proper object of a curriculum theory of adult education.

From a certain point of view, on the other hand, legislation to extend access to provision is of necessity progressive, for as was sug-gested earlier the imputation of limitless adult learning needs is an important element of professional ideology as it finds expression in the literature. From a theoretical point of view, it is being argued here, legislation may be of curriculum consequence or not. And whether such consequences are desirable or not is a matter of value judgement.

Now these social theoretical and value-related issues are precisely what social policy analysis opens up in proportion as an 'ideology of legislation' tends to close them down. Social policy analysis permits a view of legislation as reactionary as well as one of it as progressive, because it focuses upon the social, cultural and political construction of policy in a context, as Pinker put it, of normative social theory. If, therefore, the focus of adult education theory is to be upon the social, cultural and political construction of the content of adult learning then social policy theories may prove suggestive in this area too.

Social Policy Analysis

In a collection of essays on the subject Martin Rein has described a personal approach which seems to raise most of the procedural issues in the context of a normative theory.[9] There is, he says in the first place, some honesty and truthfulness in scepticism, provided always that it does not degenerate into cynicism and is underpinned by some faith and hope:

> In other words, I believe that scepticism is valuable because it questions facile beliefs and facile interpretations of facts, and requires one to be serious about the practicality of ideals and their implication. This defence of scepticism presupposes an underlying commitment to ideals — otherwise why does it matter whether people are facile and impractical or not?[10]

Just what this scepticism entails is described by Rein in six principles which he argues should determine our approach to social policy. The first of these is to treat the question of purpose as unresolved, and here he is thinking of such concepts of 'needs' which, it has been suggested, are of little theoretical significance however largely they figure in an ideology of provision:

> The study of social policy is basically concerned with the range of human needs and the social institutions created to meet them. Yet we have no adequate definition of 'need', and much confusion prevails about the distinctions between 'need', 'preference' and 'social problems'. Moreover, the institutional arrangements meeting these 'needs' seem infinitely varied and have a rapid rate of obsolescence. What is accepted in one decade as truth may be challenged in

another.[11]

There are no permanent solutions to problems of social policy, in other words, because both problems and purposes are continually being redefined. The assumptions of the analyst must therefore be that the objectives of any public policy are 'multiple, ambiguous and conflicting', and its goals should never simply be accepted as given.

The analyst should, says Rein, attend to practice as well as policy:

> One way of coping with ambivalent purposes is through vagueness and ambiguity. If one examines the purposes of most social legislation one usually finds that the moral and ideological objectives, the goals of social policy, are open to many interpretations. Ambiguity seems to be essential for agreement.[12]

The study of policy is inseparable from the analysis of practice, for only in this way could the manifest and latent functions of policy be identified. For example, and referring to his own research, Rein cites the functions of youth training programmes which, manifestly providing skills, effectively defer the entry of youth into the labour market. Policies such as this, he is saying, may be taken to be technical solutions to problems without regard to their ideological significance. Conflicting distributional principles, such as universal or selective provision (which underpinned Pinker's 'institutional' and 'residual' social welfare models) represent conflicts of ideology which are only apparently resolved at the level of practice.

For these kinds of reasons Rein argues for a historical perspective in policy analysis. Our knowledge of policy issues is not cumulative, and there is a sense in which it is impossible to learn from experience in these matters, given conditions of more or less permanent social change. So there is a general tendency in social policy for it to develop in a cyclic rather than a linear manner:

> Since the problems are in essence intractable, and can rarely be resolved without sacrificing some strongly held values, the issues tend to be recurrent. Each generation takes up the same issues again and seeks to re-define them in the light of its own political, economic and social reality.[13]

History suggests that it is almost impossible to conceive of social policy in liberal democratic societies as any kind of once-for-all establishment of social priorities among conflicting claims without internal contradictions. For this reason, says Rein, social policies develop rather as a succession of fads or fashions, first one and then another being pursued.

Since social policies are developed in a context of competing interests and purposes, accepted patterns contain 'the contradictions and limitations which make it politically acceptable'. It is as important therefore to distrust orthodoxy as it is to be sceptical of fashions, and policy analysis will distance itself from prevailing trends simply on the grounds that since there are no permanent, unchanging problems there are no permanent, unchanging solutions either: 'When community care and de-institutionalization become the accepted ideology of the helping professions, the benefits of institutional care need to be reassessed.'[14]

The contrast between the values which inform policy and those which are embedded in practice suggests to Rein that the analyst should approach social policy as a moral critic. His scepticism entails a view of policy as an outcome of conflicting interests and principles in which some come to prevail over others and in which debates about means conceal issues which are of an ideological as much as a technical kind:

> To understand goals we need to consider them not as philosophical abstractions of the common weal, but as a reflection of the interest of specific social groups. It is therefore useful to review goals concretely in terms of the actors who cherish them and of what is at stake for them when they forsake, compromise on, or achieve their ends.[15]

What may seem therefore to be a technical issue as to how best to achieve a universally desired goal may conceal the fact that, in the absence of such a goal, policy decisions represent a triumph of some interests and principles over others: 'I am inclined therefore to treat debate about means as masked ideology.' The outcome of public policy is, after all, the distribution and redistribution of incomes, services, resources and so on, and in this sense – and in conditions of inequality – it is almost impossible to conceive a policy the outcome of which was universal and equal benefit.

Finally, Rein illustrates what he describes as his 'value-critical' approach to policy analysis by considering the importance of the relation of knowledge to policy studies, the kind of information upon which decisions are made and the kind of political response which empirically-based studies attract. Again, it must be concluded that the ideological element of policy-making is such that a decision directly derived from knowledge and evidence is difficult to envisage:

> Knowledge is not used simply to influence policy actively. The process is more complex; as policy evolves, knowledge is used selectively to justify actions reached on other grounds. Moreover, knowledge and policy are interactive, being as much influenced by as influencing the current agenda for reform. While the active role is accepted as the dominant model, in practice social science both justifies policy decisions and interacts with them.[16]

It is easy to see, therefore, that policy analysis either in the 'normative theory' or 'value-critical' mode gives ready access to an idea of social policy as retrogressive or reactionary as well as progressive, and that this is not inherent in a view of adult education provision as an object of legislation: the curriculum, unlike the structures of provision, is a description of the practices of teaching and learning. And between the policy and the practice, as has been seen, we may be permitted a legitimate degree of scepticism. For what people learn, the knowledge-content of their learning, is not determined by legislation directly. It is not so determined in some instances of schooling even, but in the case of adult education it would seem quite impossible to legislate for a curriculum. It is in this kind of area that the elements of distinctive theory are to be sought. But it would be quite mistaken to suppose that legislation for adult provision exhausts the possibility of theoretical analysis of the adult curriculum as an object of social policy, particularly in view of the kind of policy analysis models at present under review. We are able to think of it, for example, in ideological terms in the same way that we can think of schooling not only as an object of legislative provision but as constituing, and constituted by, an ideology of the curriculum. Legislation for adult education provision is presumably no more exempt from critical and ideological analysis than legislation for anything else, and the curriculum assumptions inherent in such provision are the outcome of the same kind of social processes as those of any kind of provision.

One of the most important contributions of the social theoretical approach to policy has, as has been seen, been to challenge the view that it could be analysed in purely scientific, technical or value-neutral and ideologically free ways. Another contribution, which reflects closely certain developments in the sociology of education, has been to call into question the whole basis of progressivism in modern society and to draw attention to the persistence of poverty and inequality. In Rein's terms this is a tradition which has sceptically explored the ideology of the welfare state in relation to its practices and to people's experiences of it. Such a tradition, as represented by Richard Titmuss or Peter Townsend, amounts to a critical theory of the ideology of progressivism in the context of social welfare. But it is suggestive too in other contexts. Adult education, it is argued, is by its very nature a progressive force in society. The analytic distinction between legislation and social policy, however, gives grounds for a more theoretical view of adult education, and one which in an important sense transcends its ideology.

Peter Townsend's definition of social policy avoids the contentious issue of needs:

> Perhaps most commonly social policy is defined as policy concerned with the public administration of welfare, that is, the development and management of specific services of the State and of local authorities, such as health, education, welfare and social security services, to remedy particular social problems or pursue social objectives which are generally perceived and agreed as such.[17]

As a definition, however, Townsend suggests that this is very limited. For one thing, it is based not so much upon the functions of government as upon the analysis and classification of formal administrative divisions. In fact, he is saying, the analysis of such divisions does not of itself constitute a genuinely theoretical view of the functions of government in relation to social change:

> There may be unintended social by-products or effects of Government policies in defence, industrial ownership, industrial relations, trade, employment and the administration of law. These could either reinforce or undermine social service policies. They cannot be ignored in any discerning account or application of social policy.[18]

Substituting functional for administrative categories, says Townsend, gives us a more realistic picture of social policy than that which is derived solely from such categories. It is a reason for reinforcing the distinction between legislation and social policy, not only in relation to their objects but to the way in which they may be analysed. To concentrate upon legislation is to abstract a particular category from functional social policy: to look, say, at legislation concerning paid educational leave and perhaps comparing one country with another in this particular respect, does not provide a 'discerning account' of paid educational leave as social policy unless many other factors are taken into account. For legislation for paid educational leave could quite easily be undermined by the unintended (or indeed intended) consequences of legislation concerning employment or industrial relations. By the same token it could be made more effective. From a theoretical point of view, legislation which is intrinsically 'progressive' may, in a context of 'regressive' social policy, have little effect upon social change.

Another reason why the standard definition of social policy is limited, says Townsend, is that it limits policy functions to the domain of government. Again, we must look for a definition which transcends formal legislative categories:

Government policy is no more synonymous with social policy than Government behaviour is synonymous with social behaviour. Institutionalized social polices cover a wider range than those promulgated and administered by central and local departments of Government and include the indirect as well as direct welfare policies of industry, religion, voluntary associations and private companies or employers. Religious and voluntary bodies have pioneered some services later innstitutionalized by the State. Today they often run services resembling those run by the State or in more or less satisfactory partnership with those run by local authorities.[19]

Comparative social policy could not usefully be reduced to comparative legislation because the meaing of relevant concepts, of housing, health care and insurance, educational provision and so on, will vary with respect to different historical, economic and social conditions. Townsend is saying that in these ways social policy is a social construction and must be held conceptually distinct from legislation as such: it would, he says, be absurd to confuse the two. An extended definition would have the disadvantages of ambiguity and scale: social inequality, for example, frustrates attempts even to document it. Academic and mass media treatment 'will tend to revert to more reassuring administrative concepts and will concentrate on areas about which there is information'. But there are advantages in resisting such tendencies and seeking broader social structural analyses of social policy, for they will bring us closer to social realities than any account of legislation could. The student of social policy, says Townsend, should seek knowledge about the structural causes of, and remedies for, social problems. For problems, causes and remedies are all, in some sense or other, socially constructed. And although Townsends's own concerns have had to do largely with poverty, the implications for analysing education and adult education in these terms are not far to seek. In the case of schooling, structural policy analysis is already well under way:

> Much of the specialized work in sociology is in practice policy-oriented. Contributions to the sociology of education in the United States and Britain make this abundantly clear. Educational sociologists, criminologists and medical sociologists, for example, are conscious of the relevance of their work to developments in policy and often actively contribute to them.[20]

The social policy analysis of adult education in these terms seems to be at a pre-theoretical stage. There is much material, prescription and quasi-theory but little development so far of the kind of theoretical categories that Townsend is talking about. There is, on the other hand, a predominance of administrative, organisational and learning-theory categories over those of a cultural, sociological and political kind which focus upon the curriculum as the central problem of education and change. It is perhaps an indication of the dominance of the paradigm of the school curriculum that such a focus has not arisen within adult education theory. It also indicates a need for much more of the kind of sociological anaysis which tends to be 'value-critical' of received, commonsense or 'taken-for-granted' practice than do those disciplines which have so far been most influential in the formation of adult education theory. And certainly, in his own considered definition of social policy Townsend sees sociological analysis as being important:

> Policy analysis must therefore depend on a broad sociological perspective about both objectives and means. Social policy is best conceived as a kind of blueprint for the management of society towards social ends: it can be defined as *the underlying as well as the professed rationale by which social institutions and groups are used or brought into being to ensure social preservation or development*. Social policy is, in other words, the institutionalized control of services, agencies and organizations to maintain or change social structure and values. Sometimes this control may be utterly conscious, and consciously expressed by Government spokesmen and

others. Sometimes it may be unspoken and even unrecognized.[21]

As with Rein,Townsend tends to stress social policy as an outcome of conflicts of interest and principle among different social groups, including professional groups more or less directly concerned with implementation, and to see apparently technical arguments about means as in reality forms of ideological conflict. One way of illustrating conflict is by constructing models along the lines of Pinker's distinction between 'residual' and 'institutional' models of social welfare policy. This, it was argued, was a way of thinking which may be suggestive for a curriculum analysis of adult education. It may be useful to look at another classical example of social policy model-building to see whether this way of conceptualising policy can take us further in the direction of suggestive analogies.

Richard Titmuss, who was associated with social administration rather more than with a tradition of sociological analysis, showed that administration nevertheless could hardly be conceived merely as a technical resource-allocation process, and that it was located in a wider framework of social policy. In this framework a variety of mutually incompatible criteria for decision-making and evaluative choice can be discovered and conceptualised as social policy models.[22]

Titmuss set out three such models, pointing out that 'the purpose of model-building is not to admire the architecture of the building, but to help us to see some order in all the disorder and confusion of facts, systems and choices concerning certain areas of our economic and social life'. Although the models of Titmuss reproduce elements of Pinker's they are elaborated in rather different ways.

The first he calls the residual welfare model, corresponding to Pinker's own version of the market forces ideology:

This formulation is based on the premise that there are two 'natural' (or socially given) channels through which an individual's needs are properly met; the private market and the family. Only when these break down should social welfare institutions come into play and then only temporarily.[23]

This model is postulated on the assumption that morally people would be better off without the welfare state: its existence is seen in basically negative terms and the need for it as arising out of the temporarily pathological condition of society — a condition generally attributed to individuals rather than society, in fact. It stands for an ideology of individualism, argued on philosophical, social and economic grounds.

Model B Titmuss describes as the industrial achievement-perform-ance model of social policy:

> This incorporates a significant role for social welfare institutions as adjuncts of the economy. It holds that social needs should be met on the basis of merit, work performance and productivity. It is derived from various economic and psychological theories con-cerned with incentives, effort and reward, and the formation of class and group loyalties. It has been described as the 'Handmaiden Model'.[24]

Later in the book Titmuss describes this model as an occupational welfare system, and asks − in the spirit of Townsend's injunction to consider the unintended as well as the intended outcomes of legislation − what effect it has over the whole population, including the non-employed, and what effects it has upon community life and participa-tion in the administration of the system.[25]

Model C Titmuss calls the institutional redistributive model of social policy:

> This model sees social welfare as a major integrated institution in society, providing universalist services outside the market on the principle of need. It is in part based on theories about the multiple effects of social change and the economic system, and in part on the principle of social equality. It is basically a model incorporating systems of redistribution in command-over-resources-through-time.[26]

This model, Titmuss later points out, shifts the attribution of pathology from individuals to society less ambiguously perhaps than was the case with Model A: it 'sees the social services as instruments to provide for certain specified needs in society regardless of value judge-ments about individuals and families as to whether or not they consti-tute social problems'.[27]

The last model corresponds roughly to Pinker's institutional model, in which social problems were located in institutional social change as such, rather than in any particular institutional structure of society. Titmuss's formulation draws attention to the ethical principles of redis-tribution which are associated with the institutional model and with universal, as opposed to selective, welfare provision — the opposition around which Pinker's own models were polarised.

The general analogy being pursued in this chapter between social policy analysis and curriculum analysis in relation to legislation and ideologies or models or provision, may finally be applied in the case of comparative analysis. In their introduction to a recent study of comparative social policy the authors put the matter thus:

> The comparative approach involves more than merely describing the apparently similar social security, health or social work services of another country. Simple description is not enough. Putting descriptions side by side does not help us to understand why the differences are there; nor does the drawing up of league tables of who spends most on what . . . Students will need to adopt a critical attitude to the concepts and analysis used by the various people, including themselves, who attempt comparative study. They should ask how far the purely intellectual constructs, intended to illuminate and impose some order on the social phenomena being studied, make comparisons possible without at the same time distorting the realities.[28]

Social policy, it has been suggested, is a complex thing to analyse, and the complexity of it is compounded in its comparative study. Clearly it may not be reduced to legislation or administration but is the outcome, both intended and unintended, of conflicts of interest and principle in society. The ethical issue may not be avoided either, any more than the ideological, and critical analysis does not preclude the formulation of means and strategies from this approach — even though these may appear to be only raising technical issues.

The increase in legislation for adult education has been in a context of alternative conceptualisations, notably that of lifelong learning.[29] It is therefore significant perhaps that the term 'strategies', rather than policies, is often used in connection with these alternative conceptions of adult learning. They are certainly alternatives to what is traditionally understood by adult education. To talk in terms of strategies, however, does seem to imply an effort, conscious or not, to conduct an analysis at the level of technique, or to consider alternative means to a goal which is itself not a matter of ideological significance and not therefore an object of social policy analysis as this has been briefly outlined.

The distinction between aims and ideologies of adult and continuing education or, indeed or lifelong learning itself, needs continually to be borne in mind. The analysis of any social policy makes this abundantly clear. Except in philosophical terms, of course, there is no single ideology of adult education but a whole range of culturally prescribed alternatives, of which an ideology of individualism is one. Thus it would be an interesting exercise in comparative social policy of adult education to analyse adult learning in relation to dominant social and political ideologies, and look, for example, at the redefinition of liberal or individualistic ideologies of adult education in societies whose dominant social and political ideology is more collectivist. It would be interesting to consider the status of collective adult learning ideologies in societies whose dominant political ideologies are more individualistic. The materials to do this are increasingly coming to hand in alternative conceptions of adult learning such as continuing, lifelong or recurrent education. Sometimes these are presented as alternative strategies to achieve a common goal – lifelong learning, say, or the 'learning society' – which as an idea would seem to transcend otherwise irreconcilable political ideologies. Society as such, it is often claimed, changes in such a way that traditional education systems of schooling need to be replaced or supplemented by lifelong learning systems in all societies, whatever their economic, social or political ideologies. In this sense, at the level of concepts or ideas, all societies move towards a common goal – only strategies to achieve it will reflect the ideological differences which exist between them.

As the growth of legislation, both national and under the auspices of international organisations, suggests, adult learning is increasingly an object of social policy, whether or not it reflects an ideology of individualism. To what extent, though, could we analyse strategy or policy according to the categories of curriculum theory being developed here? Strategies, it was suggested, have legislation and structures of provision as their object, whereas the social policy approach is analogously concerned with the object of adult learning itself: the curriculum of socially constructed knowledge.

To what extent are strategies for lifelong learning likely to have as their object a transformation of the social, cultural and political construction of knowledge, of its redefinition, redistribution or re-evaluation in these terms? After all, as has been pointed out, legislation as such is not progressive: its consequences, intended or not, may be socially regressive. There is no reason to suppose that legislation for adult education could be analysed in a way different from that of any other social welfare legislation, even though from an ideological point of view any increase in adult learning is necessarily progressive. In order therefore to transcend ideology and adopt a more theoretical perspective it would be useful to introduce the dimension of social policy analysis which makes it possible to think of the objects of strategies and legislation as changes in the social construction of the curriculum content of adult learning. A theoretical, curriculum or knowledge-content based analysis would help, too, to put into a single perspective the confusing terminology of lifelong learning strategies. For all of them the same kind of criteria may be sought, the same kind of question asked: what are the curriculum consequences for any strategy as a form of social policy? To what extent does it envisage a reproduction or a transformation of the curriculum of schooling as a social policy of adult education? In other words, are strategies for lifelong learning directed towards the transformation of the knowledge-content of adult learning or only of traditional forms of adult education?

A stage has now been reached where it is possible to formulate a hypothesis. For by combining social policy and curriculum analysis we could compare and distinguish between adult education and lifelong learning. Adult education, as an object of legisation and structures of provision, and reflecting an ideology of needs, access and organisation for provision, has generally little curriculum reference along a reproduction-transformation scale, and is functionally related to the curriculum of schooling in various ways. Lifelong learning, as an object of social policy, may have this kind of curriculum reference depending on what kind of strategy is adopted.

Strategies for Lifelong Learning

The recent publication of a collection of papers written by international experts under this heading[30] provides a good opportunity to illuminate the curriculum analysis hypothesis. In the first place, though, it ought to be remembered that the common pursuit of an ideal may only superficially obscure ideological conflicts. Remembering Rein's procedural injunction for social policy analysis 'to treat debate about means as masked ideology' we may reasonably expect common themes and purposes to be stressed at the expense of the different ideologies inherent in different strategies for lifelong learning. So the need to create a political, professional, public and, indeed, international consensus concerning the desirability of lifelong learning[31] has to be considered together with the fact that adult education is a site of philosophical and ideological conflict. This is a point put across effectively in a recent collection of papers addressed to this subject, and which raises the issues both of the public image of adult learning and the ways in which adult educators see their work in different contexts. Both issues surely constitute potential obstacles in the way of a consensus about the need for lifelong learning:

> Adult education is often mistakenly perceived as being a fairly traditional conservative activity dealing with unexceptional subject matter of a professional, vocational, remedial, or hobby nature. The content of adult education programs is usually noncontroversial, avoiding sensitive issues and steering clear of disputations about values. Not surprisingly, observers of practice and programs in this field frequently get the impression that adult educators are people who never get involved in disputes, men and women who adroitly avoid arguments as they seek community approbation for their programs and institutions. In fact, adult educators are a quite contentious lot who spend a great deal of time embroiled in arguments among themselves about purposes, methods, audiences, and procedures.[32]

It seems reasonable to suppose that lifelong learning is potentially as contentious an idea as that of adult education turns out to be in practice. On the other hand, as ideas, lifelong learning and adult education are some distance apart; contributors to the development of an idea of lifelong learning may be as much concerned to distance it from that of adult education as adult educators have sometimes been to distance their activities from those of schooling. But these efforts, it is suggested, are not entailed by the logic of educational ideas so much as by the ideological contexts of schooling and adult education: the 'distancing' efforts which, as outlined in Chapter 2, culminate in 'adult characteristics' theory are in part a function of local cultural and ideological conditions which sometimes permit concepts of adult schooling or 'adult pedagogy' and sometimes do not. Nevertheless, the nature of adult education in relation to strategies for lifelong learning has been complicated by a terminology which seems to keep pace with legislation itself.

So the editors of the symposium of views on strategies for lifelong learning usefully provide a note on terminology at the outset of their published volume, where the following meanings prevail:

Lifelong learning to indicate a basic *concept* and social *goal*: the opportunity for individuals to engage in purposeful and systematic learning during the periods of their lives when this opportunity is most relevant.

Recurrent education to indicate a *strategy* of provision that makes these recurrent opportunities possible.

Continuing education to indicate the post-initial *stage* of this process: i.e. after a substantial break from initial education.

Continuous education to indicate systematic learning closely based on everyday work.

Higher education to indicate final degree study and beyond.

Adult education to include all systematic learning provision for adults, other than full time higher education.[33]

The curriculum hypothesis is concerned with the degree to which such terms are seen to entail changes in the definition, distribution and evaluation of knowledge as an object of social policy. On the surface, and not to make substantive issues out of what are presented as convenient definitions, lifelong learning is seen as an object of social policy without necessary consequences for the knowledge content of adult learning. Recurrent education is a strategy of provision with the same kind of implications as that which has been traditionally called adult education: its object is legislation to widen the access of adults to learning opportunities. There is nothing about these definitions of lifelong learning and recurrent education which is at first sight inconsistent with established social constructions of knowledge: they may or may not, in other words, transform the curriculum of schooling. The definitions of continuing, higher and adult education seem to reflect primarily administrative categories, and it can only be assumed that they are more likely to reproduce rather than transform the curriculum of schooling. Paradoxically, the only term which does imply curriculum transformation is the least familiar, that of 'continuous education', with its suggestion of the continuity of working and learning experience.

So the terms which have become familiar in the process of making lifelong learning and associated ideas objects of social policy give in themselves little indication of the degree to which they entail a transformation of the knowledge-content of adult learning, or whether on the contrary they could be accommodated to the reproduction of the curriculum categories of schooling. Strategies having legislation as their object may or may not embody social policies for the redefinition, redistribution and re-evaluation of knowledge. As before, exercises in 'distancing' the new ideas from old ideas of adult education will depend for their validity upon establishing criteria around the knowledge-content of the curriculum.

There is, no doubt, a problem constituted by the need to make all of these ideas attractive to governments, a need which would seem *prima facie* to rule out the possibility of doing anything other than redefining the case for reproducing received categories. As a strategy, for example, recurrent education may sound sometimes as though it functions simply to reinforce the existing work and education systems and to add little therefore to traditional definitions of vocational education:

> It is a handy strategy for planning in which consequences for educational policy may be estimated. From a political point of view it is attractive that recurrent education
> — emphasizes close ties between education and the world of work;
> — permits education to be better adapted to the requirements of the labour market;
> — may relieve the pressure on higher education caused by the broadening of the secondary system;
> — may narrow the educational gap between generations.[34]

In these terms there would be little possibility, supposing it were thought a desirable goal, of doing anything but reproducing the curriculum categories of schooling. Indeed, these attractions of recurrent education could themselves constitute a strategy of progressive schooling itself. At another extreme, though, lifelong learning may have a potential to transform politics and decision-making in modern technological societies in a direction of openness and participation. A learning society, it is argued, is one where barriers to the transfer of educational solutions in such societies are recognised and overcome:

> . . . if policymakers, developers and adopters are aware of these barriers and assume a posture of inquiry and continuous lerning in their work, they stand a good chance of influencing and guiding the development of society in a positive way, and in a way that enhances local diversity, responsiveness and pluralism, at the same time that it garners, where possible, the efficiency and effectiveness benefits we seek from technology.[35]

In these various ways the connection of lifelong learning strategies with economic and social policy is made manifest, although its curriculum and ideological implications, for reproduction and control or transformation and change, are not always explicit and will vary from one strategy to another. One measure of curriculum significance, however, is a stress upon 'continuous learning', as opposed to 'continuing education' — as suggested above, the first of these may be a genuinely transforming curriculum category, unlike the second, which is merely an administrative one. Even more directly than in the case of the political and decision-making consequences of a learning society, some strategies for lifelong learning, especially those based upon the 'continuous learning' idea, clearly do envisage a transforming curriculum. Geoffrey Bock, Karen Cohen and Myron Tribus make the distinction quite clear in their paper on adult distance learning in engineering:

> In continu*ing* education the learner lays aside his or her daily work and attends sessions where the material discussed may have no direct connection with the learner's immediate working problems . . . On the other hand, in continu*ous* education, the work itself is the basis for the educational programme. The learning process begins by helping to define the problem uppermost in the user's mind. This process then follows a well charted path of defining and re-defining the problem, understanding the context within which it must be solved, deciding upon the general principles which should be used, formulating the specific method of solution, and evaluating the utility of the result.[36]

Continuous education, as a strategy of lifelong learning, has the curriculum process, the knowledge-defining issue, at its heart and therefore constitutes at least potentially the kind of transforming curriculum development which other strategies — having legislation rather than knowledge as their object — do not. It is surely not without significance that the authors see themselves as concerned with engineers as 'knowledge-based professionals' and see the 'knowledge-base' of professions growing and changing.

Summary

In developing curriculum theories of adult and lifelong education it is important to distinguish between legislation and social policy. Adult education legislation has for its object structures of provision for adult learning. The analysis of social policy, on the other hand, is concerned with all the ways in which policy is itself a social construct and therefore suggests an account of legislation in more theoretical terms and in a more problematic context of ideology. The curriculum content of adult learning, in so far as it is socially constructed, is thus more appropriately conceived as an outcome of policy rather than of legislation.

Models of social policy can be suggestive in the context of this curriculum: in terms of 'residual', 'institutional' or 'redistributive' models of social welfare, a variety of curriculum models of adult education can be derived so that, for example, adult learning which is functionally related to schooling ('residual' in some sense) may be distinguished from intrinsic adult learning situations ('institutional' in some sense).

Strategies for lifelong learning (a common theme of legislation) may or may not constitute social policies for the transformation of the curriculum categories of schooling. Although often ostensibly addressed to institutional rather than residual situations, addressed, that is, to learning situations arising from social, economic and technological change, it does not necessarily follow that strategies for lifelong learning always succeed in transcending administrative categories. This is generally the case with the strategy of 'continuing' education. And in such cases they reproduce rather than transform the curriculum categories of schooling. Nevertheless, the idea of lifelong learning is a potentially transforming one, and some strategies distinctly reflect this.

Notes and References

1. See Nell Keddie, 'Adult Education – An Ideology of Individualism', *Adult Education for a Change*, ed. Jane Thompson (London: Hutchinson, 1980).

2. See, for example, B.W. Kreitlow and associates, *Examining Controversies in Adult Education* (San Francisco: Jossey-Bass, 1981), Chapter 3.

3. Colin Titmus and Alan Pardoen, 'The Function of Adult Education Legislation', *Comparing Adult Education Worldwide*, Alexander M. Charters and associates (San Francisco; Jossey-Bass, 1981), p. 161.

4. Ibid., p. 136.

5. Ibid., p. 161.

6. Robert Pinker, *Social Theory and Social Policy* (London: Heinemann, 1971), p. 98.

7. Ibid., p. 99.

8. Ibid.

9. Martin Rein, *Social Science and Public Policy* (Harmondsworth: Penguin Books, 1976), Chapter 1.

10. Ibid., p. 20.

11. Ibid., pp. 20-1.

12. Ibid., p. 22.

13. Ibid., p. 24.

14. Ibid., p. 26.

15. Ibid., p. 29.

16. Ibid., p. 34.

17. Peter Townsend, *Sociology and Social Policy* (Harmondsworth: Penguin Books, 1976), p. 2.

18. Ibid., p. 3.

19. Ibid.

20. Ibid., p. 10.

21. Ibid., p. 6.

22. Richard Titmuss, *Social Policy: An Introduction* (London: Allen and Unwin, 1974), Chapter 2.

23. Ibid., pp. 30-1.

24. Ibid., p. 31.

25. Ibid., pp. 140-1.

26. Ibid., p. 31.

27. Ibid., p. 48

28. B.M. Rodgers with A. Doron and M. Jones, *The Study of Social Policy: A Comparative Approach* (London: Allen and Unwin, 1979), p. xi.

29. See above (p. 94-5).

30. Per Himmelstrup *et al.* (eds), *Strategies for Lifelong Learning: A Symposium of Views from Europe and the U.S.A.* (Esbjerg: University Centre of South Jutland, Denmark, and the Association for Recurrent Education, UK, 1981).

31. Ibid., Chapter II.

32. B.W. Kreitlow and associates, *Examining Controversies*, p. xiii.

33. Per Himmelstrup *et al., Strategies for Lifelong Learning*, p. 6.

34. Ibid., p. 20.

35. Penelope L. Richardson, 'The Political Decision-making Process in a Technological Society', *Strategies for Lifelong Learning*, ed. Per Himmelstrup *et al.* p. 213.

36. Geoffrey E. Bock, Karen C. Cohen and Myron Tribus, 'Continuous Education as Recurrent Education: A New Approach to Teaching Adults at a Distance', *Strategies for Lifelong Learning*, ed. Per Himmelstrup *et al.* p. 76.

5 AGENTS OF PROVISION AND AGENCIES OF CURRICULUM DEVELOPMENT

Introduction

The curriculum of adult education, it has been argued, is more appropriately conceived as an object of social policy rather than of legislation. There is no necessary connection between legislation for provision and change or transformation in the knowledge-content of learning. Nevertheless, there are obviously connections, intended or not, between changing structures of provision and changing structures of knowledge, and individuals and groups are differently placed in relation to the social processes of knowledge-change. The overwhelming majority of people experience change as being in some sense beyond their control, and it could hardly be denied that important elements of the curriculum of adult education and of lifelong education itself are determined by social, economic and technological change and the need for people to accommodate themselves to it. There is an important view of curriculum development therefore to the effect that change is led by economic and technological development, with the corollary often that such changes and the need to assimilate them somehow transcend politics and ideology and provide the grounds for a truly international concept of lifelong learning.

The need to accommodate to structural social change as a basis for lifelong learning came through strongly from the international Brandbjerg Seminar.[1] Among important trends are changes in people's experience of work, leisure and education, such that the traditional kinds of distinctions between these aspects of our experience are tending to break down and merge together. As one contributor put it: 'The *overlapping* between work, education and leisure is, in fact, a dominant feature of any description of such activities in our societies'.[2]

In such a situation the concept of lifelong learning makes better sense than traditional concepts of schooling. Such changes in social structures and institutions also have implications for the social construction of knowledge and hence for the curriculum of adult learning:

> Concrete knowledge tied to present conditions may prove far less important than general readiness, basic openness, and solidarity toward others. Potentially, these are educational products. But we may still have to learn how to produce them.[3]

The association of lifelong learning with social openness, political participation and ideals of democratic citizenship[4] clearly illustrates the ways in which it is conceived as an object of social policy. As the strategies to achieve it suggested, however, it is by no means clear whether, if at all, participation and citizenship under new technological conditions of society come about in association with changes in the definition, distribution and evaluation of knowledge. Instead of a hard analysis of knowledge as a problem of social construction, together with the roles played by groups in a dynamic and highly differentiated process, there seems a view of the autonomous growth of knowledge. It is a non-political view, reflecting perhaps the 'institutional' policy model analogy described in the last chapter. The autonomous growth of knowledge makes curriculum development processes somewhat superfluous in that accommodation to change is inevitable. It constitutes a version of avoiding the ethical issue: technological change itself rather than the traditional 'needs' concept becomes the 'logical stop'. So not only is there a view here of knowledge as autonomous (growing and developing like the 'forms' of knowledge according to its inner logic) but of the curriculum development process as reflecting a necessary accommodation to the growth of knowledge itself. This autonomous-institutional model of curriculum development seems therefore both to depoliticise knowledege itself and to leave little scope for the idea of the adult curriculum as truly an object of social policy and as an outcome of processes and conflicts in the way that critical curriculum theory describes. So perhaps such a view of the inevitability of lifelong learning, which seems to render the whole idea of curriculum development and its agencies relatively superfluous, would be a good starting-point at which to examine the issue.

The Autonomous-Institutional Model

The autonomous growth of knowledge and its institutionalisation in systems of lifelong learning, together with the rather bland assumption that this would somehow constitute a process of social and political democratisation, tend to permeate much discussion of the idea. But the issue of modernisation and of structural and functional adaptation was raised at the Brandbjerg Seminar in a context of lifelong learning by William M. Cave,[5] and his analysis will serve as a good example of what is called here the autonomous-institutional model of curriculum development. Arguing that 'Modernization stems initially from an attitude, a belief that social and cultural change is desirable and that society can and should be transformed', Cave goes on to suggest that: 'The process by which this transformation has taken place may be discussed in terms of the adaptation of a given set of institutions to changing functions.'[6]

A universal 'drive' or 'passion' for modernity characterises almost all nations. It is a complex and uneven process, but, argues Cave, it is associated with definite structural features such as high levels of differentiation and 'social mobilization', and 'a relatively large-scale, unified and centralized institutional framework'. He observes that education as a key to this process is amost universally given priority, and it is associated with a shift in attention from physical capital to human resources:

> This shift suggests the need for new structural forms capable of responding to the evergrowing list of adult education concerns and priorities in all modernizing nations. In effect, the shift of emphasis from the formation of physical capital to improvement of existing human resources may be accompanied by an increase of government activity in such areas as national institutes or centres for adult education, residential centres, national training institutes for key adult education personnel, and so on. Along with this shift, the emergence of learning structures tuned to the modernizing process seems an inevitability.[7]

'The process of modernization', continues Cave, 'reflects an inexorable trend.' It is a process raising many issues, not least that of the functions and dysfunctions of institutionalisation itself. But Cave is clear that the scope for purposive and planned change is limited: 'much of what is commonly referred to as social change is not the result of any purposive direction'. It follows that 'organizations and institutions are set up and structures arise to adapt to the largely uncontrolled changes taking place'. Adult education institutions, that is, exist in functional relations with other social institutions and adapt to 'fit' into a wider social system which apparently changes under its own momentum. Since social change consists of functional adaptation:

> The central problem confronting planners is the recognition and identification of the nature of these changes, so as to be able to conceptualize the appropriate innovations and accompanying structures that will capitalize on their dynamic quality.[8]

According to such a view as this, change consists of the structural adaptation of institutions, and the object of the transformation is the structure itself: 'From linguistic structures to kinship groups and stratification systems, all known structures are systems of transformation.'[9] Change and modernisation are in fact synonymous with institutionalisation:

> In a very real sense, the *institutionalization of lifelong learning* is tantamount to the *institutionalization of change* since both require the development and crystalization of new institutional settings together with the internal transformation of the societies or groups within which it occurs.[10]

Characteristic of the sociological perspective from which it is derived Cave's analysis postulates social systems in which irreconcilable conflicts of interest and principle are logically precluded by the idea of system itself. The system is, in other words, logically incapable of generating needs which it could not meet. Social systems are self-regulating, homeostatic and constantly moving in the direction of harmony, reconciliation and integration:

> Thus, when we speak of the institutionalization of adult education, we mean those enduring patterns of roles and collectivities, values, sanctions, expectations, and so forth which provide a unifying pattern and integrative quality to the social system.[11]

This is an extreme example of the 'institutional' model of social policy analysis, and it would seem, as did the 'needs-meeting' model of adult education already referred to, to make redundant what are ordinarily understood as the more innovative processes of curriculum development. For under conditions of institutionalised lifelong learning as described by Cave, this process is exhaustively described as structural adaptation to modernisation. The 'hidden curriculum' of adult education is disclosed as a form of social control, as potential sources of dysfunctional conflict are first accommodated (under 'flexibility') and then, in turn, institutionalised.

Here then the agency of curriculum development is the social process of modernisation itself, which is inevitable. The social system is understood as a system of institutional structures which exist and change in their own terms independently of planned change and despite the 'apparent sense of autonomy' experienced by planners.[12] It is a sociological perspective which has been challenged, no more so than in the context of the sociology of education, because it is excessively abstract, attributing some kind of autonomy to the 'social system' itself and an unrealistic consensus to the normative system of society. It is a traditional perspective which deals with the problem of conflict by effectively removing education, knowledge and development from the context of politics and ideology. We seem a long way here from the view of the curriculum as a social definition, distribution and evaluation of knowledge, and of a view of the process of selection from a range of culturally possible – not inevitable – alternatives. In this process of selection, which permits the possibility of real conflicts around the social construction of knowledge, agencies of curriculum development can be conventionally discerned. So it would be useful to turn now to the view that the development process is not so much a function of autonomous social systems in modernisation but rather of relatively autonomous, identifiable agencies. It is a view which may also bring the problem of knowledge back into a more prominent place.

Curriculum Development and Educational Innovation

Turning to the idea first in a context of schooling, the contrast with the autonomous-institutional model just described in a context of life-long learning is immediately apparent. The context remains one of institutions, but on the assumption now that social institutions reflect deliberation, planning and genuine choices amongst cultural and ideological alternatives:

> The term 'curriculum development' is considered as comprising those deliberately planned activities through which courses of study or patterns of educational activity are designed and presented as proposals for those in educational institutions.[13]

Courses and curricula necessarily include, say the authors of this text, Philip H. Taylor and Colin Richards, 'selections from a society's stock of meanings and embody a variety of views, implicit or explicit, about purposes, knowledge, children, society, teaching and learning'. Those who play any part in the curriculum development process do so from the standpoint of different conceptions and ideologies to which they subscribe and which are of the utmost importance for the design of courses and the way they are likely to be received by teachers and learners:

> No matter what ideologies are involved, curriculum development
> implies a degree of systematic thinking and planning in which indivi-
> dual decisions about content, teaching and learning are taken, not in
> isolation, but in relation to an overall design or framework.[14]

This approach does seem to rescue the idea of curriculum development from the limbo into which the view of lifelong learning as
modernisation seemed to cast it. It is seen now as a process having the
distribution of knowledge at its centre, constituted by deliberation and
planning, and reflecting conceptual and ideological views of knowledge,
teaching and learning.

Consonant with the view developed in the last chapter, that the
curriculum is more profitably regarded as an object of social policy
than of legislation, the agents and agencies of development are
extremely diverse. And not only is this true of different kinds of
societies but it is true of schooling as much as of adult education:

> Individuals, groups, national institutions, central governments
> and international organizations are some of the agents and agencies
> who are involved in curriculum development. In no country is
> curriculum development the prerogative of a single institution or
> individual. Those actively involved in such development vary from
> one national context to another, since who can engage in curriculum
> development depends in part upon how the curriculum is defined
> and how its function is perceived.[15]

The cultural and political relativism of the curriculum development
process is not necessarily transcended by universal and inevitable
modernisation, and it is difficult to categorise agents and agencies for
precisely this reason. The authors of this text propose two dimensions:
'the salience of curriculum development among an agency's functions (and an agent's roles), and the "arena" in which an agent or
agency operates'. By 'arena' is meant the scope of intended effective-
ness – national, provincial, regional, local or some other such 'target
group' idea. In adult education, for example, the salience dimension
seems particularly relevant for comparative or classification purposes,
since many agents or agencies of adult learning are not primarily concerned with it: it is only one of a number of concerns. But beyond
comparison and classification lies the significance of this kind of theor-

etical perspective of seeing the curriculum and the curriculum development process as an object of social policy rather than of legislation. It
certainly helps, as the authors suggest,[16] to avoid superficial generalisa-
tions about the degree to which the curriculum is subject to central
government control in countries as different, for example, as Britain
and Sweden. The curriculum is a social, cultural and political construct
in a way that legislation does not, and could not adequately convey.
Educationists concerned more directly with the elucidation of curriculum practice[17] tend to see agencies of curriculum development
primarily as adjuncts of the teaching function or as support for schools.
Stenhouse, for example, puts it like this:

> We have in Britain a wide range of supporting agencies: Her Majesty's
> Inspectorate, local advisory services, teachers' centres, research and
> development units, in-service training agencies and initial training
> institutions. It is my thesis that they and the schools should be
> united in a common research and development tradition.[18]

A broader, more theoretical than prescriptive, perspective upon
curriculum development is possible however. John Eggleston, for
example, points out that the relatively recent concept of planned curriculum change, 'the attempt to impose a rational order on a previously
spasmodic and often unordered process of updating knowledge',
reflects a movement in social policy itself:

> A widespread belief in the desirability of a planned social system
> that could alleviate if not eliminate the handicaps and hardships of
> social and economic inequality arose in most Western societies in the
> late 1950s.[19]

It had even been supposed that redistribution of educational opportunity could be a way of socially engineering changes in the class structure. However, there are limits imposed upon progressive legislation by
the social construction of the curriculum as an object of social policy,
and Eggleston expresses more clearly the real relations between
modernisation, the curriculum development process and ideology:

> The process is a continuing one; an inevitable corollary of technical,
> economic and social change. The curriculum in mathematics changes
> in the face of computerization; the science curriculum responds to
> an age of nuclear physics; language changes with the advent of new

media of communication. But change in the knowledge content of the curriculum opens up the prospect of change in the nature of social control; the process of adjustment loosens the established pattern of the definition, distribution and evaluation of knowledge, however momentarily, to new or existing groups who seek to make it more responsive to their views and their conditions.[20]

This focus upon the politics of the knowledge-content of the curriculum is therefore somewhat different from the needs-based ideology of adult education or the modernisation-function approach to lifelong learning. But in fact the same kind of forces operating to change the curriculum of schooling will inevitably be experienced in the context of adult education. Denis Lawton has identified three kinds of social pressures which continue to influence the curriculum in modern societies. These are economic and technological changes, ideological changes, and what he describes as the 'secular/rational pressures on education'. By this last he means the consequences in terms of the questioning of traditional authority for teaching and learning roles and, by further implication, for the curriculum development process itself. In fact, Lawton locates adult education along with the community functions of schooling as a response to what he calls the secular/rational social trends, where the aims of the curriculum are intellectual and aesthetic self-cultivation — reflecting a rather traditional view of it perhaps.[21] Elaborating later he argues:

> Of the very greatest importance is that one function of the school would be to convince pupils before they leave that education is not something which ends with the end of schooling, but is something which ought to be pursued for the whole of one's life. The blurring of the division between school and non-school, education and real life, is one of the very highest priorities.[22]

But of course the problem of curriculum development as described by writers such as Eggleston, Stenhouse and Lawton is essentially a problem of schooling. It is clear, though, that their focus is more or less directly upon knowledge, culture and ideology, and the practices of teaching and learning.

There are, however, possibilities of more general theories of change and innovation in education contexts which are not necessarily restricted in scope to schooling and which employ concepts derived from a variety of social science sources. The issue has been reviewed recently by Tom Whiteside,[23] who subjects the crucial concept of strategy to critical analysis, which is not without relevance to the way the concept has been used in adult education and lifelong learning literature. There is, says Whiteside, a gap between the *myths* about the nature and extent of educational change and its *actual* nature and extent. It is Townsend's point about the myth and the reality of redistribution under social welfare policy in a different setting.

Strategies for bringing about educational change were often based upon the work of social scientists committed to social planning in the new technological society. Whiteside outlines three broad types of strategy for effecting social change and suggests that 'all efforts to induce change employ a combination of these strategies'. The first is called the 'empirical-rational' strategy, 'rooted in the image of the practitioner as a rational man'. According to this, change comes about when those occupying key positions in the process (in this case, teachers) gain awareness and understanding of innovations:

> The underlying assumption is that reason determines the process of initiating innovations and that scientific investigation is the best means of extending knowledge, from the initial basic research to the final practical application.[24]

It is a view of change which, as Whiteside says, relies on a high level of social consensus about the desirable directions of change, as well as raising problems in the area of information and the application of theoretical findings in practical situations. In the context of lifelong learning it is sometimes, as a strategy, not without a certain rhetorical significance: the sheer reasonableness of the idea in itself seems to some to be sufficient grounds for advocating it. Often this strategic thinking is associated with a view that change will come about given 'the political will'.

A second kind of strategy is termed power-coercive: 'In this mode', explains Whiteside, 'change occurs by the deliberate restructuring of the situation by a superordinate having the necessary authority.' Such a strategy, underpinned by political, legal and economic sanctions which remain latent, has become inconsistent with wider social values relating to the exercise of authority (Lawton's 'secular/rational pressures') and, besides, power does not invariably invoke compliance especially when it represents a challenge to professional ideology. Furthermore, 'the environment into which an innovation is introduced will determine how the innovation will be altered and adopted'.

Referring to the Teacher Corps programme in the USA, Whiteside continues:

> The very fact that the issues had become sufficiently political to require public legislation meant that the programme would be subjected to compromise from the start. The lack of consensus within the society on the need for change, or the appropriate direction or vehicle for change, compromised the programme's legitimacy and integrity.[25]

This point further elaborates the distinction which has been drawn between social policy and legislation approaches to adult and lifelong education. The curriculum is located in a socially constructed context of culture, power and ideology in which resistance to innovation can take a variety of forms which leave it sometimes virtually impervious to legislation and the exercise of coercive authority. At the same time, a comparative study of adult education must sometimes have reference to strategies of innovation which are of this kind.

The third kind of innovation-strategy which Whiteside describes is called the 'normative re-educational'. Failure of rational persuasion in the face of traditionally held ideas and beliefs led to an increased concentration on the perceptions, attitudes and behaviour of individuals concerned with processes of change. The view that it is individual people who are most directly concerned with such processes led to an innovation-strategy which 'concentrates on the people variable as a point of entry rather than on the goals, structure and technologies of the organization'.

We are now in a positon to consider the issue of curriculum development as a category of educational innovation in rather broader theoretical terms. The agencies of change are constituted by the kinds of pressures and forces which Lawton described, while the strategies of innovation reflect the kind of possibilities outlined by Whiteside. This would seem to be as true of adult and lifelong education as of schooling. But it is also true perhaps that the agencies of curriculum development in the case of adult education are distinctly different from those of schooling. If lifelong learning as a function of the modernisation process is inevitable, then the whole concept of strategy loses much of its significance. If, on the other hand, innovation and change are subject to deliberate planning then lifelong education ceases to be something of a world-historical process and becomes an object of fairly mundane strategies, such as staff development, which is presumably an example of Whiteside's 'normative re-educational' innovative strategy model.

There are, therefore, some important theoretical issues around the concepts of strategy, policy, educational innovation and curriculum change and development. Strategies of lifelong education, it was suggested, do not necessarily have the transformation of the curriculum of schooling as their object —they may or may not reproduce its knowledge-categories. This is partly because, like legislation, strategy tends to have structures of provision as its object, either 'residual' provision which is a function of schooling, or 'institutional' provision which is not. As we have seen, too, strategies like legislation can be defeated by all kinds of social processes. Curriculum change, on the other hand, is an outcome of social processes, an object of social policy, and subject to a different kind of logic. Consequently, the relation between educational innovation and curriculum change or development is contingent and not always easy to grasp. But clearly we must hold on to this kind of analytic distinction in order to make sense of the point made by the radical curriculum theorists that educational 'progressivism' does not necessarily constitute curriculum change as an object or outcome of social policy: a redefinition, redistribution or re-evaluation of knowledge. In the case of theories of schooling such analytic distinctions are explored both as theoretical categories and as a source of empirically-verifiable hypotheses. But in the case of adult and lifelong education, innovation and curriculum development are easily confused, and the potential for establishing a distinctive theory is not yet realised. It is a potential important to realise if we are to see the real relation between ideas of adult education, recurrent education, lifelong learning and so on.

The hypothesis it is now possible to formulate, therefore, is that in the case of adult and lifelong education there is a crucial distinction to make between agencies of curriculum development and agents of educational provision. The former consist of social forces, processes, trends, pressures, etc. with a potential for changing our conceptions of knowledge and transforming its social and political significance; their potential is therefore either to reproduce or transform the curriculum categories of schooling. Agents of educational provision, on the other hand, have a much more limited potential to achieve these kinds of things and in some ways are only capable of reproducing the curriculum categories of schooling itself: they present examples of educational innovation but not of curriculum development, and of development strategies defeated by the reverse social forces, processes, trends, pressures, etc. which reproduce curriculum categories of schooling. Amongst these social forces may be located the professional ideology of needs, access and provision which, it was suggested, characterises the organisation of adult education itself. So for the sake of argument, and to propose the kind of hypothesis which it is necessary to formulate as a basis of curriculum theory in adult education, the distinctions between agencies of curriculum development and agents of provision, and between curriculum development and educational innovation, will be elucidated in the comparative contexts of British adult education and American lifelong learning. The distinctiveness of the agencies and agents of these contexts from that of schooling should also become more apparent, thus shifting the basis of theory from unsatisfactory 'adult characteristics' approaches towards the curriculum content of learning; towards the agencies and agents of 'adult knowledge' itself.

Innovation Without Development

In 1978, Graham Mee and Harold Wiltshire produced one of the very few studies of adult education in Britain with a real significance for the development of curriculum theory of adult education.[26] The object of this study was non-vocational provision for adults by the local education authorities of England and Wales. It was a survey of provision financed by the Department of Education and Science, with the intention of describing, analysing and classifying such provision and, in the authors' words, relating it to the growing body of organisational theory, although, as they continue in their Foreword:

> . . . as we visited more institutions, talked with more people and became more familiar with our material we began to see the task differently: institutions seemed more various, more complex and more resistant to classification and quantitative analysis than we had imagined — and organisational theory did not seem to be of as much direct help as we had expected.[27]

But although there were reservations about its usefulness it is important to understand that the perspective of this study was that of organisation theory, and an appendix to the book was concerned with 'Adult education and the sociology of organisations'.[28] So it is a study conducted from the standpoint of the organisation and provision of adult education rather than with the content of adult learning: the interests of the authors, as they describe in their Foreword, shifted somewhat from institutions to the people who worked in them, 'so that this report has turned out to be at least as much about adult educators as about institutions and organisations'. But although the primary concern of the authors was with structures of provision and professionalism, the provision, that is, of learning opportunities for adults, it is not without relevance for the study of what adults actually learn − the true object, it is being suggested, of a curriculum theory of adult or lifelong education. From the point of view of provision, the curriculum is analysed. Within the framework of adult education it is difficult to see how it could be analysed from any other point of view. In England and Wales provision is the relevant legislative category:

> The Education Act of 1944 lays upon Local Education Authorities the responsibility for providing, or securing the provision of, adult education and most of it (perhaps seven-eighths) is in fact directly provided by them as part of their programme of Further Education.[29]

Legislation, it has been said, has provision, not knowledge, as its object. So the curriculum, or knowledge-content of what is learned is problematic. From the point of view of organisation theory it will surely remain rather obscure: legislative categories determine the perspective whereby the curriculum may only be conceptualised in terms of what institutions teach. Along these lines, Mee and Wiltshire devised a significant and in many respects pioneering analysis and typology.

They established a typology of institutions, therefore, along the following dimensions:

1. Formal linkages (with Colleges of Further Education, Schools, Youth Service, Leisure Services − or with none of these);
2. Staffing (full-, part- and spare-time; status);
3. Environment (demographic; economic; educational);
4. Size (number of courses, of students, of student hours);
5. Teaching accommodation (own, hired, borrowed and shared premises);
6. Management (degree of autonomy; professional and lay participation);
7. Philosophy (dominant concept of purpose).[30]

In terms of these seven variables, and making the kind of reservations inseparable from an exercise in typology, the authors distinguished five major types of adult education institution. The first they described as 'Specialised' ones, in which 'adult education is conceived as a distinguishable and separate sector of education, needing to develop its own organisation and institutions and capable of doing so . . . It is in institutions of this group that adult education finds its greatest degree of independence and autonomy.' The second type of institution is the College of Further Education 'in which adult education is a recognised sector of their work making a substantial contribution to total student hours, and which are used by the providing authority as a main agency for the promotion and organisation of adult education in the area served'. The third type is the Community School or College: 'Adult education is conceived, along with youth service, as continuous with schooling and as one of the functions of the school, which is then usually designated a Community School.' The fourth type Mee and Wiltshire describe as 'Adult plus Youth', where 'adult education is conceived, not as an aspect of the work of other educational institutions (as in Further Education Colleges and Community Schools) but as a specialised and dispersed sector of education which can best be developed jointly with a similar specialised and dispersed sector'. Finally there is a type called 'Leisure', where 'adult education is conceived as an aspect of entertainment or recreation rather than education and thus comes within the purview of a Recreation and Leisure Services Committee or the like'.

Curriculum analysis of the subjects taught in such institutions was based on the following subject classification:

1. Craft and Aesthetic Skills
   1.1 Courses related mainly to personal care and the household economy
   1.2 Courses related mainly to leisure-time enjoyment
2. Physical Skills
   2.1 Courses related mainly to the maintenance of health and fitness
   2.2 Courses related mainly to leisure-time enjoyment
3. Intellectual and Cognitive Skills
   3.1 Language courses
   3.2 Other courses
4. Courses addressed to Disadvantaged Groups.[31]

The subject distribution[32] of local education authority provision reveals that 53 per cent of courses are concerned with type 1 subjects, 24 per cent with type 2, 18 per cent with type 3, and 5 per cent with type 4, although when adjusted to include provision by the responsible bodies (Workers' Educational Association and university extramural departments) the distribution shifts somewhat away from the craft, aesthetic and physical skills towards the cognitive and intellectual skills end of the spectrum.

Of more present concern than the actual and by now rather obsolete data, however, is the kind of theoretical perspective within which they have meaning. From the point of view of organisation theory they are meaningless and, as Mee and Wiltshire make plain, only leave us with questions to ask:

> Is this a credible picture of the way in which the people of England and Wales spend that tiny part of their leisure which they give to publicly provided adult education? If it is, it provokes many questions: How does the curriculum come to be the way it is? By what consensus and what means are its general outlines and proportions maintained with such consistency in many different places and circumstances? Is it an expression of a native cultural tradition? Is it a good way of spending the very small amount of public money given to adult education? Is it a reasonably well-balanced programme — *mens sana in corpore sano*? Or is it irrelevant to the problems which we face, as individuals or as a society?[33]

No answers to these questions are possible, say Mee and Wiltshire, save those of our own subjective speculation. They are, however, the kind of questions which a curriculum theory of adult education must, in principle, be capable at least of addressing. The curriculum of adult education is explicable in theoretical terms once the categories of organisation theory are transcended and it is conceived as a learning content, or as a distribution and evaluation of knowledge and skills in a context of culture and politics: in these terms at least the curriculum of adult education might constitute an object of hypothesis. The core curriculum, derived from an analysis of the programmes of institutions is, after all, significantly identifiable:

> Two subject groups, 1.1 and 1.2 in the survey group — which between them account for 53.1% of the total curriculum — show a surprising consistency of provision over most types of institutions,

and two others — 2.1 and 3.1 — a fair degree of consistency. To-gether these seem to constitute a core curriculum which is common to most institutions.[34]

Again, however, Mee and Wiltshire find this surprising and, indeed, perplexing. Given the relative autonomy of institutions, their largely non-examined courses, their differences in structure and philosophy and the independence of the professionals who plan the provision, why is there a 'core curriculum' at all?:

> They can in theory teach what they like, yet three-quarters of their work is in fact basically similar. There seems to be some sort of national consensus that these are the kinds of things that institu-tions of adult education ought to be offering the public and that there is something wrong if these subjects are not given something like their due place in the programme.[35]

Adult educators apparently conform to this consensus, and it is difficult to see how it operates in the absence of a nationally organised student body demanding such a curriculum, 'in short no organised or easily identifiable adult education public'. The reasons for this, how-ever, are not far to seek. The fact is that organisational categories, although useful to have, could not frame answers to these questions, puzzles and paradoxes: they are the wrong language in which to pose them. The issues raised are issues of the learning content of, rather than the structures of provision for, adult education. An important theor-etical issue which does arise from the questions raised in this study concerns the extent to which such apparently autonomous agents of provision as the organisers of adult education could actually engage in curriculum development at all. Is it a realisable potential or are we really only talking about educational innovation after all?

In Chapter 7 of their study, Mee and Wiltshire deal with the capacity for innovation in the institutions they surveyed, and investigated four dimensions as a measure of this capacity:

> Was a particular programme more, or less, traditional in content?
> Were many or few things being attempted?
> How much development work was undertaken?
> Did a head of centre believe innovation to be an important aspect of his work?[36]

Indicators of innovation were taken to be the proportion within a programme of non-staple subjects (i.e. courses other than those constituting the 'core' curriculum), graded courses, daytime activities, courses shorter than two terms, and courses for the disadvantaged. All of these kinds of subjects and courses were discovered to be the least represented in traditional adult programmes. As far as information was available, the authors of the study would claim these as the 'directly educational' fields of possible innovation, alongside other developments of a social and recreative kind which may have been going on.

On the educational innovation index the institutions which demonstrated the greatest capacity were specialised institutions having full-time staff and independent accommodation, which were large urban or suburban institutions; further education colleges with full- and part-time staff in which adult education constituted a separate department in shared teaching accommodation, which were medium to large institutions; and community schools which were recently established, very large, multi-purpose institutions having relatively small adult education programmes with part-time staff and shared accommodation, and which were located in urban inner-city or rehousing areas.

Institutions having the least capacity for innovation seemed to be: specialised institutions having either mainly or almost wholly spare-time staff and borrowed teaching accommodation and in small urban or small rural situations; community schools which were long established as small and medium-size rural and suburban institutions with part-time staff and shared teaching accommodation; and 'adult plus youth' smalller urban institutions with spare-time and some part-time staff in borrowed with some shared premises.

Innovation is a function to a large extent of scale and urban setting, but also of full-time staffing. To some extent, the authors point out among other reservations, the educational innovation scale cannot adequately represent the work of institutions such as community schools whose provision is not all of the 'directly educational' kind. They offer three kinds of explanations of differences in capacity for innovation. The first has to do with the individual: the scope for innovative approaches contained in specialised institutions in which the autonomous role of the principal or the head of the centre proves decisive in these matters. The second kind of explanation is concerned with the organisation itself: the number of staff is related to the degree of specialisation which in turn creates new possibilities for innovation and development. Also of organisational significance for innovation is the degree of control exercised over premises and accommodation which in turn creates some of the conditions of autonomy which innovation requires. Finally, there is the environment of a centre, 'the socio-economic mix of its catchment population, its density, etc.' And although any attempt to measure environmental variability was abandoned, some kinds of correlation are possible:

> . . . it has to be acknowledged that broadly urban situations, as opposed to rural ones, offer many more opportunities for innovation because of their greater density and heterogeneity of population. Thus an urban environment provides, for example, critical masses of students requiring a particular subject, or more than one grade of activity in a subject, or an activity for a specific type of handicapped person.[37]

Nevertheless, the environmental factor, in respect of the capacity for innovation, turns out to be less important than staffing level: 'The critical determinant here appears to be the level of staffing; the spare-timer with little time, little support and often no opportunity to specialise, is in most cases unable to demonstrate much innovative behaviour.'

The reasons why the attempt to measure environmental variability as a factor of the capacity for innovation had to be abandoned are significant, because they tend to confirm a view of the inadequacy of organisational categories of administration and provision to move beyond educational innovation to a view of curriculum development as concerned with the knowledge-content of adult learning.

Mee and Wiltshire found it, as they say, 'surprisingly difficult at times to establish a direct relationship between environmental and institutional characteristics' and they gave three reasons for this. First, it is very difficult to define the catchment population for any particular institution: its students may be concentrated in the immediate neighbourhood but they may also travel considerable distances. Secondly, the institution through its policy and programme will select its students from the possible catchment population: 'the institution defines and to some extent creates its own population and its own environment'. Thirdly, even when this catchment population can be defined, it is very difficult to match it with demographic, economic or educational statistics: 'the statistical units are usually too big, and rarely coincide with the adult educational ones'.[38]

This seems to get to the heart of the matter, which is the demonstration that agents of provision may be concerned with educational innovation, but whether this amounts to curriculum development is quite another matter. The agents of innovation in adult education as analysed in this study are constituted by the institutions and personnel of the service. But the agencies of curriculum change and development are constituted by precisely those factors of the environment which proved impervious to the organisational/provision approach. For in so far as the curriculum describes the social construction of knowledge, and curriculum development describes the ways in which this construction changes, the innovative capacity of the institutions of provision is no indication of their capacity to transform the categories of schooling as regards the knowledge content of adult learning.

That is not to say that such institutions as are described here are actually redundant to curriculum transformation: the community schools, for example, surely constitute the capacity for reflecting the social construction of knowledge in a community and for an instrumental role in its transformation. But this, as has been suggested, depends upon a view of such a construction of knowledge — not the provision of courses in itself. We should need to know, in other words, about the degree to which a concept of community impinged upon the knowledge-content of what was learned in community institutions. The kind of educational innovation which Mee and Wiltshire identified with such institutions, at least a particular sub-category of them, was 'almost wholly in the direction of work for the disadvantaged'. And whilst respecting the caveat concerning the range of functions of community institutions, for we are dealing with 'directly educational' provision, it could hardly be suggested that this constitutes curriculum development in terms of the transformation of the (community) construction of knowledge. Indeed, in the absence of detailed evidence about the knowledge-content of courses it is only possible to conclude that such provision reproduces the curriculum categories of schooling, in the sense of what has been called the 'residual' as opposed to the 'institutional' adult curriculum.

The provision of courses not only proves inadequate as an indication of curriculum development directions, but it is an approach to educational innovation which suggests the role of the institutions of provision themselves in the social construction of knowledge. For, as Mee and Wiltshire point out, the policy and programme of the institute itself is selective. Since it can only serve a minority, the question remains, which minority will it recruit and serve? 'Through the choices and decisions, often small in themselves, which combine to provide an answer to that question the institution defines and to some extent creates its own population and its own environment.' We could go further than this and say that the institution defines and to some extent creates the content of adult learning: this is a contribution of provision itself to the social definition, distribution and evaluation of knowledge. But from the fact that agents of provision function to promote educational innovation it does not follow that they function to promote curriculum development of a kind that transforms the curriculum categories of schooling. On the whole, at least according to the organisational analysis of this particular study, they do not.

If we now reverse the direction between the educational innovation which is a function of institutional provision (agents of change) and the social forces, trends and pressures which institutionalise knowledge (agencies of development) we arrive at some such conception as a learning society which, more often than not, underpins the idea of lifelong learning. In fact this is a conception of the transformation of the curriculum categories of schooling which can be usefully compared and contrasted with the kind of provision that has just been described. But instead of comparing it in the form of lifelong learning associated with Cave — where it was apparently synonymous with the inevitable process of modernisation itself, and therefore not an object of rational planning — it may be more to the point to consider it in a framework of existing institutions which could be such an object.

Institutionalisation of Development

One of the problems of Cave's 'autonomous-institutional' view was that it was based on a theory of change as a kind of structural adaptation. As such it conveyed an inadequate sense of the conflicts and contradictions which are associated with change in the real world, the ways in which established forms and forces actively impede development so that, in the real world, change is a matter of gains and losses. Many exponents of lifelong learning as a condition of the learning society would not, therefore, regard its onset as inevitable in the face of institutional resistance. It is, in other words, as common to speak of educational institutions as agents of resistance to development as well as of educational innovation. And this is a view which seems also to be a prerequisite of any curriculum or knowledge-oriented theory of education. The learning society, and the idea of lifelong learning with which it is often associated, are in fact conceptions of knowledge and its social transformations and processes:

The obsolescence of knowledge, the rapid growth of new knowledge, the shifts in national priorities, the multiplication and complexity of social problems, and the close relationship between the application of knowledge and social progress all lead to the conclusion that lifelong learning is not only desirable but necessary.[39]

This is a concept of knowledge as constituted by forces and changes in society, rather than as a function of educational provision, whether innovative or not; it is a view of curriculum development as an object of social policy; it is a view of the transformation of traditional curriculum categories. Above all, it is a view of lifelong learning which entails one of traditional institutions as engaged in reproducing traditional categories and which therefore envisages not the inevitability of a learning society but rather the difficulties of establishing one in the face of existing institutional systems.

This account of the learning society from the standpoint of the USA and its educational systems, a report of explorations supported by the Kellogg Foundation and written by T.M. Hesburgh, P.A. Miller and C.R. Wharton Jr, indicates an important distinction between curriculum development and educational innovation and between social policy and administrative categories:

If the United States is to become a learning society, significant changes are necessary in attitudes toward the design of education. Terms like *continuing education* or *adult education* are too conventional and administrative in meaning to encompass the comprehensive responses called for in attitudes and national policy.[40]

This is a view, therefore, of the planned institutionalisation of learning in the face of the failure of educational innovation to locate learning and knowledge in a wider, socially-constructed setting than that of conventional institutions of school and college. An important dysfunction of educational innovation, for example, and not only in the USA, has been the so-called 'overcredentialed society':

Too many jobs require entering credentials out of all proportion to the skills needed to perform satisfactorily. The lockstep, traditional mode of formal education makes continuous learning unduly difficult, because in the past it has almost always been implicit that learning is both the province of formal educational institutions and of youth.[41]

In other words, it would be only too easy for adult and lifelong education to reproduce discredited categories of schooling unless changes in the social distribution of knowledge are regarded as the object of curriculum development.

This particular exploration of lifelong learning, however, is fairly distinctive in that it contains a chapter on the curriculum implications of this view of the centrality of knowledge-change for all adult learning.[42] Basically, these implications are of the functional relation of the curriculum of lifelong education and that of schooling and undergraduate education, especially in a context of vocational education. As will be seen, these kinds of curriculum integrations have been taken much further, and not in a context of vocational education alone. But its significance is, quite simply, that lifelong education depends upon a transformation of the curriculum categories of schooling and subsequent 'initial' education. The relation of lifelong education and schooling is thus a functional relation quite unlike that of adult education and schooling. This latter relation, expressed by either a 'residual' or an 'institutional' adult curriculum, is not a knowledge-transforming one in the way that some strategies of lifelong education have been seen to be, but enshrines administrative and provision-based categories which, it has also been seen, tend to reproduce the curriculum categories of schooling itself. The paradox of theorising on the basis of 'adult characteristics', it may be remembered, rests precisely upon this point, namely, the greater the stress upon 'adult' as a distinctive category, the greater the tendency to reproduce those of schooling in terms of the knowledge-content of learning. More often than not, this came about because such quasi-theories of adult education evacuated the curriculum-knowledge ground in favour of the ideology of needs, access and provision.

The curriculum implications described in this particular view of lifelong learning need only brief mention, since they have been much more fully explored elsewhere in the literature of the subject:

A substantial part of the university's undergraduate curriculum in every subject matter area should be redesigned to help students learn how to carry out a program of self-education and lifelong learning.[43]

The implications for the attitudes of teachers and students are fairly clear: they amount to a more collective and co-operative view of knowledge processes, and something of a democratisation of the role relationships involved in institutionalised learning. And it amounts to a view of 'openness' in terms of knowledge and the curriculum, not just in terms of a relatively accessible learning system such as is constituted by the Open University or other distance-teaching institutions. In addition to changes in the attitudes of teachers and students, changes in the format of courses would also be required as a prerequisite of lifelong learning or the 'learning society':

> Course content should reflect the growing concerns that education be both liberating and flexible. Problem-solving should be emphasized; resources available both in and out of the classroom should be used by the learner to analyze and cope with critical issues in his or her field of interest. Work-study, cooperative-education, and similar programs can help integrate formal education with career and community experience.[44]

These are implications of the idea of lifelong learning, therefore, for the aims and content and methods of learning which are actually inconsistent with existing practices of education; the whole issue of evaluation of courses and assessment of learning, for example, is raised by a form of curriculum development which is directed at achieving more than merely reproducing the knowledge-content of the curriculum of schooling.

This means, among other things, that institutional and administrative categories of schooling, further, higher, adult education, etc. become redundant in curriculum terms and can easily come to constitute actual obstacles to the achievement of a learning society. This comes about through a failure of institutions to reflect new conceptions of knowledge; the kind of adaptation required on the part of institutions is not to abstract conceptualisations of the 'modernisation process' but to those agencies or forces which themselves are transforming the social construction of knowledge:

> The responsibilities among institutions for inculcating skills and attitudes favoring lifelong learning differ according to institutional type and purpose; these different responsibilities should be recognised and appropriate steps taken to meet them.[45]

This particular view of the institutionalisation of curriculum development for lifelong learning is concerned particularly with the consequences of the idea for higher education institutions of the USA, and with the integration of the agents of provision for it. It happens to illustrate the points both that agents of provision stand in relation to agencies of curriculum development so that they may either reproduce or transform the curriculum of schooling, and also that the object of the idea of lifelong learning is not limitless access to institutionalised provision so much as changes in the social construction of knowledge itself. So it is not surprising that a lifelong learning strategy should have such changes as its object in considering 'general education and core curricula', precisely the concepts which defeat analysis by way of the organisational and administrative categories of adult or continuing education. In other words, although access to institutionalised provision on the part of adult learners is a major strategy for achieving the so-called 'learning society'[46] it is increasingly seen as a strategy having implications for curriculum development and transformation as distinct from the capacity for educational innovation demonstrable in traditional agents of adult and continuing education.

This relation between access and transformation, or between agents of institutional provision and agencies of curriculum development, may finally be illustrated in a different context, that of adult education in European socialist countries.[47] Dusan M. Savićević takes six major determinants of the adult education systems of nine such countries, for purposes of comparison, as follows:

1. The nature of social organization
2. The development of science and technology
3. The democratization of education in general and adult education in particular
4. Acceptance of the philosophy of lifelong education
5. Linking labor and education as factors and ways of the all-round development of a personality
6. A professionalization of adult education based on social needs and scientific research.[48]

The first of these determinants refers to the fact that in socialist countries the aims of education — for children, youth and adults — have not been resolved so much by conceptual analysis as by 'the nature of the organization of society and the Marxist philosophy and ideology'. This certainly anchors the whole enterprise in a view of the social construction of knowledge, a fact reinforced through the second of these determinants, which puts the modernisation process in quite a different perspective from that sometimes associated with lifelong learning:

'From the standpoint of adult education, the scientific-technological revolution and the changes it brings about are always viewed through social frameworks.' These determinants of adult education systems clearly have to do with philosophical and ideological conceptions of knowledge, although it is interesting that the democratisation of education is associated, just as in non-socialist societies, with legislation having increased access to provision on the part of adults as its object. Thus for present purposes the third determinant is particularly significant, acceptance of the philosophy of lifelong education being consistent with the Marxist philosophy and ideology: 'This fact has contributed to the closer linking of the system in which education is acquired by children, youth, and adults.' It does not follow from this that the institutionalisation of lifelong learning constitutes a transformation of the curriculum categories of schooling in the way suggested by the 'learning society' strategies mentioned above (the capacity for this varies between the socialist countries' systems which are subsequently described in the article). But it does seem to leave open the issue of agents of provision and agencies of social change, or educational innovation and curriculum development, and still leaves scope for analysis in terms of the capacity of adult education or lifelong learning to transform or to reproduce the curriculum of schooling, to constitute a 'residual' or an 'institutional' educational provision and so on:

> Schools of various levels — from primary schools to faculties of universities — are coming to be regarded not as institutions meant for only one age group but as institutions for lifelong learning. This in no way implies elimination of special institutions for adult education.[49]

Which leaves open the major theoretical question about the exact sense in which adult institutions are special, that is, in terms of their importance for the knowledge-content of learning. Of course it may be that the social transformation of knowledge in socialist societies is effected by the material and cultural transformation of the social relations of production, and that consequently the philosophy of lifelong learning may have a different significance in socialist and non-socialist societies. But if this is true then it is because of the cultural and political and ideological significance of knowledge itself, rather than because of differences in legislation and systems of institutional provision. On the whole, it seems rather doubtful that a common philosophy of lifelong learning could be pursued by societies having different — and opposed — social constructions of knowledge as elements of political ideology. The learning society ideal was based upon some kind of democratisation of knowledge itself, and the practical tasks of implementing this would seem to be quite distinctive in socialist and non-socialist societies.

Summary

Curriculum theories of adult education, particularly in a context of life-long learning, seem to presuppose some analytic distinctions of the kind sketched in this chapter: in particular a distinction needs to be made between the agents of provision which can be the object of legislation and which may engage in educational innovation, and the agencies of change which constitute a potential source of curriculum development of a knowledge-transforming kind. On the whole, traditional adult education is not a curriculum development process, in the sense that it does not transform the categories of schooling, which in fact it often reproduces. It has, however, capacities both for educational innovation *and* curriculum development as a strategy for lifelong learning. Conceptions of the 'learning society', as well as strategies for lifelong learning, can be analysed along these lines, and it may be particularly suggestive to compare societies having different social and political systems in respect both of their adult education, lifelong learning and other progressive ideologies, and the capacity of their forms of provision to transform the curriculum categories of schooling through the knowledge-content of adult learning.

Notes and References

1. Per Himmelstrup *et al.* (eds), *Strategies for Lifelong Learning*, Part I.
2. Kjell Eide, Changing Realities of Work, Leisure, Education' in *Strategies for Lifelong Learning*, ed. Per Himmelstrup *et al*. ibid., p. 28.
3. Ibid., pp. 44-5.
4. See above, Chapter 4, note 35.
5. William Cave, 'The Inter-relation of Modernization and Institutional Change', *Strategies for Lifelong Learning*, ed. Per Himmelstrup *et al*., Chapter 9.
6. Ibid., p. 174.
7. Ibid., p. 177.
8. Ibid., p. 179.
9. Ibid., p. 187.
10. Ibid., p. 181.
11. Ibid., p. 184.

12. Ibid., p. 178.
13. Philip H. Taylor and Colin Richards, *An Introduction to Curriculum Studies*, p. 48.
14. Ibid.
15. Ibid., p. 52.
16. Ibid., p. 57.
17. Lawrence Stenhouse, *An Introduction to Curriculum Research and Development*, Chapter 12.
18. Ibid., p. 185.
19. John Eggleston, *The Sociology of the School Curriculum*, pp. 119-20.
20. Ibid.
21. Denis Lawton, *Social Change, Educational Theory and Curriculum Planning*, Table on p. 127.
22. Ibid., p. 134.
23. Tom Whiteside, *The Sociology of Educational Innovation* (London: Methuen, 1978), Chapter 4.
24. Ibid., p. 46.
25. Ibid., p. 49.
26. Graham Mee and Harold Wiltshire, *Structure and Performance in Adult Education*.
27. Ibid., p. vii.
28. Ibid., Appendix A, p. 114.
29. Ibid., p. 2.
30. Ibid., pp. 18-24.
31. Ibid., pp. 29-30.
32. Ibid., Table 5.2, p. 33.
33. Ibid.
34. Ibid., p. 41.
35. Ibid.
36. Ibid., p. 42.
37. Ibid., p. 54.
38. Ibid., pp. 21-2.
39. Theodore M. Hesburgh *et al.*, *Patterns for Lifelong Learning* (San Francisco: Jossey-Bass, 1973), p. 3.
40. Ibid, p. 4.
41. Ibid., p. 7.
42. Ibid., Chapter 2.
43. Ibid., p. 10.
44. Ibid., p. 11.
45 . Ibid., p. 12.
46. See, for example, *Future Directions for a Learning Society* (New York: College Entrance Examination Board, 1978).
47. Dusan M. Savićević, 'Adult Education Systems in European Socialist Countries: Similarities and Differences', in *Comparing Adult Education Worldwide*, ed. Alexander M. Charters and associates, Chaper 3.
48. Ibid., p. 39.
49. Ibid., pp. 42-3.

THE LIFELONG CURRICULUM

Introduction

In the last chapter it was suggested that adult education in a context of lifelong learning has been embraced as a philosophy or ideal in societies having different or actually opposed kinds of social and political systems. What kind of an ideal is it, it may be asked, that is consistent both with Marxist philosophy and ideology and with the accessibility of institutions of higher education in the USA? The cultural, political and ideological significance of knowledge is a factor which contributes to the diversity of societies, and at first sight at least it is difficult to see that lifelong learning could in reality have a common meaning in curriculum terms at all. Not only may knowledge itself be differently defined, distributed and evaluated, but the agents of provision (as objects of legislation and access) may have quite distinct significances: adults could not, under a lifelong learning idea, have access to the same kinds of knowledge or institutions in these terms. There may well be universal economic and technological forces which in all societies come in some way to constitute agencies of curriculum development. But however much modernisation is universally desired, and despite even its inevitability, it is a process having quite different cultural meanings, political significances and institutional expressions. Lifelong learning as an idea seems to share with adult education theory a propensity for outworn borrowings from the social and political sciences — in this instance, possibly, some kind of 'convergence theory' of world development. But when the cultural and ideological diversity of the knowledge-basis of the curriculum is taken into account, together with all the other factors whereby this is translated into forms of educational provision and institutionalised learning systems, then it is easy to see why a term such as lifelong learning tends to be neglected in favour of something else (continuing or recurrent education) which is more culturally and ideologically appropriate to local conditions.

The theoretical and cultural diversity of the school curriculum — the different ways in which the knowledge-content of learning is organised in different societies — has been succinctly put by Brian Holmes. In arguing that there are serious obstacles to the harmonisation of the secondary school curricula of the EEC countries he points out that:

It is preeminently through the curriculum that the accumulated wisdom, attitudes and knowledge of national states are passed on. Economic cooperation may be possible, political unity tentatively discussed, but the diversity which exists in Europe is enshrined in national curricula.[1]

In all such societies, he argues, professional educationists such as teachers, academics and the trainers of teachers, defend the national tradition according to an idea of professional responsibility, and effectively control the content of education. A special difficulty for Britain is that curriculum theory of secondary schooling is debated on assumptions going back to Aristotle:

The forms of knowledge approach of the early Paul Hirst, and Denis Lawton's selection of data from culture provide very similar answers to the question, 'What knowledge is of most worth in providing a sound general education?' The English reply has usually been, 'Those essential subjects or disciplines which can be recognised from their internal coherence and have been legitimised by teachers and by tradition.'[2]

The answer of the French has been different and its effects more encyclopaedic, so that 'the history of curriculum reform in Western and Eastern Europe, excluding Britain and the Soviet Union, has been one of trying to get rid of Greek and Latin and marginally to reduce the numbers of required subjects'. In the case of Soviet polytechnical theory, the intentions behind its encyclopaedic scope are to make explicit practical and socio-economic implications of what is taught in the content of the school curriculum: 'In other words, in Eastern Europe as in Western countries the intellectual concern of university linguists, historians, mathematicians and scientists have dominated the curricula of secondary schools.'[3]

The situation is different, says Holmes, in Britain. For here, at least in many primary schools, the influence of the utilitarianism of Spencer and the pragmatism of Dewey has resulted in quite a different kind of theory:

According to this theory the selection of content is made in the light of the knowledge pupils are likely to need to tackle the problems of living as adults: knowledge which contributes to earning a living, raising a family, participating in civic affairs, dealing with moral questions and to spending leisure time profitably.[4]

Holmes identifies four curricular theories which compete for recognition and acceptance by European teachers and which prescribe alternative approaches to the aims, content and methods of schooling. And they are theories which could not simply be reduced to expressions of national and political ideology:

> Finally, while it is appreciated that school history will tend to follow national or political orthodoxies it is not so often realized that, for example, French school mathematics is informed by Descartes, English mathematics by Euclid; and, in so far as national styles of thinking inform mathematics education, the French are analytical and the British argue logically from self-evident axioms. In other words, those theoretical traditions which make radical curriculum reform difficult in most countries are likely to make the harmonization of curricula in the EEC an impossibility in the foreseeable future.[5]

To pursue in depth the issues raised by this kind of argument would be to pursue that of the way in which, in any society, knowledge is defined, distributed and evaluated. By implication, the roles which groups such as teachers and academics and others professionally concerned play in these processes would be illuminated. In this kind of context the role of professional ideologies, such as that of needs, access and provision attributed earlier to traditional adult education, would be demonstrated as an important factor in the 'social construction' of knowledge itself. It is, after all, important that these matters, which Holmes touched upon in the comparative curriculum theory of schooling, are seen not simply as matters of legislation, access and provision but as ways of thinking and of conceptualising the knowledge-content itself. With schooling too, legislation, access and provision are important for, as has been pointed out, the fact that schooling is compulsory does not put an end to major ideological controversies over access to it. But it is important not to conflate one kind of issue with another here: to solve a problem of access in institutional terms is not necessarily to solve it in knowledge-distribution terms. It follows that barriers to access must be conceptualised in these terms too, so that we could think of them as constituted as much by the social construction of knowledge as by the material conditions of life.

Holmes suggested in the case of many British primary schools some kind of functional relation between schooling and adulthood in curriculum terms, such that the content of learning is determined to some extent by projections of 'adult need'. It would seem at first sight that an element of the ideology of adult education was itself reflected in the curriculum content of schooling. However, the precise form of this functional relationship needs to be elucidated, since it by no means amounts to a curriculum of lifelong learning. For the curriculum of schooling to incorporate an element of preparation for adult life is not only, as Holmes said, something characteristic of British primary education, but it remains an important and controversial concern of educational reform in other sectors too.[6] A recent paper, for example, proposes 'adult preparation' in these terms:

> . . . schools need to secure for all pupils opportunities for learning particularly likely to contribute to personal and social development. Religious education clearly has a contribution to make here, and study of personal relationships, moral education, community studies and community service all provide one range of contexts in which such development may be furthered. Careers education and guidance, preparation for working life, work experience, an introduction to the environmental, economic and political concerns likely to face any adult citizen, all provide another of great importance.[7]

The discussion paper, presented by HM Inspectorate of Schools in England and Wales, sees these curriculum implications for secondary schools in terms, of course, of school subjects and the appropriateness of the 'stages' in schooling where they might best be learned. It is strictly a view of children's learning needs and not one at all of adult learning. In fact it is a view of schooling which is a counterpart of the 'adult characteristics' approach to adult education, taking 'adulthood' in a range of typically adult situations — family, work, community — rather than taking adulthood in a learning relationship to the social construction of knowledge. In such a passage we can witness this construction of school-knowledge and the part played in it by professional educationists. More important for present purposes is the projection of what has been variously described as 'front-end' or 'banking' conceptions of education whereby it is a process of learning completed, more or less once-for-all, by the onset of adulthood; childhood is defined as a learning category, but adulthood is not. So in stressing the differences between these categories in terms of knowledge and learning, there would seem to be no possibility of a *mutual* functional relationship between schooling and adult learning: it is rather a one-way relationship, one of preparation and anticipation; 'adulthood' is functionally related to schooling in terms of the appropriateness of certain subjects, but in terms of the knowledge-content of learning, schooling and adulthood are logically distinct categories.

In the absence of the possibility of a mutually functional relationship between schooling and adult learning, then, the 'preparation for adulthood' element of the school curriculum — which is often advocated in the name of educational innovation and reform — is not the same thing as a lifelong learning curriculum, a condition of which would seem to be a mutually functional relationship between all the stages of learning over a lifetime. Indeed, the 'adult preparation' element of the school curriculum reproduces contingent categories of schooling and adulthood which reflect administrative rather than knowledge-based criteria of distinction.

One of the identifying characteristics of the idea of lifelong education as it has recently been developed by the UNESCO Institute for Education is a view of it as, in essence, a form of curriculum integration. This does not seem to have been the case so much with the related ideas of adult, continuing or recurrent education, which have generally been conceived in other terms as educational processes related to social and economic policy priorities, or as having some other ideological and educational significance. On the face of it, this does seem to suggest that this particular concept — lifelong education — has some significance in knowledge terms.

The rest of this chapter will, accordingly, be concerned with reviewing the idea of lifelong education as a curriculum integration process in the light of the view of the curriculum as knowledge transformation and reproduction, and as a description of the ways in which knowledge is constructed in social, cultural and political terms.

Evaluating the School Curriculum

The UNESCO Institute of Education developed a long-term research programme to explore and elaborate the concept of lifelong education as it affects schooling, and in 1977 reported a multinational project to establish criteria for evaluating the school curriculum in terms of the concept. This study[8] describes the work of teams in Japan, Romania and Sweden who 'developed their own versions of the lifelong education criteria and in various ways applied those criteria to their own national curricula'. It seems clear that translating a concept of 'lifelong learning' into one of 'lifelong education' meant, as was suggested at the beginning of this chapter, making some acknowledgement of the local and national conditions – and the ideological determination – of the social construction of knowledge: 'Each team developed its own, partly unique, set of evaluative criteria and then proceeded to apply these criteria in different ways and, in most cases, to different aspects of their own national curricula.'[9]

After reviewing the origins of the idea and its development from and relation to other similar ideas, lifelong education is elucidated as a system of institutionalisation in which schools would retain an important place but, in curriculum terms, would be involved in a quite different functional role with respect to adult learning than that envisaged by the 'adult preparation' approach to the school curriculum already met with:

> Under lifelong education the school would still have a central role, although its main function would shift from granting 'an education' in the terminal sense to one of preparing learners to continue their education by a variety of means, formal and informal, including self-study. Fostering motivation for later learning is seen as a vital function of the school.[10]

Preparing learners is certainly more of a knowledge-based function than preparing adults, for surely it is as possible to think of 'an adult' in as terminal a sense as of 'an education' itself, which is a characteristic and traditional way of thinking about the school curriculum as preparation.

The curriculum evaluative criteria which eventually resulted in this study needed, however, to be located in a common concept of lifelong education, and the following concept characteristics were taken as the most important ones in the light of the task:

1) *Totality*, or viewing education in all its forms and manifestations;
2) *Integration*, or coordination of educational options available at any given point in time in the lives of individuals as well as through the total life-span;
3) *Flexibility*, or variation and diversity of educational content, modes of learning, and time of learning;
4) *Democratization*, or universalism in access to educational oppor-

tunity for all members of a society;

5) *Opportunity and Motivation*, comprising societal and personal prerequistes for the development of lifelong education.

6) *Educability*, or the central goal of lifelong education in the development of the individual . . . ;

7) *Operational Modality*, or the recognition that education can proceed through formal, non-formal and informal channels and that the quality of learning is defined in its own terms rather than in terms of the means by which it was acquired; and

8) *Quality of Life and Learning*, or the recognition that the central societal function of education is that of enhancing the human experience.[11]

This is an extremely heterogeneous list of concept characteristics of lifelong education in terms of the analytic framework so far developed as a basis of curriculum theory. Some of them (1, 7, 8) seem to be purely philosophical in their implications: they perhaps amount to a definition of lifelong education 'properly so called'. As such they have the same logical characteristics of any other such analytic concept of 'education'. Others (2, 3, 4) seem to be objects of legislation and the forms of provision: their implementation would constitute educational innovation. But there is little (possibly 5) which implies lifelong learning as an object of social policy, or as involving curriculum development in a strict sense of a transformation of the knowledge-content of the curriculum of schooling. Consistent with the assertion that the school would still have a central role in lifelong education, some of these points (3, 4, 6, 8) could in fact express an ideology of schooling itself.

So the actual criteria of curriculum evaluation in lifelong education terms which were developed, and which are described in Chapter 4 of the report, can be assessed on the educational innovation/curriculum development scale derived from an idea of the curriculum as a reproduction and a transformation of knowledge in social, cultural and political contexts.

After the description of the processes by which the three national research teams, in Sweden, Romania and Japan, developed their own criteria of evaluation, a combined criteria list was produced, a list, as the authors say, 'meant to stimulate further work'. So perhaps an assessment of such a list in knowledge transformation and reproduction terms, or in terms of educational innovation and curriculum development, would amount to the kind of work it was intended to stimulate.

The combined list was drawn up at three levels of specificity. At the most general and highly abstract level are the five *clusters* or *categories*: horizontal integration, vertical articulation, orientation to self-growth, self-directed learning and democratisation. These very broad categories derive more or less directly from the concept of lifelong education as it relates to the curriculum.

At the second level are lists of *criteria*, 'referring to desirable states or conditions implied by the definition of each cluster, and which are more susceptible to national conditions'.

At the third level 'two or more *specifications* were developed for each criterion statement'. Such specifications reflect even more closely the concerns of national research teams, and are 'sufficiently specific to have the potential for stimulating debates about appropriateness and desirability'. A full list of combined criteria and illustrative specifications can be discovered as an Appendix (6) to the report: here it is only necessary to reproduce it in outline.[12]

1. *Horizontal Integration*: 'Functional integration of all social agencies fulfilling educational functions, as well as among elements of the curriculum at any given level and among learners with different personal characteristics.' The criteria of integration are between school and home, community, work, cultural institutions and the mass media, and also between subjects of study, curricular and extra-curricular activities, and between learners of different ethnic, physical, intellectual, etc. characteristics.

2. *Vertical Articulation*: 'Articulation among curriculum components at different levels of schooling and between school curricula and pre- and post-school education.' The criteria of articulation consist of integration between pre-school experiences and the school; between different grades or other levels within the school; and between school and post-school activities.

3. *Orientation to Self-growth*: 'Development in learners of personal characteristics that contribute to a long-term process of growth and development including realistic self-awareness, interest in the world and in other people, the desire to achieve, internalized criteria for making evaluations and judgments, and overall integration of the personality.' The criteria and specifications of this orientation are: self-understanding (learners are aware of responsibility for own growth); interest in human beings and in environmental world (learners interested in physical and biological environment); achieve-

ment motivation (learners motivated to improve their own abilities); establishment of internal judgment criteria (learners able to formulate opinions independently); establishment of progressive values and attitudes (learners develop flexible thinking and tolerance); integration of personality (learners explore and assimilate an ideal model for personal development).

4. *Self-directed Learning*: 'Individualization of the learning experience toward the goal of developing the learner's own skills and competencies in the planning, execution and evaluation of learning activities both as an individual and as a member of a cooperative learning group.' The criteria of self-directed learning are, therefore, participation in the planning, execution and evaluation of learning; individualization of learning; development of self-learning skills; development of inter-learning skills; development of self-evaluation and cooperative evaluation skills.

5. *Democratisation*: 'Equality of educational opportunity, opportunity to participate in decision-making and in the teaching/learning process despite differences in status, the constructive exercise of authority, and the encouragement of creativity, divergent thinking, flexibility and curiosity on the part of the learners.' Illustrative specifications of the democratisation process include: equal opportunity regardless of sex, race, religion, social background and other personal characteristics; participation of parents, community, teachers and learners in school organisation and administration; non-punitive evaluation functions and methods; encouragement of free creative activity, self-expression, spontaneity and originality.

As the authors of this report agree, 'none of the above specifications of criteria actually defines a curriculum element or indicates the nature of associated evaluation instruments or procedures'. And they go on to say that the exercise which has been briefly sketched:

> . . . should above all have made it clear that there are a variety of ways to develop evaluative criteria and that these involve both empirical and theoretical modes of analysis. It should also be evident that the principles of lifelong education are open to interpretation and that the nature of such interpretation is influenced by the cultural context in which it is made. At a relatively general level it is possible for individuals from different countries to agree on criteria for evaluating curricula.[13]

So we have some answer to the question raised earlier about the possibility of a universal ideal of lifelong learning. In this study the term lifelong education was employed — with reservations — to explore the possibilities of curriculum evaluation, but without very much reference to the problem of the content of learning itself. And it seems fairly clear that it is precisely this content of learning that is subject to the influence of the cultural context in which lifelong education is implemented.

This would seem to be crucial to the internal coherence of the whole idea. The 'concept characteristics' of the idea of lifelong education as it is developed by the UNESCO agencies in fact stand for logically distinct kinds of problems and issues, and have quite distinct implications for an analysis in terms of the knowledge-content of adult learning. Although the issue is presented as one of a universal goal, to attain which a variety of culturally prescribed means might be appropriate, the situation is not so straightforward in curriculum terms. For the key idea seems to be one not of reproducing or transforming the curriculum categories of schooling through later learning but rather one of curriculum *integration*. In other words, as far as the curriculum is concerned, the most important implication of lifelong education is integration. However, it is also made apparent that other 'concept characteristics' have to do with democratisation and popular control, and it is by no means clear that these have curriculum implications of a transforming rather than a merely integrating kind.

In other words, curriculum integration — horizontal, vertical or whatever — does not necessarily mean curriculum development: it may have no implications whatever for the ways in which, in any particular society, knowledge is defined, distributed and evaluated. The object of evaluation in these studies is not, of course, knowledge but the curricula of schooling. Since the curricula of schooling are constructed in a cultural context of knowledge-definition though, a major issue arises in introducing 'concept characteristics' of a potentially transforming kind, such as democratisation and popular control. Curriculum integration as such is a function of any schooling system, whether or not it is proposed as an element of lifelong education. Indeed the issue of integrating the stages of education arises out of the internal relations of any institutionalised system of education. And many school educators may see the integration of schooling with family, community and work situations — and adulthood itself — as a desirable goal without necessarily adopting lifelong education as an ideal, even though its advocates might argue that this is an inevitable consequence of such a view.

So the curriculum implications of lifelong education in this particular form are rather ambiguous. For example, the fifth of the eight summary principles of lifelong education which were derived for the project was, it may be recalled:

> *Opportunity and Motivation*, comprising societal and personal prerequisites for the development of lifelong education.

Presumably this does not refer to the need for institutional integration or flexibility, which are the object of other summary principles, but to cultural conditions of society itself which create for the individual the cultural accessibility of learning, in addition to accessibility in material terms. This raises key issues which were not capable of evaluation in the context of the school curriculum, even though it has been apparent for some time that there are, in fact, cultural barriers to effective schooling. More to the point perhaps, is that this principle of lifelong education raises the issue of cultural barriers to effective adult learning which the curriculum integration/evaluation approach seems incapable of addressing. Now it is precisely the issue of democratisation and popular control that would seem to take the argument beyond that of integration, because this really is about the degree to which, in any society's culture, the social construction of knowledge reflects the reality or the possibility of popular control and democratisation. Presumably this lies at the heart of the matter of lifelong education as a universal ideal achieved through diverse cultural means in different societies.

To sum up, this idea of lifelong education, in terms of the knowledge-content of the curriculum, is rather ambiguous. Its focus upon curriculum integration tends to disguise the fact that some of the summary principles of lifelong education upon which the study was based are significant for the transformation of the knowledge-basis of the curriculum and some are not, or at least are only potentially so. Democratisation raises qualitatively different issues about the curriculum which cannot be contained by integration/evaluation analysis, because it raises the question of the definition, distribution and evaluation of knowledge in society and that of the cultural barriers to learning which these may in certain conditions constitute. Further explorations of the idea of lifelong education would perhaps need more detailed elucidation of the basis of cultural relativity in the ways in which, as Holmes says, different peoples think differently about, say, mathematics. At least some account of the status-relativities of knowledge and the differential access to it of social groups and classes would make clearer the practical possibilities of the idea. However, as in the case of much educational theory, the emphasis of lifelong education tends to be upon the individual and upon concepts of personal growth rather to the neglect of concepts of the social construction of knowledge as a basis for thinking about the curriculum and curriculum development. In these terms, the idea of lifelong education is rather ambiguously presented: its capacity for development as a transformation of the curriculum categories of schooling is obscured by the focus upon integration and by an initial stress upon the evaluation of the school curriculum.

Some such limitations are, in fact, acknowledged by Rodney Skager in another study of the UNESCO project[14] on the same theme of evaluation practice:

> The work on evaluation criteria presented here obviously was strongly influenced by the emphasis on criteria relating to personal development that characterizes much of the literature on lifelong education. Still, organizational and societal factors, particularly those of a structural nature, are included as well. This emphasis on criteria relating to personal development seems logical as an extension of what has been written already. It does not mean that social and economic criteria can be ignored. These remain areas that richly deserve exploration.[15]

But the capacity of lifelong education as a basis for generating curriculum development theory must be limited in other ways too if, as Skager says, 'Strictly speaking . . . lifelong education is not a concept or theory, but a set of basic principles through which the Commission, its sponsoring agency, and its growing ranks of supporters hope to stimulate worldwide educational reform over the coming decades.'[16] The social and cultural contexts of lifelong education are described by Skager broadly in terms of develoment and modernisation and its principles reflect contemporary social forces. It is, as was seen before in a conception of lifelong learning, essentially a process of adaptation to technological change and associated structural changes in productive activity, a process in which both developed and developing societies share some common situations and problems. Into such patterns of change the individual is required to fit:

The need for a citizenry 'educable' throughout life is widely appreciated. In order to adapt, mature individuals must be willing and able to engage in systematic learning. In this sense, at least, more and less developed societies are on common ground.[17]

But developing countries have found it difficult to build up fast enough a traditional system of schooling, and have found as well that such a system does not necessarily meet their needs. Alternative but related systems to schooling are also sought by developed societies as a consequence of the effects of technology in changing old patterns of work and leisure:

The danger to the individual and to the larger society of passivity and inactivity in the face of more and more leisure is apparent. Education becomes the primary tool for promoting individual growth and self-realization.[18]

In addition to the need to adapt to development and modernisation is another factor, however, in the social and cultural context of both more and less developed countries, and that is to eliminate inequalities. The principles of lifelong education have been shaped as much, it is argued, by ideologies of equality as much as by economic growth and development. As such it is rather more than a new theory or philosophy of education, and it represents a view of the general role of education in society and politics.

This claim for the social and political significance of the idea, especially in so far as it is presented somehow as transcending ideology, would seem to suggest that the knowledge-content of the curriculum of lifelong education is crucial: 'Whatever the ideological origin of the press for change, a faith in the power of education to promote various types of equality is apparent in many if not all national societies.'[19] However, the variety of 'types of equality' which it is in the power of education to promote is surely very wide and unless some quite objective criteria of a curriculum or knowledge-based kind are developed it is hard to see just how these claims could be justified. In so far as social and political equality is a function of the reproduction or transformation of the curriculum categories of schooling then such claims depend upon elucidating these processes. But this is not achieved by evaluating school knowledge — the curriculum of schooling — according to an idea of lifelong learning or the principles of lifelong education, upon which task so much effort is being expended. The concepts of integration and evaluation are being explored in the context of schooling and 'progressive' education without apparently much direct reference to the ways in which, in different ideological conditions, schooling itself functions to reproduce social inequalities through reproducing cultural definitions, distributions and evaluations of knowledge. Certainly a capacity for transformation may be attributed to forms of learning of any kind but the connection between progressivism in schooling and the democratisation of knowledge and social equality is neither necessary nor obvious, as the radical curriculum theorists have argued. To focus upon the integration and evaluation of the school curriculum in the light of progressivism and lifelong education, in other words, at best enables us to see ways in which school knowledge could be transformed and at worst ways in which it could be reproduced. What seems to be entirely missing is an appraisal of the knowledge-content of adult learning — especially in terms of integration and evaluation. Without this, the claim that lifelong education is a response to pressure for equality as well as to modernisation is quite simply unverifiable.

Certainly for all kinds of reasons, lifelong education is quite distinct from adult education, and certainly this has to do with curriculum issues involved in the ideas. But lifelong education theory has in this instance replicated the theoretical failure of adult education. For just as it was suggested that adult education theory has often become bogged down in sterile attempts to 'distance' it from schooling, so lifelong education theorists have overstressed the differences between it and adult education. There is little sense of the dynamic relationships between the knowledge-content of schooling and that of adult learning (so that ideas of reproduction and transformation could be explored). Indeed there is little sense of the knowledge-content of adult learning at all, so that paradoxically in curriculum terms lifelong education is almost identified with (progressive) schooling itself. In knowledge terms it is not so much the ambiguities of the idea of lifelong education, which are often remarked upon, as the contradictions which characterise it in some formulations at least, where it seems to stand for little more than a synonym for progressive schooling. The further claims that are made for it in terms of democratisation and equality are impossible to verify or substantiate in the absence of a thoroughgoing analysis of the social construction of knowledge which deals in the same theoretical terms with the knowledge-content of *both* schooling and adult learning. If we cannot conceptualise the integration and evaluation of adult learning in the same terms as that of the curriculum of schooling then the idea of lifelong education will continue to be one of paradoxes and contradictions.

Perhaps the whole approach of definitions, principles and concept-characteristics is inappropriate for the theoretical elucidation of lifelong education where, despite appearances to the contrary, the curriculum focus is as neglected as it has been in adult education. Nevertheless, this approach has constituted a theoretical underpinning of the studies of the school curriculum carried out for the UNESCO Institute for Education. The principles of lifelong education were proposed during the 1970s[20] and they are, in the words of Rodney Skager, eclectic and inclusive:

> They are also grounded on egalitarian values. The principles define ultimate ends, but avoid being prescriptive about means. Taken together, they present a holistic view of education operating within an idealized 'learning society' — a society in which individuals engage in personally and socially meaningful learning throughout their lives and in which the means of learning are distributed by various institutions and made equally available to all.[21]

Such principles, argued Skager, are especially significant for evaluating the curriculum of schooling, since evaluation, whilst seen as a vital function, is 'one which in the past has often functioned to promote and maintain social elitism and unwholesome competition among learners'. Under lifelong education the learner has more control, both individually and co-operatively, over the learning process. So self-evaluation, flexibility and non-punitive methods are part of the definition of lifelong education, and the emphasis of traditional schooling upon assessment of attainment is replaced by one upon 'the assessment of capacity for future attainment': 'A unifying theme for evaluation is the concept of "educability" and the ways in which it might be enhanced in learners.'[22] This is seen as a major problem of schooling rather than of adult learning, and it is a reflection of the curriculum priorities of lifelong education and of the kind of functional relationship which it predicates between schooling and adult learning, so that adult learning is rather dependent upon what schools teach. As one of the most influential originators of the idea, Paul Lengrand, put it:

> Whatever the volume and depth of any campaign undertaken on behalf of adult education, success can only follow if equally resolute action is taken to amend the structures, curricula and methods of

the first stages of education, those designed for children and adolescents.[23]

No doubt this is true, in so far as some kind of functional relationship must exist between schooling and adult learning. But it tends to leave unexamined the actual contradictions between political structures and lifelong education ideals, which arise out the way in which, in any society, knowledge and the content of learning are socially constructed. The picture of the functional relation of schooling and adult learning that has been built up by both curriculum reformers of schooling and by advocates of lifelong education is one of dependence (of adult learning upon schooling) or else anticipation (by the school curriculum of adult life). The point that is lost — as it tends to be on the part of much educational progressivism — is that the transformation or restructuring of the knowledge-content of learning is a social process of cultural, political and ideological significance. It is not one that could be contained in either schooling or adult learning as such, even though major initiatives in the process may be taken there. If lifelong education was an idea of the transformation of knowledge associated with its claims to democratisation and popular control then it must involve a view of knowledge in just these terms as a social process. The functional relation of the knowledge-content of schooling and adult learning would, in these terms, be mutual or more organic, rather than being one of dependence or anticipation. The concepts of evaluation and integration, which have been used to express a UNESCO conception of lifelong education and applied to the school curriculum, are based on a view of knowledge which precludes an organic functional relation of school knowledge and the content of adult learning (with which it can hardly be said to deal). More important for its claims to be connected with democratisation and popular control, lifelong education would seem to be predicated upon a view of knowledge which is not one of social and ideological construction and which therefore gives little purchase upon the possibility of a transforming or a restructuring curriculum. The concept of 'educability', for example, which is taken as a unifying theme for evaluating the school curriculum in lifelong terms, may be problematic in terms of the social construction of knowledge and function ideologically more as an instrument of social control than of democratisation. It has done so historically, and in the absence of such a concept of knowledge, related to processes of reproduction and transformation, there is no reason to suppose that these things would change under a system of lifelong education.

The content of the school curriculum, for purposes of lifelong evaluation, is conceptualised therefore in perfectly conventional knowledge terms as the mastery of specified learning goals and skills. The familiar taxonomies devised by Bloom and Gagné constitute the received analysis of the school curriculum :

> This structural conception of learning leads to an analytical approach to the construction of curricula in which discrete learning steps leading to more complex objectives are identified and carefully sequenced . . . Whenever attainment of curriculum content is required of the general population, there is the implication that 'attainment' refers to a state very similar to mastery, and that such attainment can be assessed objectively. In other words, to require that content be 'attained' assumes that educational goals can be spelled out in some sort of concrete fashion, and that it is possible to make reasonably accurate distinctions between states of attainment and non-attainment.[24]

The content of learning consists, therefore, of specific and objectively measurable knowledge and skills, mastery of which is the object of educational evaluation : it is a fairly traditional philosophical and psychological view of knowledge and learning, and one made familiar to generations of schoolteachers in training. There is no scope for substantive knowledge transformation, since both aims and content of learning are 'given'. The only scope is for a methodological redefinition of educational goals, so that the concern is not with the transformation of knowledge but with the 'transformation of instructional content', which turns out to be quite another matter.[25]

Of course, Skager accepts the hypothetical situation which evaluation of lifelong education proposes, but argues that its principles are actually embodied in established progressive educational practices :

> Fortunately, while lifelong education as a total, organizing system does not exist anywhere, its component elements have been evident for some time in various forms and degrees. There is little that is new about lifelong education other than the fact[1] that it is a comprehensive scheme for organizing an entire society educationally.[26]

This is a massive claim, and it is important to understand the context in which it is made. In fact this particular conception of lifelong education arising out of evaluation analysis is more accurately described as educational innovation rather than curriculum change or development: it leaves the direction of innovation firmly in the hands of those who have by tradition been responsible for the educational organisation of society. In spite of a technical focus upon the curriculum of schooling there is little sense of the organic relationship of the knowledge-content of learning over the whole of an individual's lifetime in a context of society, culture and politics. Perhaps even the term 'lifelong education' reflects a view of knowledge and learning profoundly individualistic, lifetimes being attributed to individuals rather than to anything else. A claim to the comprehensive educational organisation of society must, in the end, be made out with some reference at least to the social organisation of knowledge which determines the content of both schooling and adult learning.

This content, however, seems to be determined by the analytic concepts of the idea of lifelong education itself, which are in any case not very clear. At least, they are as clear as the concepts of progressive schooling, with which lifelong education is coming to seem more and more synonymous through ideas of open goals and autonomy:

> The general concept of open educational goals incorporates the more specific concept (though it is still inclusive enough) of self-directed learning. Lifelong education now badly needs to define its concepts, especially those that suggest goals of the open variety . . . Open educational goals have been most fully articulated in the unifying concept of educability. With respect to the latter, self-direction in learning seems to be the key component concept. At the level of the individual and the instructional process the facilitation of self-direction is absolutely vital to the implementation of lifelong education.[27]

It is not really the clarity of the concepts which is at issue, however, for as many commentators have said, these are hardly new concepts in any case. What is really needed is more direct reference to the content of learning and the ways in which this relates to the comprehensive educational organisation of society and to the growth of democracy and popular control which, it is claimed, lifelong education expresses.

At this level of analysis the idea is most disappointing, for the content of learning is itself simply conceptualised in terms of educational goals and evaluation. Whatever the content of lifelong learning, apparently, the task will be to assimilate it to traditional educational processes:

. . . lifelong education's central concern with the enhancement of educability and especially the cluster of open goals relating to self-direction in learning introduces a mainly new subject matter for evaluation. This subject matter can be assessed at present only in a rudimentary fashion. Constructs referring to the personal characteristics of self-directed learners and to the dimensions of learning situations that enhance self-direction need to be stated as precisely as possible. Without precision in this area, it will be impossible to build evaluation instruments and procedures that have any chance of being valid measures of the phenomena they are meant to address.[28]

In other words, the 'content domains' of lifelong education will be specified in terms of techniques for evaluating learning within these domains 'in terms of content mastery'. So the need is for further elucidation of lifelong education in terms of accreditation and certification, assessment of self-direction in learning, qualitative research strategies and so on.

A picture of lifelong education has now been built up which is so individualistic in its assumptions as to be almost wholly devoid of reference to the problem of knowledge and its structural and ideological representation in society. This despite the consistent assertion that lifelong education is somehow connected with democratisation and egalitarian change in society. The idea does not project a social concept of knowledge at all, and the knowledge-content of learning itself is reduced to a projection of evaluation problems and techniques. However, there is an account of lifelong education which is much more directly concerned with the curriculum in terms of knowledge, and from it we may obtain a clearer view of the real nature of the lifelong curriculum.

Curriculum Integration

In the case of James B. Ingram's study of curriculum integration and lifelong education,[29] the subtitle is not without significance: 'A Contribution to the Improvement of School Curricula'. For it is indeed a view of lifelong education with little reference to adult learning, and the greater part of the study is concerned with the issues of curriculum integration as they affect the curriculum categories of schooling. It is, in other words, a view of lifelong education as anticipated by such categories, and although this functional relationship is not spelled out, but left implicit in the absence of a view of adult learning, it deals more explicitly with the problem of the knowledge-content of the curriculum than did the evaluation studies which were also the outcome of the UNESCO programme. This is as close as the idea of the lifelong curriculum has so far come to descriptions in knowledge terms. But far from elucidating the functional relation of the curriculum content of school-in and adult learning, and the ways in which the reproduction or transformation of this content is effected, the study is concerned primarily with the transformational potentialities of schooling and school knowledge as such. It is, as the author claims, basically a demonstration of the compatibility of progressive schooling and the idea of lifelong education rather than of their functional relation. It is therefore as much an argument for educational innovation in schooling as for the development of a lifelong education curriculum.

Integration, as Ingram points out, has emerged as a 'focal concept' of lifelong education, and it is this, rather than evaluation, which now needs for present purposes to be analysed in a context of reproduction and transformation. 'Lifelong education and curriculum integration have developed as two separate educational notions and practices', says Ingram. As a result they are distinguishable in many different respects:

> Lifelong education is a more global concept than curriculum integration. The one is general, the other more specific. Lifelong education encompasses a great variety of educational aspects and a wide spectrum of practical possibilities, only one of which is curriculum integration. Variations with regard to time are also significant. Lifelong education embraces the whole of the lifespan; curriculum integration is a problem that arises mainly in the years of schooling ... [30]

This seems quite a crucial problem, and one which this emerging view of lifelong education seldom addresses: how far is curriculum integration possible or desirable in a context of adult learning? If it is not possible, what are the implications for the idea of lifelong education? Is integration a desirable curriculum category of adult learning or are other quite distinct and transformational categories more appropriate? If integration is a desirable curriculum category of schooling but indifferent with respect to the content of adult learning, what are the consequences in respect of the functional relation of these stages of learning? If such questions are not answered then either the idea of lifelong education will remain, as its critics would claim, excessively utopian and abstract, or else it will tend to be reduced to a view of educational innovation and progressive schooling, in which the term 'lifelong' is simply one of a range of compatible ideas: democratisation and popular control have already been noticed. The UNESCO curriculum view is being developed in such a way as to reproduce curriculum categories of progressive schooling. These may, no doubt, constitute transforming categories in knowledge terms, and clearly there is much more to an idea of lifelong education, but the theoretical elucidation of the idea has far to go and at some point must confront the problem of the knowedge-content of adult learning directly. Otherwise analytic concepts of evaluation and integration will continue to lack substantive reference in a lifelong context.

One consequence of this, which has been noted, is a tendency to think of lifelong education as itself a kind of strategy for achieving democratic social goals:

> It is one of the principal tenets of lifelong education that appropriate opportunities should be available for all throughout their lifetime. This implies that educational provision at any one period should not prejudice an individual's chances of furthering his educational development at any other time. To do this lifelong education aims not just to supplement schooling but to transform it. It is in connection with this process of transformation that the concept of integration assumes significance for lifelong education.[31]

Now this seems to be at the heart of the matter: the exact nature of the transformation of schooling which lifelong education is claimed to achieve. In the first place, it may be observed that the curriculum of schooling can be transformed in a progressive way whilst leaving the social construction of knowledge (which determines the content of adult learning) relatively unchanged. This is precisely what radical curriculum theorists have pointed out, that progressive or 'transformed' schooling may be as much an instrument of social control as of social change: it may leave unaffected the definition, distribution and evaluation of knowledge in society. And this is because, although having the potentiality to do so, progressivism may or may not involve a political view of knowledge such as is required to effect the kind of social transformations claimed for it. Progressive education may be a necessary condition of achieving a democratic ideal of lifelong education, but it is probably not a sufficient one.

This is especially the case where progressivism is identified, as it is here, with the integration of learning experience over time (vertical integration) and as between all the possible agencies of learning experience in society (horizontal integration). Integration of schooling with learning experience in the home, the community, the media and so on will produce democratic outcomes to the extent that the home, the community and the media (and later the workplace) themselves constitute democratic sources of learning experience. Otherwise we are simply talking about the integration of individual learners into the prevailing normative systems of home, community, media and workplace: again the connection with political democracy would seem to be contingent, for totalitarian systems may often reasonably be thought to embrace lifelong education as integration — it has much in common, presumably, with what under such conditions would be called 'political' education.

The case cannot be made out, in other words, with such scant reference to the content of adult learning and with a view of knowledge lacking in the kind of social, cultural and ideological dimensions which an aim of political transformation entails. The case that is made out for integration by Ingram is, therefore, strictly pedagogical: its reference is entirely to a concept of progressive schooling. He makes it out in eight contexts: the need to keep pace with rapid social change and with the 'knowledge explosion' which formal schooling must cope with; the need for schooling to be associated more closely with society in its value systems, relevance to working life and home environments; the need for openness and for schools to break down barriers to learning and knowledge; the need for schools to teach 'knowledge that is useful' for living, and for theoretical subjects to be learned in a context of practical activities; the need to develop operational learning as a function of life, so that dealing with life experience becomes the proper object of learning rather than the traditional subject-content of the school curriculum; the need to develop a 'consensus for action' or, in other words, an education for 'the whole man' in which a wide range of different aspects of development and experience (arts and sciences, the moral and the technical, the religious and the secular) are brought into a concerted and co-ordinated learning experience; the need to 'facilitate the educational development of the individual' or to establish the 'primacy of the person', for although schools perform academic and social functions, 'this third function is the most important of the three and the other two should be subservient to it'; finally, there is the need for the 'enhancement of educability' both manifest and latent, based upon 'an unfaltering faith in the enduring educability of the individual and in the individual's potential for self-realisation'.

These are the kinds of needs which curriculum integration in schools can help to meet and which, says Ingram, are consistent with the idea of lifelong education:

> They put the person and not the system at the centre of education; they advocate a greater cohesion of school and society; they recognise the inevitabilty and ubiquity of change; they recommend an open and practical approach to teaching and learning; and they view education as a cooperative enterprise requiring the coordination of the efforts of all those who contribute to it.[32]

Whereas lifelong education seems to be an abstract idea of principles, guidelines and values, curriculum integration refers to educational practices which have been developed in the classroom in response to problems for teachers which have arisen there. It has been rather a piecemeal development, and Ingram suggests that, since the two ideas are mutually compatible, lifelong education might constitute some kind of necessary theoretical underpinning for the curriculum integration of schooling:

> At present curriculum integration tends to be self-justifying and a more realistic appraisal of its potential might be possible were it viewed from the perspective of lifelong education . . . Lifelong education would appear to provide some theoretical support for the idea of curriculum integration, focus attention on what may be its key features, and, rather than leave it as an end in itself, give it greater purpose in the wider context of education.[33]

In view of the absence of any reference to the curriculum content of adult learning, however, it is difficult to grasp the idea of a lifelong education curriculum in terms other than those of progressive schooling, which Ingram proceeds to elaborate through the process of integration.

The radical critique of progressive schooling is based upon a rather different view of knowledge than that which informs this particular concept of lifelong education. The curriculum integration approach which has been outlined in this chapter seems to be predicated upon the political and ideological neutrality of knowledge, and sometimes upon a view of knowledge beyond human control: the inevitability and ubiquity of social change as a basic assumption, unless it is much more critically treated, conveys a view of passivity on the part of those who experience it and educational institutions which are shaped in response to it. It conveys little sense of the social construction and uses of knowledge and of the conflict and struggle out of which its definition, distribution and evaluation emerge in the end. The inadequate knowledge-reference of this kind of lifelong education idea is certainly what gives rise to the criticism that it is ambiguous as between different cultural, political and ideological contexts, but perhaps it would be more accurate to speak of it as an idea characterised as much by contradiction as by ambiguity.

What, for example, constitutes 'knowledge that is useful'? The answer depends to some extent upon how knowledge is to be socially used and there are no wholly objective criteria. In the history of education in Britain, for example, 'useful knowledge' as appropriated by educational institutions was contrasted with the kind of 'really useful knowledge' as an object of learning which radicals identified as the real need of the working class. In progressivism can be traced, perhaps, the appropriation by schooling of 'really useful knowledge'.[34] The progressive credentials of the integration model of lifelong education would certainly be vulnerable to such an analysis, and its claims about democratisation and popular control subject to question.

In fact Ingram carefully distinguishes the epistemological from the social functions of curriculum integration, which latter he describes entirely in terms of making a better 'fit' between schooling and society.[35] This projects rather a 'reified' view of society rather than a political one, and political action is conceived entirely as something that occurs within educational institutions in the course of curriculum integration.[36]

So it is integration in a highly pedagogic mode: structural integration of knowledge and functional integration of schooling and society. The knowledge-content of the lifelong curriculum is conceptualised in wholly pedagogic terms: learning to know, learning to do and learning to be.[37] The relation of schooling to education itself in terms of goals is conceptualised in terms of alternative pedagogies: 'The one set is scholastic, the other more broadly related to the purposes and practicalities of life.'[38] The social organisation of knowledge is itself thought of in apolitical terms as a rather technical problem of knowledge management:

. . . the way in which knowledge is organised for curriculum purposes and the administrative structure of the system that provides the curriculum are inexorably intertwined . . . the micro-system of the school is but part of the macro-system of society and . . . the child at his desk in the schoolroom is, as it were, at the fulcrum of these various interacting forces that characterise the social organisation of knowledge.[39]

But the power struggle that consequently arises is conceived here in terms of politically disembodied forces expressing alternative peda-gogies: the social construction of knowledge finds expression, for example, in the differential incidence of curriculum integration in primary and secondary schooling.[40] It is a view of the social institu-tionalisation rather than the social construction of knowledge.

This is, therefore, a concept of lifelong education constructed accord-ing to pedagogic categories and without substantive reference to the knowledge-content of adult learning. Consequently it remains basically an alternative conception of schooling to that of traditionalism, and accordingly curriculum integration is a factor contributing to an alter-native and preferable preparation for adult life which schooling could achieve.[41] It is a strategy of anticipation, a 'front-end' or 'banking' idea of education rather than a really new paradigm. But it raises important issues. Does the integration model of lifelong education reproduce the curriculum categories of progressive schooling, as adult education has tended to reproduce those of traditional schooling? Or could it do more in a context of the politics and ideology of knowledge? In other words, what are the possibilities of integration and transformation of the curri-culum of adult learning, especially since these are limited in the context of schooling itself?[42] These issues have been addressed by alternative ideas of lifelong education.

Summary

The lifelong curriculum poses the issue of the precise nature of the functional relation between the knowledge-content of schooling and of adult learning. As a universal ideal, lifelong education has been pre-sented as somehow transcending politics, being capable of finding expression in a range of political and cultural conditions. It has also been presented as something associated with development, change and the 'knowledge explosion', and with democratisation and egalitarian-ism. However, it is in some respects a contradictory ideal, since not only do societies constitute alternative constructions of knowledge but the reconstruction or transformation of knowledge would seem to be an inevitable corollary of the kind of progressive social changes associated with lifelong learning. And this is a political issue which is not reducible to technical considerations of pedagogy.

The UNESCO concept is excessively pedagogical in its categories of evaluation and integration, lacking reference either to the content of adult learning or to the obstacles to change constituted by prevailing definitions, distributions and evaluations of knowledge. Consequently it reproduces highly individualistic categories of progressive schooling rather than transforming the knowledge-content of learning over a lifetime (where the functional relation of schooling and adulthood is organic or mutual). Its knowledge-reference does not have the kind of implication for curriculum development which its social claims would entail. So strictly speaking there is no basis here for a lifelong curriculum, in concepts of anticipation, reproduction and integration, which would transform the curriculum categories of schooling as such. On the contrary, the integration of education and society is conceived in functional terms so that lifelong education, at least in this conception of it, does not constitute the new paradigm that it has sometimes been claimed to be.

Notes and References

1. Article in the *Times Educational Supplement*, London, 3 October 1980.
2. Ibid.
3. Ibid.
4. Ibid.
5. Ibid.
6. See, for example, David Hargreaves, *The Challenge for the Comprehensive School* (London: Routledge and Kegan Paul, 1982).
7. Department of Education and Science, *A View of the Curriculum* (London: HMSO, 1980), p. 18.
8. Rodney Skager and R.H. Dave (eds), *Curriculum Evaluation for Lifelong Education* (Oxford: Pergamon Press for the UNESCO Institute for Education, 1977).
9. Ibid., p. 2. In fact, the Swedish researchers retained as a significant distinction that between 'lifelong learning' and 'lifelong education' (pp. 9-10).
10. Ibid., p. 8.
11. Ibid., pp. 8-9.
12. Ibid., pp. 50-5.
13. Ibid., p. 61.
14. Rodney Skager, *Lifelong Education and Evaluation Practice* (Oxford, Pergamon Press for the UNESCO Institute for Education, 1978).
15. Ibid., p. 22.
16. Ibid., p. 3.

17. Ibid., p. 4.

18. Ibid.

19. Ibid., p. 5.

20. See Edgar Faure *et al.*, *Learning to be: the World of Education Today and Tomorrow* (Paris: UNESCO, 1972); Paul Lengrand, *An Introduction to Lifelong Education* (London: Croom Helm, revised edn, 1975); R.H. Dave (ed.), *Foundations of Lifelong Education* (Oxford: Pergamon Press for the UNESCO Institute for Education, 1976).

21. Rodney Skager, *Lifelong Education and Evaluation Practice*, p. 5.

22. Ibid., p. 6.

23. Paul Lengrand, *Introduction to Lifelong Education*, p. 78.

24. Rodney Skager, *Lifelong Education and Evaluation Practice*, pp.55-6.

25. Ibid., pp. 80-1.

26. Ibid., p. 127.

27. Ibid., p. 125.

28. Ibid., p. 128.

29. James B. Ingram, *Curriculum Integration and Lifelong Education* (Oxford: Pergamon Press for the UNESCO Institute for Education, 1979).

30. Ibid., p. 5.

31. Ibid., p. 7.

32. Ibid., p. 19.

33. Ibid., pp. 20-1.

34. See Richard Johnson, 'Really Useful Knowledge: Radical Education and Working-class Culture, 1790-1848', *Working-class Culture: Studies in History and Theory*, ed. John Clarke *et al.* (London: Hutchinson, 1979), Chapter 3.

35. James B. Ingram, *Curriculum Integration and Lifelong Education*, pp. 53-5.

36. Ibid., p. 89.

37. Ibid., pp. 62-5.

38. Ibid., p. 64.

39. Ibid., p. 81.

40. Ibid., pp. 91-2.

41. Ibid., p. 101.

42. Ibid., p. 88.

7 GELPI'S VIEW OF LIFELONG EDUCATION

Introduction

In recent years the name of Ettore Gelpi has been added to those of Ivan Illich and Paulo Freire as among the most important contributors to educational debate especially as it has influenced discussion of adult and lifelong education. A major purpose of this chapter is to review Gelpi's concept of lifelong education and to evaluate it in the light of the criteria being developed for a theoretical elucidation of curriculum analysis in this field. The question is, therefore, one of the implications of these more radical cultural and political views of education for the knowledge-content of adult learning and its capacity to transform or reproduce the curriculum categories of schooling. What, in other words, are the assumptions about the social construction of knowledge which underlie these more recent theories and which distinguish them both from traditional adult education ideologies and from a view, discussed in the last chapter, of lifelong education as a form of curriculum integration? It is important, too, not to ignore the different assumptions and approaches of writers of such diversity as Illich, Freire and Gelpi, and to elucidate the sense in which Gelpi's own work represents a definite advance upon that of his predecessors in this more radical tradition.

The curriculum integration model of lifelong education explored in the last chapter seems to be predicated upon an apolitical concept of knowledge. Other views of it, such as those associated with a 'recurrent' strategy, seem to be predicated upon a view of knowledge in a context of inevitable and ubiquitous change and development — change running apparently out of human control and knowledge 'exploding' without apparent reference to the social, cultural and political conditions in which it is created. Such views of lifelong education, it was suggested, could hardly constitute a new paradigm of education in curriculum terms. Despite the theoretical 'distancing' of adult education from schooling, and the innovative characteristics of lifelong or adult education legislation, in knowledge terms adult and lifelong education tend to reproduce the curriculum categories of traditional and progressive schooling. This they are inevitably bound to do in so far as they fail to underpin their claims to democratisation, egalitarianism and popular control with a transformational analysis of the knowledge-content of learning.

172

There can be little doubt that writers such as Illich, Freire and Gelpi have been attempting, in their different ways, to construct a new paradigm and to engage in such a transformational analysis which has as its object the nature of knowledge itself. Certainly such an analysis is not without significance for traditional ideological categories of needs, access and provision. The point is that in such writers these are categories which tend to be located much more in knowledge-analysis, in such a way that the superficial progressivism of educational innovation is exposed by the same logic as that employed by radical curriculum theorists in their critical analyses of the curriculum of schooling. Illich, Freire and Gelpi have demonstrated the political problem of knowledge and education and, in different degrees, the ways in which institutions give expression to the political construction of knowledge and, as such, constitute obstacles to the transformation of knowledge. It is not necessary, as Gelpi himself makes clear, to associate institutionalism with repression; but it is necessary, according to all these writers, to understand education as much in terms of the politics of knowledge as of the politics of educational institutions.

So as well as drawing attention to the political character of the knowledge-content of learning, our writers are also concerned with the potentially repressive institutionalisation of culturally and politically contingent categories. It is significant that a radical view of education tends often to see the categories of 'adult' and 'child' in this light, in particular. To think of childhood and adulthood as political categories, rather than as categories of educational methodology which find expression respectively in pedagogy and andragogy, is not unfamiliar in the history of radical education. There is a sense in which this distinction – traditionally held crucial for the development of adult education theory – is an institutionalised invention of education systems, reflecting all kinds of historical conditions to do with culture and class, family and work, the divisions of professional labour and so on. Certainly such a view could be expressed from the standpoint of the history of radical education in Britain, where the child-adult distinction is of significance not in educational so much as in class and political terms: in the political appropriation by the state of childhood itself and the incorporation of childhood learning into schooling. This draws attention to the need for the critical-historical perspective upon the social construction of knowledge which is not conspicuously a feature of the history of education, which normally takes the form of the history of educational institutions and legislation. It is, in other words, a history of 'provided' education, as Richard Johnson's study of radical education suggests.[1] Nevertheless, as he says, we have recently witnessed 'the rediscovery of popular educational traditions, the springs of action of which owed little to philanthropic, ecclesiastical or state provision'. And there is a sense in which Illich, Freire and Gelpi could be said to be engaged in a similar task of rediscovery, one which implies the same kind of political analysis of knowledge, the same kind of scepticism of progressive legislation and innovation, and the same kind of approach to the processes of institutionalisation and professionalisation which create the categories of child and adult.

The knowledge-content of learning was certainly an important aspect of radical education, as it must be of lifelong education if it is really to count as a new or alternative paradigm to existing systems of education. Radical education in early nineteenth-century Britain was first of all associated with a 'running critique of all forms of "provided" education'. But, as Johnson says:

> The second main feature was the development of alternative educational goals. At one level these embraced a vision of a whole alternative future — a future in which educational utopias, among other needs, could actually be achieved. At another, radicalism developed its own curricula and pedagogies, its own definition of 'really useful knowledge', a characteristically radical *content*, a sense of what it was really important to know.[2]

To what extent does the radical lifelong education of the writers presently under consideration compare with this radicalism of the early Industrial Revolution? The early form certainly incorporated an alternative curriculum knowledge-content to that of 'provided' forms of education and constituted therefore a transformation of that of schooling. However, these radical alternatives were themselves incorporated into a system of state provision. And one of the mechanisms by which this was achieved was through the professionalisation of pedagogy, or the invention of 'childhood' as the most fundamental site of human learning. This is why, as was previously suggested, the invention of 'adulthood' as a site also of learning and the further professionalisation of andragogy paradoxically constitute a reproduction rather than a transformation of curriculum categories of schooling. It is important to understand the significance of the professionalised institutionalisation of childhood and adulthood in these terms in a context of either adult or lifelong education. It was seen how, in the last chapter, the idea of lifelong education functioned merely instrumentally to improve the curricula of schooling, without reference either to the content of adult learning or to the social construction of knowledge in 'alternative' or 'provided' forms.

It seems that radical lifelong education must have some features in common with the earlier forms of radical education such as Johnson describes. These are concerned with the possibility of alternative knowledge-contents and the institutional significance of the categories of childhood and adulthood, and they are the most important reasons why these concepts of lifelong education are consistently distanced from adult education as such. In different ways, writers such as Illich, Freire and Gelpi are led by the logic of the idea of a new paradigm of education to think of institutionalised pedagogy as a historic mechanism of the incorporation of 'really useful knowledge' into state systems of education. It has proved only too easy to conceptualise the functional relation of schooling and adult learning in such a way as to reproduce the whole process of incorporation experienced by earlier forms of radical education: whether it is called adult, continuing, recurrent or lifelong education, only the transformation of the knowledge-content in conditions which really de-institutionalise the child-adult dichotomy could actually achieve the visions of radical educationists early or late. This must indeed follow from any attempt to locate the knowledge-content of learning in settings other than formal and age-specific institutions and functional systems. With the early radicalism Johnson puts the matter thus:

> . . . radical movements developed a vigorous and varied educational practice. The distinctive feature was, at first sight, an emphasis upon informing mature understandings and upon the education of men and women as adult citizens of a more just social order. But radicals were also concerned with men and women as educators of their own children and they improvised forms for this task too. It might, however, be truer to say that the child-adult distinction was itself less stressed in this tradition, or in parts of it, than in the contemporary middle-class culture of childhood. This is one reason why, in what follows, no large distinction is made between the education of 'children' and 'adults'. Such a distinction is not found in nature by education, but has actually, in large part, been constructed.[3]

The construction of the child-adult distinction and the professional construction of pedagogy and andragogy, together with the social and political construction of the knowledge-content of education itself, is therefore an important focus of curriculum theory of radical lifelong education. It stands in fairly stark contrast to theory construction in adult education which has focused consistently upon the distinctiveness of adulthood as a learning category, upon the nature of provision appropriate to such a category, and upon the 'liberal' view of knowledge as that which transcends politics or is indifferent to it. Histories of adult education are characteristically histories of provision of knowledge which is 'useful' in this way. From the radical point of view the history of education is the appropriation of 'really useful knowledge' by the education system of the state, thus creating the conditions in which theories of both schooling and adult education must now seek viability. Richard Johnson describes the shift in strategy on the part of radical educators away from an alternative substitute to 'provided' education towards better access on the part of working-class people to the state system of education:

> From the 1850s and more surely from the later 1860s, the strategy of substitution − of an alternative working-class sytem − was replaced by the demand for more equal access to facilities that were to be provided by the state. This became the main feature of popular liberal politics and then of the Labour Party's educational stance . . . The consequences of this adaptation were immense: it involved, for instance, accepting, in a very sharp form, the child-adult divide, the tendency to equate education with school, the depoliticization of educational content, and the professionalization of teaching. In all these ways the state as educator was by no means a neutral apparatus.[4]

The theoretical paradigm of adult education is determined, more often than not, in such terms. Conceptualisation of aims, content and method takes place around the problem of the access of working-class people to provision: it is not the *problem* of the social construction of knowledge or of 'adulthood' or of the 'teacher' that comes to the fore but the *solution* to the problem of access (in terms of openness, distance learning, community education and so forth) that constitutes the starting-point of theory.

Perhaps it is because writers such as Illich, Freire and Gelpi have problematised adult and lifelong education in this kind of way that they have attracted attention from those working in that field. They have, in various ways, rejected the ideology of needs, access and provision in favour of a much more political view of the knowledge-content of learning and a much more sceptical view of the institutionalised apparatus of learning to which, in the end, the ideas of needs, access and provision must have a more or less direct reference.

Illich

On the face of it, Illich's view of institutionalisation is the most radical, for he is talking of deschooling not only education but society itself, using the school as his paradigm. 'Not only education but social reality itself has become schooled', says Illich, and he tries to show in a chapter of *Deschooling Society* called 'Phenomenology of School' how childhood itself is a product of institutionalised schooling:

> Childhood as distinct from infancy, adolescence, or youth was unknown to most historical periods. Some Christian countries did not even have an eye for its bodily proportions. Artists depicted the infant as a miniature adult seated on his mother's arm. Children appeared in Europe along with the pocket watch and the Christian money-lenders of the Renaissance. Before our century neither the poor nor the rich knew of children's dress, children's games, or the child's immunity from the law. Childhood belonged to the bourgeoisie. The worker's child, the peasant's child, and the nobleman's child all dressed the way their fathers dressed, played the way their fathers played, and were hanged by the neck as were their fathers. After the discovery of 'childhood' by the bourgeoisie all this changed.[5]

Although Illich can hardly be said to give much account of the processes by which all this came about, his point is that childhood is a product of the institutionalisation of schooling. For, as he says, 'if there were no age-specific and obligatory learning institution, "childhood" would go out of production'. So the 'disestablishment' of schools could contribute towards ending the association between learning and childhood which is perpetuated in our everyday and common-sense view of education, together with the view that learning is the result of teaching. The institutionalisation of schooling, however, casts the teacher into a repressive role so that, in Illich's words, 'the claim that a liberal society can be founded on the modern school is paradoxical'. But deschooling society means not reforming the educational establishment so much as grasping the hidden curriculum. This is not, in Illich's view, the class-based hidden curriculum of education theory but rather that which 'serves as a ritual of initiation into a growth-oriented consumer society for rich and poor alike'. He certainly seems to take issue with some of the assumptions upon which a view of lifelong education is often based — future societies which are based upon knowledge or information explosions, limitless consumerism, institutionalised value-consensus, inevitable and ubiquitous change and so on. These he characterises as the myths which the hidden curriculum of schooling perpetuates. For Illich, at least, a lifelong education system may amount to nothing more than the reproduction of this kind of hidden curriculum of schooling. So inevitably we look to him to give an account of that kind of knowledge-transformational curriculum which is here being identified as the distinguishing feature of radical lifelong education. What kind of 'really useful knowledge', in short, could withstand incorporation into the curriculum categories of schooling, of the state educational system?

Illich does not provide a particularly original epistemological critique of the school curriculum — most of these points have been made by critics of traditional schooling — but he does conceptualise it in terms of his major concern which is with consumption and consumerism:

> School sells curriculum — a bundle of goods made according to the same process and having the same structure as other merchandise . . . The distributor-teacher delivers the finished product to the consumer-pupil, whose reactions are carefully studied and charted to provide research data for the preparation of the next model, which may be 'ungraded', 'student-designed', 'team-taught', 'visually-aided', or 'issue-centered'.[6]

Illich goes on to expound his idea of education as a form of consumerism under which knowledge is packaged and marketed along the same lines as any other commodity. It is a view not without relevance to post-school education, reflecting as it does in Illich's mind myths of limitless progress, unending consumption and schooling as the 'World Church' of our decaying culture: 'No one completes school — yet. It never closes its doors on anyone without first offering him one more chance: at remedial, adult and continuing education.'[7] In other words, schooling works according to the logic of consumerism itself and has an inbuilt tendency to create rather than meet educational need. Out of such a contradiction arises Illich's view of the real need which is to deschool society or transform it from an association for consumption into something else.

Schooling is only one modern institution whose 'hidden curriculum' is one of manipulation in the direction of a false consumerism, but it is the most important. This is because only schools manifestly function to form critical judgement in conditions of dependence upon teaching, and they are the best example of 'institutionally packaged need' and of the way in which, in modern societies, consumption is inevitably linked with dependence:

> The discovery that most learning requires no teaching can be neither manipulated nor planned. Each of us is personally responsible for his or her own deschooling, and only we have the power to do it. No one can be excused if he fails to liberate himself from schooling.[8]

This view of the de-institutionalisation of society on the part of individuals is a romantic, not to say heroic, vision, as critics of Illich have often asserted. He is a thoroughgoing individualist, and his reputation among adult educators is due in much greater measure perhaps to this romantic individualism than to the force of the deschooling analysis with which his name is irretrievably linked. Learning, says Illich, 'can only be a personal activity'. If so, the content of learning could only be determined in personal terms. But this does not prevent him from talking about it in other terms:

> If we do not challenge the assumption that valuable knowledge is a commodity which under certain circumstances may be forced into the consumer, society will be increasingly dominated by sinister pseudo schools and totalitarian managers of information.[9]

It cannot be said that Illich anywhere tackles the problem of knowledge and the content of learning in such a way that we could distinguish 'valuable' or 'useful' or 'really useful' knowledge. As we shall see, a major problem of his analysis is that it fails entirely to account for the social production of knowledge and the way in which its social construction determines the ways in which it is 'consumed'.

From the standpoint of his analysis of the inherent 'consumerism' of schooling, however, Illich has much to offer in terms of a critique of received ideas which tend to operate at the level of adult education as much as of schooling itself. In the course of his famous distinction between manipulative and 'convivial' institutions, for example, he is

led to think of schools as 'false public utilities', as institutional processes which 'tend to pile up at the manipulative end of the spectrum'.
But above all, manipulative institutions depend for their existence upon
the creation of spurious needs and demands which create further scope
for expert and professional exploitation:

> Just as highways create the impression that their present level of cost
> per year is necessary if people are to move, so schools are presumed
> essential for attaining the competence required by a society which
> uses modern technology . . . Schools are based upon the equally
> spurious hypothesis that learning is the result of curricular teaching.
>   Highways result from a perversion of the desire and need for
> mobility into the demand for a private car. Schools themselves pervert
> the natural inclination to grow and learn into the demand for
> instruction.[10]

As has been suggested, the concept of need has been rather uncritically incorporated into an ideology of adult education and other concepts of post-school learning, and that of demand is likewise associated
with a market-consumpton model of provision. Illich's analysis of the
way in which, in modern societies, demand and need are essentially
creations of what he calls manipulative institutions is therefore potentially relevant in the case of adult and lifelong education itself: the
assimilation of adult learning institutions to institutionalised social
norms is a corollary of the process of reproducing the school curriculum. Such institutions may be located somewhere along the
convivial-manipulative continuum according to their mode of opera-
tion and professional style: in so far as they could be said to 'market'
adult education to its 'consumers' as a 'commodity' then in Illich's
terms they are in the business of creating as well as responding to need.
So his name must be included among those who analyse educational
'progressivism' as a form of incorporation: 'The free-school movement
entices unconventional educators, but ultimately does so in support of
the conventional ideology of schooling.'

But paradoxically, although he sees schools as political institutions,
Illich's view of knowledge itself is relatively unproblematic, and unlike
other radical critics of education systems he provides little sense of
knowledge as itself full of contradictions or even as itself a kind of
manipulative institution. His view of the deschooled society as one of
learning networks or webs deliberately avoids the issue of the content
of learning in favour of methodology:

The planning of new educational institutions . . . must not start with the question 'What should someone learn?' but with the question, 'What kinds of things and people might learners want to be in contact with in order to learn?'[11]

Four networks 'could contain all the resources needed for real learning', says Illich, and these would consist of reference services to educational objects, skill exchanges, peer-matching, and reference services to educators-at-large. This all represents a view of *how* we do, or could, learn − in what Illich would call a 'convivial' or non-manipulative way. It falls very far short of a view of the fundamentally political construction of knowledge, and to many it amounts to a utopian and idealistic vision and little more: 'Only hindsight', says Illich at one point, 'will allow us to discover if the Great Cultural Revolution [of China] will turn out to have been the first successful attempt at deschooling the institutions of society.' Hindsight, however, has allowed us to discover aspects of deschooling which Illich himself could hardly have contemplated. And yet had his grasp upon the real curriculum problem been stronger, perhaps a more sophisticated analysis − and a more accurate prediction − would have been possible. For all the rhetoric, Illich's view in the end is romantic and highly individualistic and conveys no sense of the collective and political construction of the knowledge-content of learning, which constitutes such a limitation upon the possibilities of individual deschooling efforts.

As Gintis, in his well-known and conclusive critique of Illich's thesis[12] expresses it, the trouble with deschooling is that it is an idea constructed exclusively around that of consumption. In treating the problem of consumption in the way that he does, Illich in fact treats as pathological the *normal* institutional conditions of capitalism. In his negative critique he fails entirely to account for the construction of knowledge in the relations of production. As far as adult and lifelong education is concerned, the institutionalisation of knowledge − as schooling − which is a function of these relations puts the matter in an entirely different light: a deschooled society precludes the transformation of the curriculum categories of schooling. The deschooling thesis does not provide the kind of political and ideological analysis of knowledge which is necessary to think of adult or lifelong education in terms of curriculum reproduction or transformation. On the contrary, Illich's view itself reproduces some familiar categories of bourgeois and progressive educational ideology. Since Illich's book the radical theory of lifelong education has been more securely based in an analysis of the ιowledge-content of the curriculum.

Freire

Illich was only implicitly critical of adult and lifelong education for not challenging the 'consumption model' of education which schooling projects in modern societies: he had no analytic framework, as we have seen, for postulating the transformation of the curriculum categories of schooling because he failed to locate these categories in the social relations of production. The writings of Paulo Freire, however, take the argument some way further.

Just as Illich is remembered for developing an idea of deschooling, so Freire has become well known for his association of schooling with political reaction and education with revolution:

> Because men are historical beings, incomplete and conscious of being incomplete, revolution is as natural and permanent a human dimension as is education. Only a mechanistic mentality holds that education can cease at a certain point, or that revolution can be halted when it attains power. To be authentic, revolution must be a continuous event. Otherwise it will cease to be revolution, and will become sclerotic bureaucracy.[13]

Freire's account of culture, education and revolution is more intellectually sophisticated than Illich's, and informed by Hegelian dialectics and existential 'authenticity'. He is also better able than Illich to conceptualise oppression in terms of the imposition of criteria of knowledge: such is the nature of knowledge that for Freire teaching and learning are in contradictory relation, and it is with this contradiction that authentic education must begin. So it is important to understand that for Freire his familiar idea of 'banking education' describes the inauthenticity of schooling — its incapacity to resolve the contradiction that lies at the heart of the educational relation of teaching and learning. Thus the critique of schooling is not simply that it represents a 'front-end' or 'mechanistic' idea of education but that it stands for an inauthentic account of education in terms of the problem of knowledge. It is not difficult to see that in these terms lifelong education itself could be 'inauthentic', and in so far as inauthenticity is constituted by the reproduction of the curriculum categories of schooling many ideas of lifelong education (probably all the ideas of continuing or recurrent education) are really, in Freire's terms, inauthentic: the fact that they are addressed to adulthood is irrelevant.

Nevertheless, in Chapter 2 of his *Pedagogy of the Oppressed*, where he develops this idea of 'banking education', Freire is clearly more concerned with the social relations of education and the ways in which these express the contradictions of teaching and learning, than he is with the content of learning itself. The idea, like that of Illich's learning networks, is addressed more to the methodology of learning and only indirectly to the problem of the knowledge-content as a social construction. There is obviously some relation between the teaching-learning contradiction and the construction of knowledge, but Freire does not enter deeply into the issue:

> In the banking concept of education, knowledge is a gift bestowed by those who consider themselves knowledgeable upon those whom they consider to know nothing. Projecting an absolute ignorance onto others, a characteristic of the ideology of oppression, negates education and knowledge as processes of inquiry.[14]

The question arises, as it does with Illich, as to whether Freire really confronts the institutionalisation and construction of knowledge in the social relations of production or whether in fact he is led to analyse too exclusively the contradictions in the social relations of teaching and learning.

As with Illich, Freire's categories imply rather ambiguous consequences for adult and lifelong education. Adult education may itself constitute a pedagogy of the oppressed, integrating them into the structure of society rather than transforming the structure: 'The banking approach to adult education . . . will never propose to students that they consider reality critically.' And as for a model of lifelong education based upon vertical curriculum integration, this is for Freire quite explicitly a banking concept of education. Only its opposite, 'problem-posing education', could really resolve the teaching-learning relations contradiction:

> . . . problem-posing education, breaking the vertical patterns characteristic of banking education, can fulfill its function of being the practice of freedom only if it can overcome the above contradiction.[15]

Freire does have a view of the 'true knowledge' and 'true culture' which banking education could not achieve, and he is concerned with education as revolutionary action and as transformation. But when he comes to talk about the content of what is variously described as 'authentic' or 'problem-posing' or 'dialogical' education it tends to collapse into the new methodology of teaching and learning:

> . . . preoccupation with content of dialogue is really preoccupation with the programme content of education. For the anti-dialogical banking educator, the question of content simply concerns the programme about which he will discourse to his students; and he answers his own question, by organizing his own programme. For the dialogical, problem-posing teacher-student, the programme content of education is neither a gift nor an imposition — bits of information to be deposited in the students — but rather the organized, systematized, and developed 're-representation' to individuals of the things about which they want to know more.[16]

As in the case of Illich, the scale of social transformation envisaged by Freire seems to warrant further analysis of the processes by which individuals come to want to know more about anything whatever. Like Illich too, Freire's analysis is by implication very critical of ideologies of traditional adult education and developing ideologies of lifelong education. He is critical, for example, of superficial needs-analysis, he is aware of the oppressive potential of development and the need to distinguish it both from transformation and modernisation. He is aware of the political limitations of community action and other apparently progressive developments:

> One of the characteristics of oppressive cultural action which is almost never preceived by the dedicated but naive professionals who are involved is the emphasis on a *focalized* view of problems rather than on seeing them as dimensions of a *totality*.[17]

Freire sees also the implications of this for community leadership role-training as a further instrument of oppression and alienation, in so far as it 'hinders the emergence of consciousness and critical intervention in a total reality'. And nor would he restrict his analysis to peasant society; rather, he sees cultural action for freedom as expressing the same objective for the 'urban oppressed' as it does for the oppressed of the Third World for whom he has so eminently spoken.

The influence of Illich and Freire upon adult education thinking is rather taken for granted and yet in some respects must be accounted paradoxical, since their work is hardly compatible with existing theory and practice of adult education and it seems actually to contradict the principles upon which recurrent or lifelong education is coming to be based. Clearly, neither of them is interested in such methodological procedures as andragogy: in the social and political contexts with which they are concerned, consumerism and oppression create a kind of universal dependence in which the distinction between childhood and adulthood is of little significance – who grows to adulthood in such conditions?

Both Illich and Freire, however, developed negative social and political critiques of schooling, and their influence may be accounted for in these terms. Thus they can be located in that traditional theory of adult education which has been concerned with 'distancing' from schooling, even though they have 'distanced' their own ideas from those of adult education too.

It cannot be said that either Illich or Freire developed an explicit curriculum theory of lifelong education, since neither of them provided an adequate analysis of the social construction of knowledge in the first place: learning networks and generative themes of 'problem-posing' education add little to a theory of knowledge not already contained in progressive education. So their analysis of knowledge, so crucial to curriculum development theories, remained curiously unproblematic.

It has been an achievement of Ettore Gelpi to pursue the analysis of lifelong education beyond these negative critiques, to synthesise some contradictory elements and, in short, to point the way to a knowledge-based curriculum theory of adult and lifelong education.

Gelpi

Broadly speaking, Gelpi's view of lifelong education is one of the transformation of the knowledge categories of schooling as these are reflected in the social relations of production, and he is consistent in his conception of the social construction of knowledge as a function of these relations. He has been engaged, in other words, in developing the critique of Illich by Gintis which has already been referred to. The contradiction attributed by Freire to the social relations of teaching and learning is similarly analysed by Gelpi as an expression of the social relations of production: a normal, not a pathological condition of certain societies in certain historical conditions. The liberal-progressive critique of schooling and education, which is reflected in much of the literature of adult, recurrent or lifelong education and which lingers even in the work of Illich and Freire, has tended to treat as pathological what are in fact normal conditions of modern societies.

It has also been Gelpi's achievement to locate lifelong education in a truly international and comparative perspective of development and to bring into relation an analysis of oppression in developed and developing countries, and in urban as well as peasant conditions, through a view of the division of labour in society which ultimately sets the terms in which a discussion of educational concepts must take place. It is clearly a very different view from the two conventional polarities of the development of the self-concept on the one hand and the 'knowledge explosion' modernisation-concept on the other.

Above all, Gelpi's view of lifelong education is dialectical and is capable of accounting both for the reproductive and the transformational potential of lifelong education. He is thus able to avoid the more euphoric tendency of some advocates to exaggerate the capacity of education to contribute to the solution of social problems as well as the opposite tendency to undervalue the autonomous liberating capacity which education also must possess by virtue of its knowledge-transforming categories.

In taking a dialectical view of the potential of lifelong education both for liberation and social control, therefore, Gelpi has presented a more sophisticated and more profoundly political account of the matter, for it does contain contradictions inadequately analysed by either Illich or Freire. He also understands the dialectical relation of theory and practice, so that the contradictions of lifelong education can only be explored and resolved in the context of comparative practice: operationalising the idea is the only way to grasp its logic.

Ralph Ruddock has recently translated and edited some of Gelpi's writings on lifelong education and the following points about them are taken from that source, in particular from volume 1, which is concerned with principles, policies and practices.[18] A much more extensive and systematic account of Gelpi's view than could be attempted here can be found in a further monograph on the subject by Timothy D. Ireland.[19]

For Gelpi above all there exists a possibility of transformation through education, which is always a process characterised by relative autonomy even though absolute autonomy in relation to prevailing social forces is out of the question:

If we think of lifelong education in terms of this dialectic, we shall be able to escape the false choice between the idealised approach (lifelong education seen as a global new response to the educational and cultural needs of our society) and the negative approach (lifelong education seen as a new form of manipulation), which is in fact also an idealist approach.[20]

But in fact there is an almost total international consensus on lifelong education which Gelpi, in his capacity as chief of the UNESCO Lifelong Education Unit, was well placed to know. It is an object of social policy, as this was earlier distinguished from legislation for educational innovation: 'Radical change in social, moral, aesthetic and political affairs is often the outcome of a process of self-directed learning in opposition to the educational message imposed from without.'[21]

As a social policy, 'education for change' cannot be a neutral matter for, as Gelpi makes clear, not only is adaptation to change and development a potential mechanism of exploitation: it is a site of conflict around the curriculum itself, so that self-directed learning from the standpoint of development, 'becomes an obstacle because it means individual control of the ends, contents, and methods of education'. The strategy of lifelong education, Gelpi is saying, cannot be reduced to the traditional processes associated with educational innovation, and there is an important sense in which lifelong education is not a matter of educational innovation at all. The rapid increase in educational legislation in a 'lifelong' context is no real indication of the social policy situation. In order to understand the importance of the idea it needs to be seen as an object of social policy analysis which goes beyond legislation to the social origins of change itself, which Gelpi characteristically sees in terms of struggle and conflict among the elements of society:

> It was and it will be the revolt of young people and of workers, the seizing by citizens of responsibility for their political life, the displacement, often distressful, of migrants, women demanding new roles — these have provoked and will again provoke new educational strategies. Proposals for changes in education will also come from advanced industries, from political forces whose fortunes are tied up with economic growth and with change of a kind, from intellectuals whose freedom and participation in their society cannot be separated from the struggle for greater liberties.[22]

The policy and practice of lifelong education, says Gelpi, will be worked out against the background of these forces, and obviously it may or may not be a progressive development in society so much as an instrument of control or incorporation, or the organisation of leisure in response to continuing conditions of alienated labour. 'To escape from this ambiguity', says Gelpi, 'we must dismiss the idea that lifelong education and deschooling are the same thing.' It is not schooling as the object of legislation so much as a social policy having divisive and oppressive educational outcomes that must be the main target of the lifelong strategy.

But just as we have mistaken the appearance of legislation for the realities of social policy so, in the comparative context, argues Gelpi, we have mistaken the institutions for the reality of education:

> The weakness of our work as educationalists is clearly revealed by our timid efforts in comparative education. It is the schools and the universities that receive attention, or the institutionalised forms of adult education. We have not been prepared at the national or the international level, to do more than analyse the purely institutional realities.[23]

Always, he insists, the contents, the practice and the methodology of lifelong education must be located in 'the productive educational and cultural realities' of countries whose legislation claims to enshrine it as a principle.

The policy of lifelong education, says Gelpi, is therefore quite distinct from the idea of deschooling and quite distinguishable from legislation for educational innovation. It depends much more upon the analysis of the division of labour in society, the social relations of production which express this division and the processes by which the curriculum categories of all educational institutions reproduce or transform the social distribution of knowledge.

Gelpi's view of lifelong education cannot therefore be contained within the framework of traditional pedagogy: 'Its temporal and spatial dimensions exceed those of the school and of classical adult education'. An important area of research, he suggests, should be those educational innovations carried out in the name of lifelong education but not, perhaps, really challenging the distribution of knowledge in terms of, say, professional or institutional exclusivity. The fact is that educational theorising and planning tends to be divorced from cultural, social and political factors which in the end largely determine what happens. Gelpi's view of what constitutes educational planning is therefore very far from the view of lifelong education as a concept for integration or evaluation of the school curriculum: 'The oppression of one social class by another, the conflicts between rural and urban regions, the subordination of pre-industrial societies by industrialised societies, are significant problems for educators and for educational planners.'[24]

The division of labour Gelpi is talking about is an international one and it is this factor, rather than a ubiquitous modernisation process, that confers a universal relevance on the idea of lifelong education: always he is concerned with the social conditions of learning, so that even such initiatives as alternating work and education, community education, non-formal education or lifelong education itself, may lack significance through the failure to locate them in social, political and cultural contexts. 'We need to know', says Gelpi, 'why educational institutions so often have no meaning for people and why workers have difficulty in using them even when they are available to them.' The fact is that, as he says, the structures of production are implicated in the process of recurrent education and, for too long, 'too many progressive educators have failed to take into account the world of production, which is in all reality so significant for personal and social development'. The real relationship between education and work, postulated as a theoretical basis of recurrent education, cannot be grasped in pedagogical terms, as Gelpi points out in a discussion of lifelong education and Asian cultural development. This has implications for a professionalism quite unlike those of Illich's critique:

> Educators should receive an initial and continuing training in the sociology, psychology and culture of the working world; at this level, thinking about modernisation ceases to be abstract and begins to be related to everyday life.[25]

Education, in other words, may be linked to cultural, social and economic transformation, 'on condition that it is based on social forces and not on structures'. Gelpi cites this as a reason for the importance of adult education which, he claims, is 'often at variance with the established structures'. Given a traditional preoccupation among adult educators with 'structures of provision' and given that these structures tend on the whole to reproduce curriculum categories of schooling, it is important to understand Gelpi's orientation to adult education. This is something he outlines in a paper on adult education in relation to development.[26]

As in the case of other writers from a Third World perspective, Gelpi takes the view that 'development' stands more for exploitation, conflict and disequilibrium than for the inevitable, ubiquitous and beneficent process of uncritical Western opinion. So in so far as adult education 'aspires to promote a balanced development' it cannot evade the issue of global struggle. The continuing division of labour which reflects unbalanced development may, however, be reproduced in various ways, among which Gelpi is inclined to include adult education:

> To affirm that adult education can be an instrument which streng-thens educational discrimination might appear to be a paradox because adult education was conceived as a means of bringing about a balance within a dualist education system. But this paradox disappears when one analyses the contents, methods and problems of adult education today: on one side education for adults in the productive sector of high technology, and on the other side adult education for the 'marginals' of the educational system (illiterate or semi-illiterate people etc.). The dual system of education is perpetuated by strengthening the elites and by discrimination in terms of social origins.[27]

This is as clear a statement as could be desired of Gelpi's view of the need to locate the content of adult education in the social relations of production and to focus upon the capacity of adult education either to reproduce or transform prevailing social constructions of knowledge. And it stands in fairly stark contrast to the kind of analysis implicit in an ideology of needs, access and provision which pays little regard either to the social construction of knowledge or to the ways in which this is located in the social relations of production.

In Gelpi can be seen the way in which the curriculum structure of adult and lifelong education — its aims, content and methods — becomes crucial to their capacity to contribute to what he would call 'balanced' development, or the struggle against the division of labour. But he argues that adult education itself can play an important role 'only if it is not content to be merely a compensatory instrument'. And by 'compensatory' he undoubtedly has in mind not only the functional relation of adult education and schooling but also the compensatory function of adult education in respect of the alienating conditions of society associated with the division of labour.

Gelpi's preoccupation with the work-system and the division of labour which actually determines the conditions of people's lives also stands in contrast with the theoretical concerns of traditional adult education with personal growth through recreative and liberal learning, which have tended to underpin 'constructive' responses to alienation and marginalisation in society. Despite the futurological vision of the 'leisure society', Gelpi continues to see the contribution of adult education to development in terms of employment, unemployment and underemployment:

> Adult education might well take this as its starting point, and for example (a) demystify vocational training as an adequate response to the problem of employment; (b) develop a new type of collective solidarity as a response to the prevailing uncertainty in the world of work; (c) prevent wage labour in the modern sector from becoming a divisive element within the working class.[28]

What these strategies would require would be an appropriation by workers of scientific and technical knowledge itself, and not merely vocational knowledge. This distinction, between knowledge for application to the material world and knowledge as structured in the relations of production, seems crucial to an understanding of Gelpi's position with regard to curriculum transformation as a social redistribution of knowledge, and it is what so emphatically distinguishes his view of lifelong education from others which can be located within the knowledge-categories of schooling. As such, these latter views reflect a traditional institutional-provision model of adult education, whereas the kind of education required by workers to achieve their aims in development must be based upon quite different assumptions: 'Knowledge in our contemporary societies does not belong to the researchers and professionals in education alone.' This democratisation of knowledge has important implications for professionalism and the structure of education too since, as Gelpi says, 'hierarchical relationships cannot be allowed to perpetuate the cultural dependence of adults on educational institutions'.

Gelpi pursues this analysis consistently into the field of educational guidance and counselling, which is so often an important element in an integrated strategy for lifelong education. Traditionally understood as an essentially individualistic procedure, counselling is characteristically envisaged by Gelpi in dialectical and comparative terms. 'The relationships between the individual and collective life', he says, 'are both complementary and dialectical, and adult education does not extend beyond these relationships.' The realities of adult education must be sought in the discriminations, exploitations and oppressions which find expression in education systems, and the contradictions which characterise the lives of men and women:

> If the education of adults is not an independent variable, but is in a dependent/independent relation to 'the relations of production' at the centre of every society, one must avoid defining adult education, guidance and counselling, in abstract terms. There must be different types of guidance related to the social and existential condition of adults in each society.[29]

Whether education is sought by adults for its intrinsic value or as a response to the 'logic of production' is a duality which Gelpi says paralyses educational debate. But in his own mind their motivation is at its most genuine when it arises from a wish to transform their working lives, to improve their living conditions and especially to take part in the management of their society. These motivations, he says, are often ignored by educational institutions 'which prefer to induce adults to adapt themselves to the needs of production, or to engage in cultural and educative leisure activities as a response to the alienation resulting from their work'. It is certainly true that some conceptions of recurrent and lifelong education are squarely based upon an imputed universal need to adapt to conditions of change and modernisation with little or no regard to the problematic nature of development in its divisive, alienating and oppressive aspects. Some conceptions, as has been suggested, have been claimed on behalf of democracy and popular control with little or no supporting analysis in terms of the social relations of production or the appropriation of knowledge for democratic purposes. It is also the case that adult education has been widely assimilated to consumerism, both in the sense of Illich's 'pathology' model and also in that of Gelpi's own view of it as a functional response to the alienating conditions of modern society. So what Gelpi's view of lifelong education involves, among other things, is a further development of the view of 'useful' and 'really useful' knowledge as these have been distinguished in the historical analysis of working-class education: 'useful' and vocational knowledge which reproduces curriculum categories of schooling, and 'really useful' knowledge which transforms them. For Gelpi, of course, this distinction, together with the motivation of adults to learn ('authentic' or 'inauthentic' as Freire might have put it) can only be grasped in terms of the significance of knowledge in the social relations of production:

Guidance and counselling within the field of adult education need to be richly informed on 'the relations of production', the labour market, and the organisation of work which so strongly conditions adult life. To inform people about educational possibilities without discussing the relation between education and work is to ignore the real problems of counselling.[30]

There is no possibility of an abstract understanding of needs, argues Gelpi, since these arise fundamentally in the social division of labour. All too often needs are predicated upon some professional or institutional criteria, whereas adult learning activities require that the contents and methods of education are brought into discussion. As he says in another context, 'Workers are not enchanted by admission to a culture and an education in which they have no control of objectives, methods or contents.'[31] Similarly, their needs could not be identified on these terms either.

Gelpi has also discussed the idea of lifelong education as related to family systems and the elderly, and in both contexts has thrown further light upon his thinking about it. Comparative study of the family, for example, displays it in the light of ambiguities and 'functional contradictions' which must be accounted for if lifelong education is to have the kind of universal significance which is often claimed for it. The cultural relativity of adulthood and citizenship, so important to grasp for developing strategies, is rooted in the divisionof labour in such a way as to render spurious the kind of philosophical abstractions upon which education theory — and some adult education theory — rests. At least this must be the case if lifelong education constitutes a universal ideal, and Gelpi's tendency — as was Freire's — is to see the childhood/adulthood issue in terms of the social relations of production rather than absolute moral categories; just as was the case when it came to understanding working-class education movements in nineteenth-century England. The economic structure of the family may determine patterns of dependency, in other words, which make absolute categories meaningless. Gelpi cites, for example, the sociology of Indian family life: 'Many a 40-year-old Indian man will go to his father or elder brother (or, when away from home, to his employer or professor) with a request for decision-making that would be permitted a 10-year-old child in the West.'[32]

However, despite the fact that, as Gelpi sees it, the relation between educational and family structures tends to reinforce institutional roles, and in particular education reinforces the culture of dominant social classes, nevertheless there are important ways in which family life itself could constitute an element of lifelong education. It gives expression to the culture of the great majority of persons, and when this culture is recognised as, in essence, an educational force, workers can be teachers and not merely 'adult students'. The most significant change would be, therefore, recognition of the role of family life in a lifelong education process 'which recognises the educational value of all experience'.

In his paper on 'Education and Later Life in Industrial Society' Gelpi develops further the argument that lifelong education describes the political struggle for the integration of 'marginal' members of society in terms of the whole of their lives: 'It is not a matter of giving older people a little culture or of providing pastimes to make the last years of their life less sad, but of pressing for the integration of these years into the rest of life as fully as may be possible.'[33]

This kind of integration is, as has been seen, a common theme of lifelong education concepts, as is the integration of formal education with all kinds of non-formal, non-institutional learning structures. But again what makes Gelpi's contribution to the debate distinctive is his insistence upon locating all of these possibilities in the social relations of production, and in the division of labour both national and global against which lifelong education will have to struggle. Thus lifelong education in the context of later life is not the same thing as education for retirement. Retirement is, according to Gelpi, 'the outcome of the organisation of work, the labour market, the remuneration of manual work and technological changes within the production system'. So, he continues, a policy for the 'third age' cannot start from retirement, for 'retirement education' simply reproduces the division of labour which lifelong education challenges. In short, the conventional ideology of adult education for later life, reflecting the needs of the elderly and the problem of their access to suitable provision is, in Gelpi's view, inadequate as an authentic lifelong response. 'The central problem', he says, 'is not participation but changing the organisation of work and its basic component, productive labour.' Too often the problem of lifelong education for later life is reduced to the production of scientific evidence of lifelong learning capacity. We need, says Gelpi, more information about concrete learning experiments in comparative cultural contexts rather than about the 'abstract components of our learning faculties'. For above all, lifelong education is policy oriented in ways that can be captured neither by science nor legislaton:

The older person can learn, the psychologists tell us; but this scientific statement is not sufficient unless it is accompanied by a policy for the third age. It is not simply a matter of providing a course for retired people in a university, or of developing cultural activities in a community centre. What is necessary is to have a policy for community life, for housing, for the organisation of work, for culture, medical assistance, leisure, etc.[34]

The role of adult education for the elderly is very important, but only in such conditions of lifelong education. And by these conditions Gelpi is raising the issue of the functional relation of adult education to schooling — the reproduction or transformation of its curriculum categories — which has been a preoccupation of this book:

Adult education has often wagered upon its ability to compete with the school system. It has been seen as lying permanently behind the front runners, and often as demonstrating that one can 'catch up' on one's primary, secondary and higher education. The perspective changes if one considers learning as a permanent process. In this case, contents, methods and means will refer more to the future than to the past. The concept of 'catching up' will no longer be the key to the education of adults.[35]

Lifelong education, in other words, is an idea of intrinsic adult learning situations whose knowledge-content is much more a function of the social relations of production than of the curriculum categories of schooling. Adult education theory and ideology has been predicated upon quite different assumptions. What Gelpi is therefore saying is that it is the curriculum categories of adult education as much as those of schooling which would need to be transformed to achieve an ideal of lifelong education.

As he is well placed to do, Gelpi has reviewed policies for lifelong education in Europe, observing that a wide range of involvement in planning now takes the issue to some extent out of the hands of educational theorists and adult educators. It has indeed become an issue which has transcended legislation and educational innovation, or 'progressivism', so that lifelong education is an object of social policy with all of the analytic elusiveness this entails. So there are important consequences for comparative study, and the perspective of structural provision is being left behind, together with the belief that education could ever be separated from systems of production:

The dialectical dimension of lifelong education is more and more accepted in pedagogical debates; social and counter-cultural forces are taken into consideration, even if the contradictory nature of these is underlined.[36]

As Gelpi says in his volume on work and education, educationists have not always seen lifelong education 'in the context of the antitheses between town and country, social classes, men and women, privileged and underprivileged countries'.[37] In this volume he explores in greater detail work and education, and the need to rethink the relationship between them. His analysis is particularly significant in its depth as a critique of currently fashionable ideas of continuing and recurrent education based upon an inadequate and unproblematic analysis of education and work, and which have led to a rather simplistic view of the capacity of education to define, compensate for, enrich or even create work. For Gelpi, in the end, it is a struggle for the redefinition, redistribution and re-evaluation of knowledge which must take place in the social relations of production as such: 'To define the new educational strategies, we will need to insist on the characteristics of the division of labour and its extension at the international level.'[38] 'Really useful knowledge' is a construction of these relations, whereas 'useful knowledge' is a projection of educational institutions and a professional ideology of needs, access and provision. This, says Gelpi, is what must be transcended: 'Hence, a new relationship between work and education is no longer a question of the access of workers to the educational institutions, rather the presence of workers as educators within these structures.'[39]

And so his view of lifelong education inevitably comes back full circle to the problem of the knowledge-content of learning itself, and Gelpi sees the relation of work and education most fundamentally in these terms, as an issue of the social construction of knowledge:

It is not only a matter of guaranteeing access to the educational systems but of reconsidering the relationship between these systems and society as a whole. 'The problem is not to deny the need to acquire scientific knowledge. Rather it is to determine:

— who should acquire knowledge? And why should it be only a minority?

— for what purpose does one learn? What control does the learner have over his immediate environment?

— how should knowledge be organised? By whom and to what end?

It is important to expose the ideological content of all learning. Sometimes this is explicit, sometimes it is much less obvious.'[44]

Gelpi's view of lifelong education is therefore one of the social construction of knowledge in the relations of production: this is what holds his view together and it is important to grasp its logic in this way. Even in the conclusions of a sympathetic commentator such as Timothy Ireland it is possible to stress its elements (the dialectical view, the advance on Illich, the international perspective, the elucidation through practice and so on) too much at the expense of this fundamental logic that binds them all together.

Summary

What Illich, Freire and Gelpi seem to have demonstrated in their different ways and from a global perspective, is the redundancy of 'adult' as a morally prescriptive category. It does not adequately describe the objective conditions of dependency, oppression and exploitation which people find themselves in. And as Freire says, this is not only true in the case of the peasant societies of the Third World, rapidly urbanising as these are. So there are some common assumptions which both constitute a unifying theme and at the same time crucially distinguish such a view of lifelong education from that based upon ideas of curriculum integration and evaluation which have also emanated from UNESCO sources. This latter approach seems to reflect more closely a current academic preoccupation with functional evaluation theory of social policy and educational programmes.

There are significant differences in the approach of Illich, Freire and Gelpi to problems of adult and lifelong education, however, and it would be a mistake to suppose that their analyses had much more than this in common. Illich's view arises out of what he takes to be the pathological consumerism of modern society. Freire's arises out of the revolutionary capacity of 'authentic' education in which the teaching-learning contradiction is resolved. Gelpi's view arises out of the struggle against the division of labour in which the knowledge-content of learning is a function of the social relations of production. Only Gelpi provides a really satisfactory account of the way in which knowledge is produced in these terms, and his is not merely a critique of schooling, because he recognises the capacity of institutions to contribute to the transformation of the knowledge-content of learning. Whereas Illich and Freire assume a rather deterministic view of both schooling and adult education as instruments of social control, Gelpi acknowledges their capacity for transformation too.

Despite their influence, all three have been very critical of the kind of ideology of adult education which expresses an uncritical or untheoretical (in Freire's terms, perhaps, 'non-dialogical') concept of needs, access and provision. But only Gelpi has succeeded in following the current of this ideology to its source in the social relations of production. The case for adult and lifelong education is not made out by 'deschooling' or 'banking' critiques *as such*. Indeed, adult and lifelong education reproduce curriculum categories of schooling more often than not. Gelpi has described the conditions in which they might be transformed.

Notes and References

1. Richard Johnson, 'Really Useful Knowledge'.
2. Ibid., p. 76.
3. Ibid., p. 77.
4. Ibid., pp. 94-5.
5. Ivan Illich, *Deschooling Society*, p. 26.
6. Ibid., p. 41.
7. Ibid., pp. 43-4.
8. Ibid., pp. 47-8.
9. Ibid., pp. 49-50.
10. Ibid., p. 60.
11. Ibid., pp. 77-8.
12. Herbert Gintis, 'Towards a Political Economy of Education: A Radical Critique of Ivan Illich's Deschooling Society', *Schooling and Capitalism: A Sociological Reader*, ed. R. Dale *et al.*
13. Paulo Freire, *Cultural Action for Freedom* (Harmondsworth: Penguin Books, 1972), p. 82.
14. Paulo Freire, *Pedagogy of the Oppressed* (Harmondsworth: Penguin Books, 1972), p. 46.
15. Ibid., p. 53.
16. Ibid., pp. 65-6.
17. Ibid., p. 111.
18. Ettore Gelpi, *A Future for Lifelong Education*, introduced and translated by Ralph Ruddock *et al.* Manchester Monographs, 13 (Manchester: Manchester University Department of Adult and Higher Education, 2 vols, 1979).
19. Timothy D. Ireland, *Gelpi's View of Lifelong Education*: Manchester Monographs, 14 (Manchester: Manchester University Department of Adult and Higher Education, 1979).
20 . Ettore Gelpi, *A Future for Lifelong Education*, vol. 1, p. 11.
21. Ibid., p. 2.
22. Ibid., p. 5.
23. Ibid., p. 9.
24. Ibid., p. 22.

25. Ibid., p. 38.
26. Ibid., Chapter 5.
27. Ibid., p. 46.
28. Ibid., p. 47.
29. Ibid., p. 51.
30. Ibid., p. 52.
31. Ettore Gelpi, *A Future for Lifelong Education*, vol. 2, p. 92.
32. Ettore Gelpi, *A Future for Lifelong Education*, vol. 1, p. 60.
33. Ibid., p. 67.
34. Ibid., p. 68.
35. Ibid., p. 69.
36. Ibid., p. 72.
37. Ettore Gelpi, *A Future for Lifelong Education*, vol. 2, p. 99.
38. Ibid., p. 4.
39. Ibid., p. 3.
40. Ibid., p. 10

8 CONCLUSION – ELEMENTS OF ADULT AND LIFELONG CURRICULUM THEORY

It is possible now to summarise the elements of a curriculum theory of adult and lifelong education – one, that is, which is addressed to problems of the aims, content and methods of adult learning in a context of knowledge, culture and power. The need for such an approach arises partly, at least, out of the kinds of claims made out for the importance of adult and lifelong education, and which are implied by the increasing amount of legislation incorporating education into social policy issues.

In the course of this process of incorporation, ideas of continuing or recurrent, as well as lifelong, education have entered into the debate. By this process also the category of adulthood in relation to education is being displaced and relegated to more of a procedural or methodological role. Social policy and legislation addresses itself not so much to a generalised and culturally prescriptive idea of adulthood but to more specific target populations of workers, women, the elderly, ethnic groups, the unemployed and so on. From this point of view a general concept of adulthood has become impractical in societies so heterogeneous that it could not convey the diversity of conditions in which people actually live and which, as Gelpi says, results in adult provision polarised around 'compensatory' education for some and 'continuing' education for others: the problem is not so much one of adulthood as inequality. To many advocates of lifelong education, adult education in its traditional forms is anachronistic or even reactionary. Curriculum-based theory contributes to an understanding of such a crisis of identity, and it may also help to distinguish theoretical from philosophical issues, with which they are all too often confused. It is a philosophical issue as to whether adult education ought to promote individual or social purposes, whether it should be regarded in instrumental or intrinsic terms, and so on. But important as these issues are, they tend to remain abstract and philosophical. Theories, on the other hand, are concerned with the actual conditions in which philosophical issues of this kind arise, and in the ways in which philosophical, moral, scientific and other beliefs find expression in practice. The necessity for curriculum theory of adult and lifelong education arises in part from the contradiction between the scale of its universal potential and the parochialism of the 'disciplines of education' and 'adult characteristics' approaches. Often it seems that the scale of the claims made is greater on the part of those who write about it than those who practise it as teachers and learners.

The object of theory is the elucidation of practice; it is not the solution of philosophical, social or moral issues. Any theory of education must, in the last resort, be a theory of practice. This is true in a variety of ways, as theorists themselves have argued. The question immediately arises as to what actually constitutes the practice of adult and lifelong education. And here it must be said that a received idea of practice has arisen out of the organisation of professional roles rather than from the inherent or curriculum characteristics of adult education itself.

So a theory of adult and lifelong education is one of curriculum practice. It is not a theory of adult learning, nor of the organisation of provision, nor even of why more adults do not participate in formal or structured learning. Important as these issues are, they give rise to theories *about* adult education rather than *of* it.

Theories about adult and lifelong education could not substantiate the claims made for its individual, social and political importance, and do not contribute much to a deeper understanding of it as an object either of legislation or social policy. It has been argued here that its importance and its theoretical elucidation depend ultimately upon a curriculum-oriented approach which focuses upon the practice of adult teaching and learning, and especially upon the content of practice in terms of knowledge, culture and power.

For this kind of reason developments in the general theory of education are relevant to adult and lifelong education practices, especially in so far as these practices relate to what was called the dominant paradigm of the school curriculum. Efforts to define 'adulthood' in philosophical, psychological or sociological terms have diverted attention from the relevance of recent education theory, and have always run up against the fact that it is both a culturally prescriptive as well as an administrative category, which between them often defeat the purposes of definition. More importantly, and in contradiction to some of the claims made out for the significance of adult education, the effect of both the 'disciplines of education' and 'adult characteristics' approaches is to depoliticise it and remove it from the processes of the definition, distribution and evaluation of knowledge in which all education is involved. In the end, the significance of adult education could only be measured in these terms of knowledge and politics which the curriculum theory of schooling itself has increasingly focused upon. The functional relation of adult learning to schooling, and the issue of whether adult education reproduces or transforms the curriculum categories of schooling, must be a central concern of theory, and it is in this sense that a theory of adult and lifelong education must focus upon curriculum problems.

The idea of the curriculum as standing merely for the content of learning has been successfully challenged by a view of it which is much more problematic. Analyses in terms of ideology, cultural reproduction and social control have implied a more radical critique of educational progressivism, and it is against this kind of background that the potential of adult and lifelong education must now be conceptualised.

Recent developments in curriculum theory have not been reflected in adult education, however, even though influential writers such as Illich and Freire clearly raise precisely the kind of issues of education, society and politics with which such developments have been concerned. Their critique has been of traditional adult education and educational progressivism as much as of schooling, and they have not been particularly concerned with elaborating distinctions. Indeed the critique of progressivism has, more often than not, taken such distinctions to be evidence for the way in which adult education reproduces, rather than transforms, the categories of schooling. The 'adult characteristics' approaches do not contribute to our understanding of the issues which are raised by Illich and Freire: they are all made from the security of a liberal-progressive position which entails an ideologically neutral view of knowledge together with a major stress upon methods and organisation. The selective use of 'deschooling' and 'banking' critiques has, in other words, not been followed up in appropriate theoretical terms at all. The consequences of following it up may have proved too difficult to assimilate to prevailing theoretical and ideological beliefs.

Three modes of the 'adult characteristics' approach were described. These were to do with adult knowledge, adult teaching and learning, and adult education organisation, and each was criticised for, among other things, its incapacity to elucidate adult education in curriculum terms: we learn nothing from them of the ways in which adult education reproduces or transforms the curriculum categories of schooling, or of its functions in the social definition, distribution and evaluation of knowledge, and there is no basis here for substantiating the kind of claims made for its potential.

The liberal-progressive ideological formulation of its potential is by way of needs, access and provision, which are dominant ideas in much of the policy literature. It amounts much more to a professional ideology rather than a philosophical statement of aims. At the level of philosophy all education involves some consideration of needs, access and provision: they are all crucial to understanding schooling. But the voluntariness of adult education, although it has therefore no unique philosophical implication, does have profound practical and professional ones. Consequently, it was argued, ideas of needs, access and provision express not so much the philosophical aims of adult educators (although not discounting them as such) as organisational and administrative criteria of a professional ideology. Their primary function is therefore to describe and justify practice, although they do not function in identical ways.

Much has been written about 'needs', and it was argued that its use in adult education ideology is indistinguishable from its use in the context of progressive schooling. As a theoretical contribution to our understanding of the curriculum too, it adds little: more often than not, needs-analysis is little more than uncritical reflection upon received ideas and practices. Its ideological function is, however, significant in that it reduces problematic and political issues to ones of technique, methodology and administration. It functions most importantly as an ideological underpinning of the curriculum development process. It was therefore argued that whereas such development must be organised around the problems of redefining, redistributing and re-evaluating knowledge in social, cultural and political conditions (if the adult curriculum is to transform the curriculum categories of schooling) a needs-meeting ideology is much more likely to reproduce schooling. In other words, needs-meeting is most likely to reinforce prevailing definitions, distributions and evaluations of knowledge if the analysis remains conducted at the level of professional ideology. So although the ideas of access and provision are of more distinctive ideological significance for adult education than that of needs, nevertheless taken together they amount to a model of curriculum development which is much more institution-based than knowledge-based. Again, the consequences of this would seem to be important in evaluating the potential of adult and lifelong education and the claims made for its social and political significance. For in curriculum terms it is possible to distinguish two modes of development: either its criteria reflect a professional ideology of needs, access and provision which leaves unquestioned the prevailing social construction of knowledge as expressed in the curriculum categories of schooling, or else they reflect rather a transformation of these categories in a new paradigm of education. In the real world nothing corresponds to the logic of either/or, so that in practice the reproduction of school knowledge in the former mode of development — by way of 'positive discrimination', outreach, community education or non-traditional strategies — always makes possible development as a social reconstruction of knowledge.

Curriculum development in adult education may therefore be evaluated in relation to the curriculum categories of schooling along a transformation-reproduction scale, and the criticism levelled against adult education from the standpoint of radical lifelong education is based upon its tendency to reproduce rather than transform the school curriculum and thus to defeat the larger claims sometimes made for its social and political potential.

Another way of conceptualising this point is to distinguish between adult and lifelong education as an object of legislation or as an object of social policy. The object of legislation is provision for adult learning. It does not, and could not, have some kind of social reconstruction of knowledge as its object. Social policy, on the other hand, is a more complex and problematic social construct, and more theoretically and ideologically ambiguous. In this it resembles the curriculum content of adult learning itself, and for this reason it makes better sense to think of the adult curriculum, in so far as it is a social construction of knowledge, as an object of social policy. It is always necessary to understand the possibilities and limitations of educational legislation in terms of knowledge, culture and power which find ideological expression in social policy. In this connection it was suggested that models of social welfare policy may illuminate the functional relation of adult learning to schooling.

So legislation for lifelong education may not necessarily constitute social policies for transformation despite appearances to the contrary. What is generally called 'continuing education' manifestly reproduces the curriculum categories of schooling. As an object of social policy, however, lifelong learning is potentially a new paradigm, and some strategies reflect this but others do not.

A further analytic distinction which seems a prerequisite of curriculum theory construction in adult and lifelong education is that which was drawn between what were called agents of provision and the social agencies of change. The agents of provision are at once the objects of legislation and the source of educational innovation, while agencies of change are social forces which constitute a potential source of curriculum development as knowledge-transformation. In other words, a distinction needs to be made between educational innovation and curriculum development. This is especially important in the area of adult and lifelong education and its relation to the curriculum categories of schooling. Generally speaking, adult education does not transform these categories and does not constitute a curriculum development process at all in this sense. Traditionally, its capacity is for progressive educational innovation. As a strategy of lifelong learning, however, it would constitute an element in such a process — at the cost, perhaps, of its distinct identity.

Progressive methods of teaching and learning do not entail any transformation of the knowledge-content of education, particularly when its content and processes are regarded in a non-political light. This is the case made out by the radical critics of educational progressivism. Whether this is true or not it is certainly an issue which lies at the heart of the idea of lifelong education. This is an idea which Gelpi says is characterised by ambiguities, but it would be nearer the mark to say it was characterised by contradictions. To say, for example, that recurrent education is a strategy for achieving lifelong education is not very illuminating when lifelong education may mean so much or so little. This was illustrated in the analysis of the lifelong curriculum which, it was argued, brings out very sharply the issue of the functional relation between the knowledge-content of schooling and of adult learning. It is possible to conceptualise lifelong learning as a transcendent idea having universal relevance for development, the growth of knowledge, democratisation, egalitarianism and so on. But it is not easy to reconcile this with the actual social conditions of different societies. It is tempting therefore to reduce the idea to one of pedagogy and organisation, and to conceive it almost entirely in terms of integration and evaluation. It becomes little more than progressive schooling extended over a lifetime, directed towards individual growth and organised through more rational systems of provision: integration and evaluation are fundamental concepts of a developing ideology of continuing and lifelong education; as such it gives expression to a functional relation of education and society, so that it is not difficult to see why societies across a wide social and political spectrum all find it acceptable as a goal of legislation.

Gelpi's view of lifelong education is quite different both from the liberal-progressive pedagogy and the analyses of more radical writers such as Illich and Freire. In so far as he has located the problem of lifelong education in the social relations of production, the struggle against the division of labour, and the social constructions of knowledge which reflect these relations and this struggle, Gelpi's work is preoccupied with knowledge, culture and power. Whether or not his view prevails, it is as close as we have presently attained to a curriculum theory of adult and lifelong education.

The development of an idea of lifelong education suggests, so far, that it is possible to innovate within a conventional curriculum paradigm, namely, that of schooling itself. The object of any curriculum theory of adult and lifelong education must therefore be to explore the ways in which its aims, content and methods transform or reproduce the knowledge categories of schooling. For unless it demonstrably transforms them, the claims of adult and lifelong education to achieve social policy objectives will remain difficult to make out.

BIBLIOGRAPHY

Advisory Council for Adult and Continuing Education (1981), *Protecting the Future for Adult Education*, Leicester, the Council.

Advisory Council for Adult and Continuing Education (1982), *Continuing Education: from Policies to Practice*, Leicester, the Council.

Althusser, L. (1972), 'Ideology and Ideological State Apparatuses', in B.R. Cosin (ed.), *Education: Structure and Society*, Harmondsworth, Penguin Books and Open University Press.

Apple, M.W. (1980), *Ideology and Curriculum*, London, Routledge and Kegan Paul.

Apple, M.W. (ed.) (1982), *Cultural and Economic Reproduction in Education*, London, Routledge and Kegan Paul.

Archambault, R.D. (ed.) (1965), *Philosophical Analysis and Education*, London, Routledge and Kegan Paul.

Archer, M.W. (1979), *Social Origins of Educational Systems*, London, Sage Publications.

Archer, M.S. (1982), 'The Sociology of Educational Systems' in T. Bottomore *et al*. (eds), *Sociology: the State of the Art*, London, Sage Publications.

Armstrong, P.F. (1982), 'The Myth of Meeting Needs in Adult Education and Community Development', *Critical Social Policy*, vol. 2, no. 2.

Ball, S.J. (1981), Beachside Comprehensive: a Case Study of Secondary Schooling, Cambridge, University Press.

Bantock, G.H. (1971), 'Towards a Theory of Popular Education', in R. Hooper (ed.), *The Curriculum: Context, Design and Development*, Edinburgh, Oliver and Boyd and Open Univeristy Press.

Bantock, G.H. (1980), *Dilemmas of the Curriculum*, Oxford, Martin Robertson.

Barton, L. *et al*. (eds) (1980), *Schooling, Ideology and the Curriculum*, Lewes, Falmer Press.

Becher, T. and Kogan, M. (1980), *Process and Structure in Higher Education*, London, Heinemann.

Becher, T. and Maclure, S. (1978), *The Politics of Curriculum Change*, London, Hutchinson.

Bernbaum, G. (1977), *Knowledge and Ideology in the Sociology of Education,* London, Macmillan.

Bernstein, B. (1971-5), *Class, Codes and Control* (3 vols), London, Routledge and Kegan Paul.

Bloom, B.S. (1956-64), *Taxonomy of Educational Objectives* (2 vols), London, Longman.

Bourdieu, P. and Passeron, J.C. (1977), *Reproduction in Education, Society and Culture*, London, Sage Publications.

Bowles, S. and Gintis, H. (1976), *Schooling in Capitalist America*, London, Routledge and Kegan Paul.

Brown, R. (ed.) (1973), *Knowledge, Education and Cultural Change*, London, Tavistock Publications.

Charters, A.N. *et al*. (1981), *Comparing Adult Education Worldwide*, San Francisco, Jossey-Bass.

Clarke, J. *et al*. (eds) (1979), *Working-class Culture: Studies in History and Theory*, London, Hutchinson.

College Entrance Examination Board (1978), *Future Directions for a Learning Society*, New York, the Board.

Cosin, B.R. *et al*. (eds) (1977), *School and Society: a Sociological Reader*, 2nd edn, London, Routledge and Kegan Paul and Open University Press.

Cropley, A.J. (1977), *Lifelong Educaton: a Psychological Analysis*, Oxford, Pergamon Press for UNESCO Institute for Education.

Dale, R. *et al*. (eds) (1976), *Schooling and Capitalism: a Sociological Reader*, London, Routledge and Kegan Paul and Open University Press.

Dale, R. *et al*. (eds) (1981), *Education and the State* (2 vols), Lewes, Falmer Press and Open University Press.

Dave, R.H. (ed.) (1976), *Foundations of Lifelong Education*, Oxford, Pergamon Press for UNESCO Institute for Education.

Dave, R.H. and Stiemerling, N. (1973), *Lifelong Education and the School: Abstracts and Bibliography*, Hamburg, UNESCO Institute for Education.

Davies, B. (1976), *Social Control and Education*, London, Methuen.

Dearden, R.F. (1968), *The Philosophy of Primary Education*, London, Routledge and Kegan Paul.

Department of Education and Science (1973), *Adult Education: a Plan for Development* (the Russell Report), London, HMSO.

Department of Education and Science (1980), *A View of the Curriculum* (HMI Series: Matters for Discussion. 11), London, HMSO.

Easthope, G. (1975), *Community, Hierarchy and Open Education*, London, Routledge and Kegan Paul.

Eggleston, J. (1977), *The Sociology of the School Curriculum*, London, Routledge and Kegan Paul.

Entwistle, H. (1978), *Class, Culture and Education*, London, Methuen.

Evans, N. (1981), *The Knowledge Revolution*, London, Grant McIntyre.

Evetts, J. (1973), *The Sociology of Educational Ideas*, London, Routledge and Kegan Paul.

Faure, E. *et al*. (1972), *Learning to Be: the World of Education Today and Tomorrow*, Paris, UNESCO and London, Harrap.

Fletcher, C. and Thompson, N. (eds) (1980), *Issues in Community Education*, Lewes, Falmer Press.

Flude, R. and Parrott, A. (1979), *Education and the Challenge of Change: a Recurrent Education Strategy for Britain*, Milton Keynes, Open University Press.

Fordham, P., Poulton, G. and Randle, L. (1979), *Learning Networks in Adult Education*, London, Routledge and Kegan Paul.

Freire, P. (1972), *Cultural Action for Freedom*, Harmondsworth, Penguin Books.

Freire, P. (1972), *Pedagogy of the Oppressed*, Harmondsworth, Penguin Books.

Gagné, R.M. (1977), *The Conditions of Learning*, 3rd edn, New York, Holt, Rinehart andWinston.

Gelpi, E. (1979), *A Future for Lifelong Education*, introduced and translated by Ralph Ruddock *et al*. (2 vols), Manchester, University of Manchester Department of Adult and Higher Education.

Gordon, P. and Lawton, D. (1978), *Curriculum Change in the Nineteenth and Twentieth Centuries*, London, Hodder and Stoughton.

Gramsci, A. (1971), *Selections from the Prison Notebooks*, London, Lawrence and Wishart.

Griffin, C.M., (1978), 'Recurrent and Continuing Education: a Curriculum Model Approach,' Nottingham, Association for Recurrent Education Discussion, Paper 3.

Griffin, C.M., (1982), 'Curriculum Analysis of Adult and Lifelong Education', *International Journal of Lifelong Education*, vol. 1, no. 2.

Hargreaves, D.H. (1982), *The Challenge for the Comprehensive School: Culture, Curriculum and Community*, London, Routledge and Kegan Paul.

Harrington, F.H.(1977), *The Future of Adult Education*, San Francisco, Jossey-Bass.

Harris, W.J.A. (1980), *Comparative Adult Education: Practice, Purpose and Theory*, London, Longman.

Hesburgh, T.M., Miller, P.A. and Wharton, C.R. (1973), *Patterns for Lifelong Learning*, San Francisco, Jossey-Bass.

Himmelstrup, P. *et al.* (eds) (1981), *Strategies for Lifelong Learning: a Symposium of Views from Europe and the U.S.A.*, Esbjerg, University Centre of South Jutland, Denmark, and the Association for Recurrent Education, UK.

Hirst, P.H. and Peters, R.S. (1970), *The Logic of Education*, London, Routledge and Kegan Paul.

Holmes, B. (1981), *Comparative Education: Some Considerations of Method*, London, Allen and Unwin.

Hooper, R. (ed.) (1971), *The Curriculum: Context, Design and Development*, Edinburgh, Oliver and Boyd.

Hostler, J. (1981), *The Aims of Adult Education*, Manchester, University of Manchester Department of Adult and Higher Education.

Houghton, V. and Richardson, K. (eds) (1974), *Recurrent Education: a Plea for Lifelong Learning,* London, Ward Lock Educational for the Association for Recurrent Education.

Hutchinson, E. and Hutchinson, E. (1978), *Learning Later: Fresh Horizons in English Adult Education*, London, Routledge and Kegan Paul.

Illich, I. (1971), *Deschooling Society*, London, Calder and Boyars.

Ingram, J.B. (1979), *Curriculum Integration and Lifelong Education*, Oxford, Pergamon Press for UNESCO Institute for Education.

Ireland, T.D. (1978), *Gelpi's View of Lifelong Education*, Manchester, University of Manchester Department of Adult and Higher Education.

Jenks, C. (ed.) (1977), *Rationality, Education and the Social Organization of Knowledge*, London, Routledge and Kegan Paul.

Jourdan, M. (ed.) (1981), *Recurrent Education in Western Europe*, Windsor, NFER/Nelson.

Kallen, D. (1980), *The Universities and Permanent Education: a Lost Opportunity*, London, Association of Comparative Educationists.

Karabel, J. and Halsey, A.H. (eds) (1977), *Power and Ideology in Education*, New York, Oxford University Press.

Knowles, M. (1978), *The Adult Learner: a Neglected Species*, 2nd edn, Houston, Gulf Publishing Co.

Kreitlow, B.W. *et al.* (1981), *Examining Controversies in Adult Education*, San Francisco, Jossey-Bass.

Lawson, K.H. (1977), *A Critique of Recurrent Education*, Nottingham, Association for Recurrent Education.

Lawson, K.H. (1979), *Philosophical Concepts and Values in Adult Education*, revised edn, Milton Keynes, Open University Press.

Lawton, D. (1973), *Social Change, Educational Theory and Curriculum Planning*, London, Hodder and Stoughton.

Lawton, D. (1975), *Class, Culture and the Curriculum*, London, Routledge and Kegan Paul.

Legge, C.D. (1982), *The Education of Adults in Britain*, Milton Keynes, Open University Press.

Lengrand, P. (1975), *An Introduction to Lifelong Education*, revised edn, London, Croom Helm.

Levitas, M. (1974), *Marxist Perspectives in the Sociology of Education*, London, Routledge and Kegan Paul.

Mallinson, V. (1980), *The Western European Idea in Education*, Oxford, Pergamon Press.

Maslow, A.H. (1968), *Towards a Psychology of Being*, 2nd edn, New York, Van Nostrand.

Mee, G. (1980), *Organisation for Adult Education*, London, Longman.

Mee, G. and Wiltshire, H. (1978), *Structure and Performance in Adult Education*, London, Longman.

Moore, T.W. (1974), *Educational Theory: an Introduction*, London, Routledge and Kegan Paul.

Musgrave, P.W. (1973), *Knowledge, Curriculum and Change*, London, Angus and Robertson.

National Institute of Adult Education (1970), *Adult Education: Adequacy of Provision*, London, the Institute.

National Institute of Adult Education (1980-), *Review of Existing Research in Adult and Continuing Education*, Leicester, the Institute.

Newman, M. (1979), *The Poor Cousin: a Study of Adult Education*, London, Allen and Unwin.

Northern Ireland Council for Continuing Education (1980), *Continuing Education in Northern Ireland: a Strategy for Development*, Bangor, the Council

OECD/CERI (1973), *Recurrent Education: a Strategy for Lifelong Learning*, by Denis Kallen and J. Bengtsson, Paris, OECD.

Open University (1976), *Report of the Committee on Continuing Education* (the Venables Report), Milton Keynes, the University.

Paterson, R.W.K. (1979), *Values, Education and the Adult*, London, Routledge and Kegan Paul.

Peters, R.S. (ed.) (1973), *The Philosophy of Education*, London, Oxford University Press.

Phenix, P. (1964), *Realms of Meaning*, New York, McGraw-Hill.

Pinker, R. (1971) *Social Theory and Social Policy*, London, Heinemann.

Reid, W.A. (1978), *Thinking about the Curriculum*, London, Routledge and Kegan Paul.

Rein, M. (1976) *Social Science and Public Policy*, Harmondsworth, Penguin Books.

Richards, C. (1978), *Curriculum Studies: an Introductory, Annotated Bibliography*, Nafferton, Studies in Education.

Richards, C. (ed.) (1978), *Power and the Curriculum: Issues in Curriculum Studies*, Nafferton, Studies in Education.

Roderick, G. and Stephens, M. (eds) (1979), *Higher Education for All?*, Lewes, Falmer Press.

Rodgers, B.M. with Doron, A. and M. Jones, (1979) *The Study of Social Policy: A Comparative Approach*, London, Allen and Unwin

Rogers, J. (1977), *Adults Learning*, 2nd edn, Milton Keynes, Open University Press.

Salter, B. and Tapper, T. (1981), *Education, Politics and the State*, London, Grant McIntyre.

Sarup, M. (1978), *Marxism and Education*, London, Routledge and Kegan Paul.

Sarup, M. (1982), *Education, State and Crisis: a Marxist Perspective*, London, Routledge and Kegan Paul.

Schon, D.A. (1971), *Beyond the Stable State: Public and Private Learning in a Changing Society*, London, Temple Smith.

Sharp, R. (1980), *Knowledge, Ideology and the Politics of Schooling: Towards a Marxist Analysis of Education*, London, Routledge and Kegan Paul.

Sharp, R. and Green, A. (1975), *Education and Social Control: a Study in Progressive Primary Education*, London, Routledge and Kegan Paul.

Skager, R. (1978), *Lifelong Education and Evaluation Practice*, Oxford, Pergamon Press for UNESCO Institute for Education

Skager, R. and Dave, R.H. (eds) (1977), *Curriculum Evaluation for Lifelong Education*, Oxford, Pergamon Press for UNESCO Institute for Education.

Sockett, H. (ed.) (1981), 'Continuing Education', *Educational Analysis*, vol. 3, no. 3.

Stenhouse, L. (1975), *An Introduction to Curriculum Research and Development*, London, Heinemann.

Stephens, M.D. and Roderick, G.W. (eds.) (1978), *Higher Education Alternatives*, London, Longman.

Tapper, T. and Salter, B. (1978), *Education and the Political Order: Changing Patterns of Class Control*, London, Macmillan.

Taylor, P.H. (ed.) (1979), *New Directions in Curriculum Studies*, Lewes, Falmer Press.

Taylor, P.H. and Richards, C. (1979), *An Introduction to Curriculum Studies*, Slough, NFER Publishing Co.

Taylor-Gooby, P. and Dale, J. (1981), *Social Theory and Social Welfare*, London, Edward Arnold.

Thompson, J.L. (ed.) (1980), *Adult Education for a Change*, London, Hutchinson.

Titmus, C. (1981), *Strategies for Adult Education: Practices in Western Europe*, Milton Keynes, Open University Press.

Titmuss, R. (1974), *Social Policy: An Introduction*, London, Allen and Unwin.

Townsend, P. (1976), *Sociology and Social Policy*, Harmondsworth, Penguin Books.

Tunstall, J. (ed.) (1974), *The Open University Opens*, London, Routledge and Kegan Paul.

Tyler, R.W. (1949), *Basic Principles of Curriculum and Instruction*, Chicago, University of Chicago Press.

Whiteside, T. (1978), *The Sociology of Educational Innovation*, London, Methuen.

Williamson, B. (1979), *Education, Social Structure and Development: a Comparative Analysis*, London, Macmillan.

World Yearbook of Education (1979), *Recurrent Education and Lifelong Learning*; ed. T. Schuller and J. Megarry, London, Kogan Page.

Young, M.F.D. (1975), 'Curriculum Change: Limits and Possibilities', *Educational Studies*, vol. 1.

Young, M.F.D. (ed.) (1971), *Knowledge and Control*, London, Collier-Macmillan.

Young, M. and Whitty, G. (eds) (1977), *Society, State and Schooling*, Lewes, Falmer Press.

INDEX